PINSTRIPES
by the TALE

Also by Marty Appel

Baseball's Best: The Hall of Fame Gallery (with Burt Goldblatt), 1977

Thurman Munson: An Autobiography (with Thurman Munson), 1978

Batting Secrets of the Major Leaguers, 1981

Tom Seaver's All-Time Baseball Greats (with Tom Seaver), 1984

Hardball: The Education of a Baseball Commissioner (with Bowie Kuhn), 1987

The First Book of Baseball, 1988

Yesterday's Heroes, 1988

My Nine Innings (with Lee MacPhail), 1989

Joe DiMaggio (for young readers), 1990

Working the Plate (with Eric Gregg), 1990

Yogi Berra (for young readers), 1992

Great Moments in Baseball (with Tom Seaver), 1992

When You're From Brooklyn, Everything Else Is Tokyo (with Larry King), 1992

Slide, Kelly, Slide, 1996

Baseball: 100 Classic Moments in the History of the Game (with Joseph Wallace and Neil Hamilton), 2000

Now Pitching for the Yankees, 2001

Munson: The Life and Death of a Yankee Captain, 2009

162–0: The Greatest Wins in Yankee History, 2010

Pinstripe Empire: The New York Yankees from Before the Babe to After the Boss, 2012

Pinstripe Pride: The Inside Story of the New York Yankees (for young readers), 2015

Casey Stengel: Baseball's Greatest Character, 2017

PINSTRIPES
by the TALE

Half a Century in and around Yankees Baseball

Marty Appel

TRIUMPH
BOOKS

Library of Congress Cataloging-in-Publication Data available upon request.

This book is available in quantity at special discounts for your group or organization. For further information, contact:

Triumph Books LLC
814 North Franklin Street
Chicago, Illinois 60610
(312) 337-0747
www.triumphbooks.com

Printed in U.S.A.
ISBN: 978-1-63727-278-7
Design by Nord Compo
Page production by Patricia Frey

For my grandsons,
Casey, Tyler (Ty), and Matthew (Matty)

Contents

Foreword

One of Marty Appel's handful of jobs in baseball and related to baseball over the decades was as executive producer of New York Yankees games on the local WPIX television station in the 1980s and '90s. That meant he was the boss, to use the term loosely here, of the beloved Yankees broadcasters, the irrepressible Italian Phil Rizzuto and the equally irrepressible African American Bill White. As Marty relates here in *Pinstripes by the Tale*, Rizzuto and White went at their jobs with a delightfully free-ranging approach. One moment that is memorable to me was when Rizzuto was talking about having picked up a suit at a neighborhood cleaners near his home in New Jersey—maybe the cleaners was Stringeni's—and then stopping at an Italian grocery store—maybe Pezzola's—and White interrupted him. "Scooter [Rizzuto's nickname]," "why is it that all your friends' names end in a vowel?" And without missing a beat, Rizzuto said, "Like you, White?"

Marty began working for the Yankees as a kid out of State University of Oneonta in upstate New York during summer break. He was assigned to answer Mickey Mantle's mail. In time, after college graduation, he was hired as an assistant public relations director for the Yankees and then, at age 24, he became the youngest head of public relations in Major League Baseball history. A dream job, perhaps, but not without its perils—which means, primarily, working for the mercurial and sometimes acerbic Yankees owner, George Steinbrenner.

As Marty writes, company heads all had two phones installed on their desks. The red ones took incoming calls only from Steinbrenner: "If you were on another call, you dropped it—you dropped whatever you were doing—and leaped for the phone. There was no second ring. He had no patience for second rings."

As for Mantle, Marty recalls someone asking the Yankees great how he felt about being famous. "It keeps me from getting a real job," replied Mantle. And Marty relates a little-known statistic: in Mantle's 18-year big-league career (9,910 plate appearances), he was hit by a pitch just 13 times. "No one wanted to risk disabling him, knowing how fragile his legs were," writes Marty. "It is an amazing statistic to behold."

Marty is the author or co-author of 24 previous books regarding baseball. One of them is *Working the Plate*, a memoir by the umpire Eric Gregg. The book title has a double meaning, since Gregg had a weight problem, due in part to a voracious appetite. Gregg was one of the umpires assigned to the 1989 World Series, San Francisco Giants versus the Oakland A's, famous now for a 10-day delay because of a California earthquake just before Game 3. Marty writes, "Gregg's colleagues blamed him for the quake by falling off the trainer's table."

Pinstripes by the Tale is an anecdotal romp through a captivating life and times of a baseball fan and baseball professional. Page after page, it's a triumph of storytelling. It's one wonderful story after another, and the reader, with a proverbial box of chocolates in their hands, says, "OK, one more." And then, "OK, one more..." followed by, "Oh, OK. Just two more..."

The book just as easily might have been titled *The Adventures of Marty Appel* and in baseball terms reminds me of Mark Twain's *The Adventures of Huckleberry Finn* or Saul Bellow's *The Adventures of Augie March* in its richness and complexities, whether traveling through Twain's Missouri or Bellow's Chicago or Appel's Yankees clubhouse and dugout. I should include John Cheever's compelling short story, *The Swimmer*. Writes Cheever, "Neddy feels young, energetic and happy. He decided to get home by swimming across all the pools in the country. He feels like an explorer.... He thinks about all the pools that lie ahead and the friends that await him."

And Marty's cast of characters are of such an entertaining variety that, as the saying goes, you can't make up people like Casey Stengel and Yogi Berra and Billy Martin and Thurman Munson and Whitey Ford and Catfish Hunter and Jim Bouton and Joe DiMaggio and Roger Maris and Roger Peckinpaugh. (Who? Marty explains in beguiling detail.) Marty was not simply the fly on the wall for so many Yankees years, but a perspicacious observer and often participant in events. There is humor galore and wondrous insights and, to be sure, human tragedy, such as when Marty learns that Munson died when the catcher crashed the plane he was piloting.

There is no official Yankees historian, but Marty, with his previous volume *Pinstripe Empire* as well as his best-selling *Munson*, among others, comes as close to that designation as ever was.

Marty and I have been friends since 1970, when he became the assistant PR director for the Yankees. We crossed paths often in a kaleidoscope of places, from my work as a sports journalist to his with the Yankees, with sports TV, with doing publicity for the 1996 Atlanta Olympics, as PR director for Topps baseball card producers to establishing his own PR firm.

Marty told me once that, in his baseball life, he identified with a quote from the old Dodgers Hall of Fame catcher Roy Campanella: "You have to have a lot of little boy in you if you play baseball for a living." In its way, to be sure, that's true, but in the baseball front offices, it can also be a particularly rugged business and you must be a mature adult—or suited with metaphoric armor—if you're going to deal with it. And to his everlasting credit, Marty did.

But the love of the game itself is at times not far from Marty's awareness—and pleasure. I recall a photograph he showed me that was taken by a friend a few years ago that underscores this point. It is a picture of Marty and his lovely wife, Lourdes, playing catch, about 60 feet apart, both wearing ball gloves. It appears to be springtime, and in New York's Central Park. While Yankee Stadium rises unseen in the Bronx several miles away, the joy on the faces of the Appels says that here, on this grassy Manhattan knoll, resides another version of baseball enchantment.

—Ira Berkow
Pulitzer Prize–winning columnist, *New York Times*

Preface:
Pregame Warm-Up

Having worked in and around our beloved game of baseball for more than half a century—and being a fan since 1955—I can tell you that in the end, it's not about the wins and losses so much as it's about the people and their stories.

The baseball universe is the players and management, the front offices, the support staff, the ballpark employees, the whole minor league infrastructure, the media, authors, historians, ballpark architects and designers, equipment manufacturers, and even the network, ad agency, and PR agency people who work on baseball accounts. And to my mind, always with a seat at the table, are the fans.

When I started working for the Yankees in 1968 as Mickey Mantle's fan mail clerk in the team's public relations department, I had an appreciation for the history unfolding around me and the interest that everything about the team held for many people. I was aware. I grew up watching, reading, and learning everything about the game, and here I was, in it.

And I remembered it all. Well, almost. For the life of me I can't remember how we got to the press box from the press dining room in the original Yankee Stadium, a journey I made hundreds of times. Did I take an elevator up and walk down an aisle to the press box? If I did, so too did Mel Allen and Red Barber and Phil Rizzuto and Bill White. How did they walk through the fans each day without getting mobbed? Maybe by the time I finish writing this, I'll remember.

But I do know that over time, over the course of working for the Yankees and for Major League Baseball, producing Yankees games for television, doing public relations for baseball-related businesses and publishers, writing two dozen baseball books, and delivering a lot of speeches, I became a storyteller. And I've loved holding an interested audience in tow while I weave a tale or a theory about the game we love. Some have suggested, especially as I write this during the pandemic, that I should bottle these stories into a podcast.

But I'm a writer, not a podcaster, and so here, my friends, are my stories. They aren't all Yankees stories, but many of them would not have happened without the associations and friendships that came from my Yankee experiences. Would I have spent an evening with John Lennon had I not known a producer at the radio station that carried Yankees games?

Nope.

So, stay with me as I wander off course from time to time, doing what storytellers do—reacting to something in a story that triggers a new one.

The stories don't necessarily connect. For the last quarter century, I've been meeting monthly over lunch with a bunch of baseball writers over a round table (as founder Larry Ritter insisted). Sometimes a story leads into another, sometimes there is a total disconnect, but that's how friends share stories, and that's basically the format of this book. We may jump from the 1910s to the 2020s, or from baseball to less-essential matters, but that's how a free-flowing conversation among people runs.

First Inning

I begin with a visit I made to Roger Peckinpaugh during spring training, 1975. It's always good to start with someone who was born during the Benjamin Harrison administration.

Even avid Yankee fans don't know who Roger Peckinpaugh was, but he was manager of the Yankees in 1914 and, to this day, remains the youngest man to ever manage a major league team. He was only 23!

He was a shortstop with a long jaw, easy to pick out in team photos. My Yankees boss, Bob Fishel, called him "ol' Lantern Jaw," and he was captain of the Yankees in 1914 when he was appointed manager for the last 20 games of the season (10–10) after Frank Chance was fired.

That was his whole managing record until Cleveland named him manager in 1928, where he lasted six seasons and was later the team's general manager. He was very popular in Cleveland, which is why Fishel spoke of him affectionately, Bob having been raised there.

Anyway, I was gathering information for my very first book, *Baseball's Best: The Hall of Fame Gallery*, and when someone told me Peck wintered in Deerfield Beach, just north of Fort Lauderdale (the Yankees' spring training site), I tracked him down and invited myself over to interview him about players from his era.

I asked him about Chance, who was part of the famous Tinker–Evers–Chance double play combo of the Cubs, and their story involved Fred Merkle and the famous "Merkle Boner" play in 1908, when Fred failed to touch second on a game winning hit and was called out. This became one of the great tales of the game.

Merkle was only 19 then, in his second year, and went on to have a fine 16-year career. But you can never escape your past, I suppose. I asked Roger about Fred, and he said, "the Bonehead?"

Some things you never live down. It was so interesting to see a baseball player of that era thinking like that, accepting what newspapers called poor Fred.

Roger, then 84, was living in a modest apartment, and I told him about my project and what I was looking for. To score points with Peck, and display my newfound admiration for him, I casually said, "You should be in the Hall of Fame, with your accomplishments!"

Well, that touched a nerve.

"Whaddya mean 'should be'?! I am in the Hall of Fame!"

Uh oh. He wasn't—and isn't. What do I say? He had a nice career—17 seasons and an MVP award in 1925 with Washington's pennant-winners (and a 29-game hitting streak for the Yankees in 1919)—but he only hit .259 with 48 homers and was never seriously considered.

With that, he got up and headed for the bedroom, opened a bureau drawer, reached down, and came back with a yellowed old newspaper from Cleveland that said, "Our Man Peck; A Hall of Famer for Sure."

(He brought the clipping with him from Cleveland for the winter?)

But yes, that was the story, and the newspaper was from the early '30s, before there really was a Hall of Fame in Cooperstown, and apparently the term "Hall of Fame" was occasionally thrown around back then. (The Hall of Fame for Great Americans, in New York, had opened in 1901 at New York University.)

Well, I had insulted the ol' Yankee manager. Here I was writing a book about the Hall of Famers, and he wasn't in it. Awkward.

But I recovered and did get some good information from him—and I was smart enough to record it, which is a pretty good tape to own.

And so, when I talk about old time Yankees who I knew, the story begins with Roger Peckinpaugh, born in 1891, who broke into pro ball in 1910 when Cy Young was still pitching.

Peckinpaugh, as mentioned, was the captain of the team prior to being named manager. Captains were common in the early days of the pro game—sort of assistant managers, taking charge of the team on the field. Peck was in fact the seventh Yankees captain (they were the New York Highlanders before 1913).

Lou Gehrig would be the ninth, and when he died in 1941, manager Joe McCarthy said, "The position dies with Lou; there will never be another Yankee captain."

This was upheld through the next 35 years, and while the honor could have gone to Bill Dickey—or Joe DiMaggio or Tommy Henrich or Frank Crosetti or Phil Rizzuto or Yogi Berra or Hank Bauer or Billy Martin or Ellie Howard or Whitey Ford or Mickey Mantle—it never did. And they did just fine without one.

Prior to the 1976 season, at a full senior staff meeting at New York's Carlyle Hotel, George Steinbrenner pointed to our manager Billy Martin and said, "Now, Billy, what I want to suggest here is your call—sometimes these things are good ideas and sometimes not, but it's up to you. I'm thinking we might do well with a team captain going into the new stadium and all, and of course I'm thinking of Munson, but it could be anyone."

Before Billy responded, I raised my hand. Although I was only 27, I was already one of the senior executives on the staff and probably had the most knowledge of the team's history.

"I'd like to point out that in 1941, when Lou Gehrig passed, Joe McCarthy said there would never be another captain—which is why there hasn't been one."

In an instant, Mr. Steinbrenner said, "Well, if Joe McCarthy knew Thurman Munson, he'd say this is the right time and this is the right guy."

End of argument. Billy nodded, and the decision to make Munson captain was done. It was pretty brilliant by the Boss.

Thurman himself was a reluctant captain. He didn't want to wear a "C" on his jersey (not that that's done in baseball) or bring the lineups out. If he was to lead by example, playing hard, that would be okay. He was already doing that.

And so, it unfolded, and Munson won the 1976 MVP award and led the Yankees to their first pennant in 12 years. And the position had been reestablished.

What it meant for me as PR man was that in the past, Munson would growl and bark if I asked him to meet a sponsor or a fan on the field before a game. He wouldn't do it. End of story. Now that he had all the responsibility of being a captain, he'd say okay.

But he wouldn't show up. I'd be standing there with a heartbroken fan, or a pissed-off sponsor, and I'd desperately call over the nearest guy in uniform for a meet-and-greet.

I liked it better the old way.

Yes, he could be exasperating. At Old Timers' Day in 1976, I wanted to shoot a photo of the four great catchers in Yankees history, thinking Thurman had taken his place among them. So, for the first time, we had Bill Dickey, Yogi Berra, and Elston Howard present to do such a photo with Thurman. (Berra had been a coach with the Mets since Thurman came up and attended only one previous Old Timers' Day at which Thurman was present—but it was too soon to think about such a photo).

I gathered Dickey, Berra, and Howard in front of the Yankees dugout during the hour before the introductions began. No Munson. I had reminded him about the photo several times.

Frantically, I ran into the clubhouse in search of our captain. I had hoped the three others would stay in place during my absence.

Finally, I found Thurman in the player's lounge, sitting in his underwear, watching a *Three Stooges* rerun on Channel 11.

"Thurman, remember the photo? Dickey–Berra–Howard? I've got them all in front of the dugout waiting for you!"

He sighed, slowly got up (he would never know how the *Three Stooges* episode ended), got dressed, and walked with me to the field.

We got the shot. And after he died, I saw a 16 x 20 framed version of it hanging in his home in Ohio.

Occasionally, we would have meetings in Mr. Steinbrenner's palatial office, and he would read us some new rules for employees. It might have to do with hours of work or perhaps some benefit that was being

My press box view of Thurman Munson (batting here in 1973) never changed in his first five major league seasons, with the beautiful backdrop of the historic original Yankee Stadium.

eliminated. When Individual Retirement Accounts were created, I learned that we weren't eligible to create one, because the Yankees had a profit-sharing plan. Unfortunately, the team hadn't shown a profit in more than 10 years, so there was nothing in our accounts. A longtime ticket department executive named Mike Rendine retired around that time only to discover that money was being removed from our accounts each year we showed a loss, depleting his total without his realization.

Mr. Steinbrenner told us that the profit-sharing plan was being ended. This came in 1976, just as the new stadium opened and just as two million people walked through the turnstiles, and when ABC Television became the second network to fund baseball's treasury. There was at last going to be a profit, except this time, no profit-sharing.

"I'm taking care of my partners first," he said. "And now you can put money into an IRA."

I would listen to the new rules and I'd think of Deputy Barney Fife of the Andy Griffith Show, telling new prisoners, "Here at the rock, we have two rules. Number one—obey all rules. Number two—no writing on the walls."

Words to live by, although Bronx grafitti artist Ray Negron was caught writing on the walls of Yankee Stadium and turned it into a four-decade career as a special advisor to the Boss and his successors.

I knew Munson had a special connection to the fans even in his rookie season, a season in which he started out with one single in his first nine games and seemed in danger of going back to the minors. Ralph Houk, who was a terrific manager for so many years, assured him that he was up to stay, and could keep the job on defense alone. Still, he spent the whole season trying to dig out of that awful start.

In those days, Yankee players on Army Reserve duty would have to miss games from time to time and head to Fort Dix in southern New Jersey for training.

That summer, Munson was absent for just such a reason, but on Sunday, August 9, he got out of his obligation in early afternoon and decided he could get to Yankee Stadium in time for the final innings of Game 2 if he hustled. He listened to the game on the radio as he sped up the Jersey Turnpike. The fans were shocked to see No. 15 step out from the dugout in the last of the sixth, and as he swung his bat in the on deck circle a terrific ovation grew from the stands. To my mind, this was the moment that Munson emerged as a special player, a fan favorite. He wouldn't be the captain for another six years, but he was the people's choice starting that very afternoon. It was a memorable moment, even though he grounded out. He got another ovation on his way back to the dugout.

I mentioned Cy Young in my Peckinpaugh story. It is remarkable that his name, attached to the best pitcher award, has endured. Thanks to that connection, he is probably better known than pitchers like Christy Mathewson, Grover Cleveland Alexander, and all the other early 300-game winners.

Cy was a 500-game winner, unimaginable today. But everyone knows his name because somehow, it emerged stronger than "Pitcher of the Year." When they took Kenesaw Mountain Landis' name off the MVP award in 2020, most people didn't even know it was on. Jackie Robinson's name is on the Rookie of the Year award, but few people say, "Who are the contenders for the coveted Jackie Robinson Award?" Does anyone call the World Series MVP the "Willie Mays Award?" Did you know the Ted Williams award goes to the All-Star Game MVP?

(And by the way, are there any awards that aren't "coveted?" When my captain's badge was retired after I headed the school safety patrol in sixth grade, that was a coveted honor.)

The first Cy Young Award was presented in 1956 to the Brooklyn Dodgers' Don Newcombe, who also won MVP that year. Cy had died in 1955, so his name was on the award from year one and his name was top of mind. Perhaps that is what it took.

I didn't see Cy Young pitch, and the photos we see of him, mostly from the tail end of his career when photography was more rampant, don't show him to be the most athletic-looking guy—maybe a bit portly. Bob Fishel didn't see him pitch either, but he did have him at a Yankees Old Timers' Day in 1955, about three months before he died. He was a little old man with a crooked little cane, and what a moment that must have been for Bob, who as I said grew up in Cleveland where Cy had his big years.

I became a fan in 1955—the 1955 World Series in fact. 1956 was my first full year of following the game—I was seven. Forty-year-old Enos Slaughter, who broke in in 1938, was still playing. I came to know Enos before he finally got elected to the Hall of Fame, and if you'd ask him, he'd say, "I played 2,380 games, had 7,947 at bats, scored 1,247 runs, had 2,383 hits…." He'd do the whole back of his baseball card for you. He memorized it all. And he finally got into the Hall, after years of campaigning for it. (Fishel thought he wasn't as much of a hustler as he was proclaimed to be…. Bob thought he detected "false hustle" there during his Yankees years, but of course, he was an aging player.)

How did it come to pass that I was born in Brooklyn and became a Yankees fan? When the Yankees lost that 1955 World Series to Brooklyn, from my window I watched people on St. John's Place in Brooklyn (where there was a trolley car line) literally dancing in the streets. Oh, what a day it was in Brooklyn history—their first world championship. (It would be their only one.)

But me, age seven, I felt sorry for the losers. I thought of the poor Yankees with sadness, and on that day, I decided I was going to be a Yankees fan and root for the underdogs. Maybe it was the way my parents explained it to me. And I suppose at seven, feeling sorry for the losers was a newly discovered emotion.

So, my entire life as a Yankees fan was sort of a mistake. The Dodgers should have been my team; I should have celebrated too; and I missed out on cheering for those great "Boys of Summer." Of course, they would have broken my heart two years later when they announced they were moving to Los Angeles. Maybe I was better off.

Through nickel purchases and wise trades, I got the full set of 1956 Topps cards, and I was on my way. (I still have them, but I once traded a duplicate '56 Mantle for a 1959 Zach Monroe, which was missing from my collection that year. A bad trade.) Kids today don't really understand the impact those cards had. When one of those guys dies today, the first image in my head is his Topps card. They were what we had before color TV and close-up lenses. Through the cards, we saw the colors of the ballparks and the uniforms. It was magical.

Color photography went back to the 1930s, but it was seldom used by professionals, because there were not many places to get them published. So, color film was used more often by amateurs with home snapshots, long before magazines started publishing in color. Topps offered fans color, and baseball images came alive as never before.

I know many kids today don't know the names of the old-time players—they never heard of Al Simmons or Pie Traynor or Tris Speaker. We knew all those guys. But for us Baby Boomers, it was a matter of catching up with maybe 40 or 50 years of history. Today's kids have a century to master. It's a lot to expect.

I come down on the side of the kids. When I was growing up, there were 16 teams and about 400 players a year, give or take a few, and we knew them all, from Hank Aaron to George Zuvernik. But today's fans are asked to learn nearly 1,200 players a year spread over 30 teams, and with Topps no longer marketing cards to kids—hey, it's a tough assignment! So, let's cut them some slack. It's a daunting task to know all the players. At least fantasy sports keeps them knowledgeable about today's rosters.

During Hank Aaron's career, it was amazing that he not only ascended to the top in home run totals, but that he led off all of baseball history in alphabetical order. Even his brother Tommie had to stand behind him. And then came the spoiler in 2004, 27 years after Hank's last game. David Aardsma, a pitcher with eight teams including the Yankees, should have been ashamed of himself.

Old Timers' Day was certainly my most fun assignment when I worked with Fishel or ran it myself for the Yankees. It was an enormous amount of work for one day of entertainment. Before we called them spreadsheets, I had my green legal pad marking invitations, responses, follow-up letters with travel instructions, ordering uniforms (half our old timers were opponents), gifts, hotels, (Casey Stengel, Mickey Mantle, and Joe DiMaggio stayed in their own preferred hotels), buses, guests, ticket needs, travel expenses, expense checks, complimentary bats from Louisville Slugger, a printed program for fans, the introductory remarks on index cards for Frank Messer to read, shipping the gifts home if preferred, the dinner (Toots Shor or the 21 Club or the Diamond or Stadium Clubs), and then thank-you notes. Getting the uniforms right was a source of pride to me, and I would work directly with the clubhouse men at opposing teams to dig up the correct vintage version. Those guys understood the importance of getting it right. You couldn't have an old Philadelphia A's player in an Oakland A's uniform.

In 1973, the legendary Satchel Paige was an invited guest. When we announced that Paige would be attending, I got a phone call from a

At top left of a 1973 Old Timers' Day "team photo" is Satchel Paige, the only non-Yankee present; I wish I knew the fate of the Monarchs uniform he wore. Bottom row, left, white cap and white shirt is ol' Lantern Jaw, Roger Peckinpaugh.

gentleman who said he owned an original Kansas City Monarchs uniform, and would I like to borrow it for the Paige appearance? Would I ever! I knew this one would be spectacular.

So Satch wore it for the player introductions. It was otherwise an all-Yankees event marking the 50th anniversary of Yankee Stadium, so he was the only one not in a Yankees uniform.

Sad to report, he took it home with him! He put it in his satchel, I suppose. The visiting clubhouse man, Mickey Rendine, gave me the bad news. I still remember that awful call I had to make to that generous fan about its disappearance. I still think about it today, more than a half-century later.

Probably the most famous legend that grew from Old Timers' Day came from the year we introduced Mantle after Joe DiMaggio. DiMag was insulted and said he would never return. The last introduction, after all, was a special honor.

Actually, that was all true; it was not a myth. Joe was indeed pissed. The reason it will always be hard to keep things like this out of the media is that there will always be insiders who are anxious to befriend a journalist, both to show they are important enough to hold insider information, and of course to befriend an important reporter as they seek to build a personal reputation in the interest of advancement. I'm not being critical, I'm just saying this is how life works, and those who spend hours trying to find the "leaker" are swimming against the tide.

Often the leaker is a very high-level team official seeking that same coziness with the press. Gabe Paul, the Yankees team president, had me run several fool's missions seeking the culprit, only for me to find out that it was him.

Anyway, in 1969, Mickey Mantle was at the height of his popularity. He retired that very spring after 18 seasons. While his last four years were quite ordinary and mortal, the body of his work and the glamour of his name were still lofty.

In retrospect, it was just sad that this great natural athlete and American folk hero had his last big year at age 32.

Mickey Mantle Day in June was one of the great events in Yankee history, with an emotional farewell before a full house, with a nearly a 20-minute standing ovation before he was finally able to speak. Then there was a final ride around the warning track in a bullpen cart driven by Danny Colletti of our grounds crew. It had been Bob Fishel's idea, and it was great.

The affection of that day still lingered as Old Timers' Day arrived two months later, the first in which Mick would participate. In keeping with the long tradition of DiMaggio being introduced last, it was decided that Mantle would be next to last.

To little surprise, the ovation for Mantle was enormous and prolonged, so much so that Messer's introduction of DiMaggio was all but drowned out. He didn't get his just due.

So, the following year, 1970, Fishel (with me in agreement) decided to do DiMaggio next-to-last, then Mantle, so that the cheers for Mantle

A little 1970 Old Timers'
Day hero worship;
Bob Fishel greets
Joe DiMaggio at the
Yankees dugout as I
look on.

didn't obliterate Joe's. Mantle's fans were obviously younger, louder, more boisterous, and the memory of Mick was fresher. It all made sense.

Until...

Until Joe was insulted by being relegated to next-to-last. I suppose if we had told him ahead of time and listened to his objection, a wiser decision might have been made. But we did it without consultation, just because it felt right, with the intent of giving DiMaggio his full ovation, in what was his first year of being introduced as baseball's greatest living player.

(The year 1969 was the centennial of professional baseball, and at a gala in Washington D.C. at the All-Star break, Ruth was named greatest player and Joe the greatest living player. It was said that he always insisted on being introduced that way, which made him seem egocentric, but in fact, it was a logical introduction to which he never objected. The story of him "insisting" was exaggerated.)

One of my Old Timers' Day assignments was prompting players when their turn arrived to go onto the field for their introduction. DiMaggio knew the drill. He didn't need me. Farm director Johnny Johnson is on the left.

After the field ceremony in '70, when he was introduced next-to-last, Joe returned to the clubhouse and hastily showered and changed into his always impeccably tailored suit and left, telling clubhouse man Pete Sheehy that it would be his last Old Timers' Day.

The news of his displeasure got out, and of course, we were humiliated and embarrassed that we had unintentionally insulted Joe. But he could be sensitive to slights. A few years later, after we had made our peace and told him he would always be last, a security person barred him from getting an early coffee in the Diamond Club because it was being set up for the evening's dinner. Oh boy. Again, there was a well publicized grievance and again we had to offer our apologies, but he left and didn't stay for the dinner.

I never stopped admiring Joe DiMaggio, but he could certainly be difficult when he wanted to be, which actually seemed to be annually. On the Old Timers' Day in 1975 when Billy Martin was announced as our new manager, Joe was again upstaged. (Martin was introduced last with the surprise announcement of his new position.) Again, we had to deal with Joe the Insulted. Bob Fishel had moved on by this point—it was my show—but bringing Martin out last was orchestrated by George Steinbrenner.

I served on the advisory committee for the Cracker Jack Old Timers' Games, held in Washington, D.C., and later in Buffalo, New York (where I actually managed the National League team in the final one, held in 1990). Joe was a participant and was actually happy to see me, a familiar face, in the clubhouse. He greeted me by name, which was always a thrill to me.

But as he was changing into his American League uniform, a local photographer started taking pictures of him, bare chested at his locker.

My 1971 Old Timers' Day watch with the foolish personalization on the back.

Joe was 75 by now, and while lithe and strong, he was still 75 and did not care for being photographed "topless." He let the photographer have it and decided right there that this would be the last time he ever changed into a uniform. And sure enough, all of his future appearances everywhere saw him don a classy suit and tie, but never again a uniform. It was a significant moment for keepers of the DiMaggio timeline. No more No. 5 on his back. (He had stopped taking a turn at bat some years earlier.)

It took me almost 30 years to fully appreciate one of my dumber moves regarding DiMaggio and Old Timers' Days.

In 1971, we gave every guest a custom-designed Yankees watch by Longines, with the top hat logo on the front and the player's name engraved on the back.

They really were beautiful and, as always, Bob Fishel approved it and had me order them for all the guests.

"While you're at it," he said, "order one for each of us; we work hard on that event."

That was really nice of him and so I did—Bob Fishel, me, Pete Sheehy, Bill Kane, and a few others. They cost about $75 each.

DiMaggio died in 1999. A few years later there was an auction of the items he left behind, and included in the auction was the watch! He had kept it all those years.

It went for a nice five-figure sum at auction, because it was Joe's, coming from his own estate sale.

Suddenly it occurred to me. *What was I thinking?* Back in 1971 I could have ordered *two* DiMaggios and *no* Appels. I could have taken the "alternate" DiMaggio home with me, and one day, sold it and financed a nice European vacation.

What was I thinking?!

In 2022, a bawdy letter handwritten in ink by Mantle (a practical joke meant to shock Bob Fishel) sold at auction for almost $250,000. I had given it away after holding it for some 30 years, never wanting Fishel to see it. It was another brilliant decision by me.

Second Inning

That final Buffalo Cracker Jack game was significant for me too. As a last-minute manager of the National League, I got to make up a lineup and make substitutions as though I was dealing with living and breathing Strat-O-Matic cards. On my roster was Tom Seaver, who was then a Yankees broadcaster. I had hired him and was his boss, as I was by then executive producer of the Yankees telecasts. Also on the roster was Sandy Koufax, a hero even to Yankees fans, who recognized that this man, who had quit while on top in 1966, was a god among baseball players.

Sandy didn't really want to pitch. He was still sensitive to that damaged left elbow, which had forced his retirement. But Dick Cecil, the game's organizer, had talked him into facing "just one batter."

Sandy started, I was the manager, and Dick McAuliffe was the leadoff hitter for the AL The agreement was in place—one batter.

But McAuliffe started fouling pitches off, and Sandy's pitch count got up to nine or ten. He was looking at me and I was rolling my arms or something, giving a signal to please hang in there for the full batter. Eventually McAuliffe walked (which might have been semi-intentional).

Now it was time to replace Sandy. Was I going to let it happen without going to the mound? Of course not. It was going to be my moment.

So dressed in my NL cap and a blue windbreaker, I headed for the mound, only to find him laughing good naturedly. I put out my hand and said, "Sandy, I don't like what I'm seeing here," as I took the ball

17

At the 1990 Cracker Jack Old Timers' Day event, where I managed the National League team and had my broadcaster Tom Seaver pitch the second inning.

from him and motioned with my left hand for Warren Spahn to come in from the bullpen. I patted Sandy on the ass, and he walked off. I had just done something that Walter Alston, his only manager, had seldom done, especially in Sandy's final glorious years in the '60s.

He was still laughing at breakfast the next morning, and people were teasing me about my showboating, which was fine. It was an exhibition and I had been an exhibitionist. Perfect, right?

Seaver, back on the air a few nights later, took time to tell the Yankees audience what "our dandy little executive producer had done" in Buffalo. He included the final score, a 3–0 win under my managing, although one of my players, Gene Mauch, the longtime manager, was quietly making substitutions behind my back.

Lee MacPhail, my old Yankees boss and now President of the American League, sent me a handwritten note questioning how I could have participated in an event in which the NL beat the AL. It was all in good fun.

When the Toronto Blue Jays played pandemic home games at that same ballpark in Buffalo in 2020–21, you can be sure my mind flashed back 30 years to the Cracker Jack game. Do you think Sandy's did too?

Let's not push it. He had better highlights to reflect on, for sure.

My friend, sportswriter Ira Berkow, came down with Legionnaire's disease a few years ago, something you don't hear about too often anymore. He had a full recovery.

The illness, under that name, dates back to an American Legion convention held at the Bellevue Stratford Hotel on South Broad Street in Philadelphia in 1976, where 182 people, mostly members of the Legion convention, came down with a respiratory illness resembling pneumonia. Twenty-nine died. It was said to have been caused by some bacteria emerging through the air conditioning system, and the historic hotel, which opened in 1904, was out of business a month later. The illness took the name Legionnaire's disease.

Well, guess what. Eight days before the American Legion checked in, the American League All-Star team stayed there. The 1976 All Star Game was played in Philadelphia as part of the nation's bicentennial celebration and, as is the custom, each league had a headquarters hotel. The Bellevue-Stratford was the AL headquarters. The registration list included Munson, Rod Carew, George Brett, Rusty Staub, Catfish Hunter, Sparky Lyle, Luis Tiant, Carlton Fisk, Willie Randolph, Chris Chambliss, Mark Fidrych, Carl Yastrzemski, and Frank Robinson. And through a quirk of fate, Legionnaire's disease could have been American League disease and taken down some very great ballplayers.

There were probably players who made the connection while watching the story unfold, but to my memory, no one in the media picked up on it. The media would have stayed elsewhere (as did I). I always thought this was one of the oddities of the game that went unnoticed.

I'm always happy when my name is linked with Sparky Lyle's in tales of the '70s, because I was the one who came up with entrance music—"Pomp and Circumstance"—when the pinstripe-painted Datsun (and later Toyota) drove him in from the bullpen. He was like a matador, entering the field to conquer the opponent, and the music (Toby Wright on the organ) got the fans excited and added some theater to the game. It had more impact than it would today because it was included on telecasts. Today, all the breaks are covered by commercials (about 90 commercials per game), and no one at home would hear the entrance music.

The truth was, Sparky didn't like the walk-up music; it created extra pressure, and he asked us to drop it after two seasons. But for those two years, our creation was much enjoyed by Yankees fans.

Another thing seldom pondered by baseball historians was the 216 stitches on the baseballs. Broken down, the essence of the game as we know it owes a lot to those stitches. They are what makes the ball curve, drop, rise, and generally dance. When someone says of a pitcher, "His ball has a lot of movement," they are acknowledging that he knows how to work the stitches. Without the stitches—if baseballs were like billiard balls—there would be little movement. Pitchers could control speed and location, but basically, the games would belong to the hitters, and it would look like batting practice.

So, what of those stitches? Here is the question for the ages: Did the founding fathers of the game, in the mid-19th century, understand what the stitches would do? Or was it simply the only way that a baseball could be constructed?

The early days of base ball (two words) generally featured underhand pitching, so curve pitching was waiting to be discovered. Candy Cummings' Hall of Fame plaque reads: PITCHED FIRST CURVE BALL IN BASEBALL HISTORY. INVENTED CURVE AS AMATEUR ACE OF BROOKLYN STARS IN 1867. Cummings was selected to the Hall in 1939. Scholarship since then seems to credit another Brooklyn pitcher, Jim Creighton (not in the Hall), who used what was sometimes called an illegal delivery, one in which he failed to "pitch" the ball underhanded with a stiff arm. Creighton, who died in 1862 at age 21, had turned heads with a delivery that created more speed by moving his elbow and wrist, and may in fact have stumbled on breaking pitches in doing so. It was said that his young death may have been attributable to internal bleeding caused by his unorthodox delivery.

If the founding fathers envisioned the game using underhand deliveries, then the value of stitches may have indeed been unknown to them. But it eventually led to the game as we now know it, where hitters being successful only three of ten times is considered a great achievement.

George Weiss was the Yankees farm director and then general manager for many years until he left with Casey Stengel following the 1960 season. His departure (and golden parachute) included an agreement that he would not become general manager of another team.

So, when the Mets were born, Joan Payson and M. Donald Grant named him president to get around the provision.

With the Yankees, Weiss had the nickname "Lonesome George." He had little personality, was not much for bantering with writers, and was thought to be a rather humorless fellow—although quite good at building pennant-winners.

One anecdote Bob Fishel told me was that a promoter came to see Weiss about having a "Cap Day" at Yankee Stadium—at which all young fans would receive a Yankees cap. (One considerably cheaper than the real thing, of course.)

Weiss was said to have slammed his fist on his desk and told the promoter, "Do you think we want every kid in this city walking around with a Yankees cap?"

While hard to believe that thinking once existed, it does ring true for those days when "rooting for the Yankees was like rooting for U.S. Steel."

(Today, the caps are seen all over the world, including, unfortunately, on a lot of people who get arrested and wear the caps on their perp walks into court.)

So, I find it somewhat fascinating that Weiss did not have much luck building a ballclub when he went to the Mets (considering all he had was a bunch of players essentially given away by other teams), but I am amazed at his success with almost every other aspect of the franchise's origin.

Think about it—his choice of manager (Casey Stengel), his choice of announcers (Lindsey Nelson, Ralph Kiner, Bob Murphy), the team's mascot (Mr. Met), its song ("Meet the Mets"), its promotions (especially Banner Day), its embrace of a "new breed" of young and boisterous fans, its encouragement of the "Let's Go Mets" chant, its popular organist (Jane Jarvis), its classic pinstripe home uniforms, its logo, its choice of the site of Shea Stadium to attract Long Island fans, its courting of the press to embrace the feats of Marvelous Marv Thronberry and other less-than-stellar performers—everything worked! Many still exist! The thing Weiss was worst at with the Yankees, he was best at with the Mets. (I know some will argue that Shea wasn't exactly a luxurious ballpark, but to Mets fans, it was "home," and I always thought their original Shea scoreboard was perfect and had all you needed.)

And a word about the man after whom the ballpark was named—Bill Shea. He was a "power broker," a term often associated with Robert Moses, but while Moses' work has come to be seen as visionary with a touch a cruelty, everybody liked Bill Shea. Brilliant and affable, he could have been an ambassador. But his greatest trait, to me, was the way he would remember names. What a gift! It is almost my worst thing, and it was one of his best. I was with him numerous times at dinners, ceremonies, etc. I never had a real conversation of any substance with him, but when he'd spot me, it was always, "Hi, Marty." I can't tell you how impressed I was that Bill Shea knew me, and that his talent for names was so grand.

Of course, one faux pas in his background was legendary. When the Mets were born, there was a ceremony at City Hall to introduce them. And with all the players sitting behind him, Bill leaned into the microphone and implored the audience to "stick with us until we get ourselves some real players."

George Pfister was the farm director of the Yankees when I joined their front office, reporting to Johhny Johnson (who would later move to the Commissioner's Office and then become president of the minor leagues.)

George was a cigar-smoking, old-school "Rickey guy," as he liked to call himself, having grown up as a minor league catcher for the Brooklyn Dodgers when Branch Rickey was growing the Dodgers' farm system.

I never saw anyone who could smoke a cigar down to its final eighth-of-an-inch, but he could do it.

He kept all his records on green oversized index cards, filed in a rolling "tub" near his desk, all hand-written. He liked to talk about his tub.

As the protector of records, he had oversight in making sure that all such records, contracts, options etc., were in proper order. Later, he followed Johnny to the Commissioners' Office where he continued to monitor all transactions, making sure everything was in perfect order.

The irony of all of this was that George himself happened to be an "illegal player," the only one I've ever heard of.

It wasn't a big deal, but it was a violation of the rules for sure.

In 1941, as the Dodgers played their final weekend of the regular season, preparing for the World Series against the Yankees, their three catchers—Babe Phelps, Mickey Owen, and Herman Franks—were all ailing for one reason or another. Manager Leo Durocher wanted them all healthy for the Series, of course, so he implored the front office to get him an able-bodied catcher for the weekend for emergency use.

That would be George, then 22. His minor league season having ended, he was sitting at home when the phone rang. It was a a few days before the final series of the season.

He did in fact suit up and got into the final Saturday game against the Phillies. He entered in the fifth inning, replacing Owen; went 0–2 (flying out to center and grounding out to first); and behind the plate he had three putouts and two assists including starting a double play and throwing a runner out at second. (Owen would have an infamous passed ball six days later in the World Series against the Yankees, turning a Dodgers victory into defeat.)

The problem was, George never signed a contract. His minor league contract was purchased by the Dodgers, but he didn't sign a major league contract. It was all done in haste, and whoever was responsible for producing a contract for him to sign (probably the traveling secretary) never got it done. And so, George Pfister's one game major league career was played without a legal contract. His appearance was deleted from official records of the 1941 season, although by the 1950s, it was reinstalled, lest the box score of that one game not proof out.

And George would go on to validate and record contracts in his tub during a long front office career.

I never got very far as a player—I was no George Pfister—but one thing I could do as a kid was play second base. If you keep your concentration on the game and anticipate the bad hop, you can handle second. I had some range and an arm decent enough for second (not short or third). I wasn't very good at going back for fly balls, but I could field grounders, make the pivot on a double play, and make accurate throws. And I loved making the final out and spiking the ball on the pitcher's mound as I left the field. Very cool. (I joined a Central Park Softball League in my fifties and played second base, but I discovered that everyone else in the league was Manny Ramirez and I soon retired, unhurt.)

I couldn't hit a lick, so forget about making my high school team.

Graig Nettles once asked me what kind of a player I was as a kid, and I said, "I couldn't hit. I think I was afraid of the ball, afraid of getting hit." And he responded, "Only hurts for 30 seconds. You can count down to zero as you go to first base." And I thought, "Why didn't any of my coaches ever say that to me?"

As a kid I wore No. 1, after my hero Bobby Richardson, and mostly played second, just like him. (He was listed as 5'9", but when I met him I realized he was more like my size, 5'7".) I felt so at home there. And learning all those little nuances of fielding, like signaling to teammates how many outs there were or holding up my forefinger and pinky to show two outs (lest the forefinger/middle finger combination look like a one from afar).

The few sportswriter games I played in at Yankee Stadium taught me some valuable lessons. First, I believe that every fan ought to somehow experience the throw to first from deep behind third base, which is made by either the third baseman (if playing deep) or the shortstop (if he moves to his right). Once you've attempted that, you will have such a greater appreciation for the throwing arms on those guys. In addition, when I played the outfield, the enormity of a triple deck major league ballpark was overwhelming. A ball hit against that background, if one wasn't used to it, was really difficult to read, much more difficult than against a high cloudless sky. And outfielders make it seem so routine, even as three of them are covering so many acres—enough to build seven or eight homes on!

I did have one "on field" highlight many years later, and to my surprise, it was as a hitter, not a fielder.

I was at a Yankees fantasy camp at Steinbrenner Field in Tampa in 2011. I was 62, and I was there at the Yankees' invitation to interview the dozen or so participating retired Yankees players for use on the team's website. My work done, and at the urging of assembled campers, I was encouraged to don a uniform (I chose to wear No. 7) and take a turn at bat.

My inspiration for this was Billy Crystal, who had taken a turn at bat in a spring training game at age 60 and hit a foul ball. He didn't embarrass himself, and I thought I might get away with it too.

With my pal Ron Blomberg coaching at third (and thus, a witness), I stepped in to face El Duque—Orlando Hernandez—who was a camp participant.

I was aware that I was standing in the same right-hand batter's box used by Derek Jeter in spring training.

I was able to black out all the extraneous noise and distractions of the day, people yelling "swing hard," and concentrate on the pitch. And Duque's very first pitch looked inviting, like the size of a softball. I lined it over the infield dirt and into short center field for a clean single. I ran to first, took a wide turn, and with the biggest smile I ever had, took myself out for a pinch runner and retired on the spot.

So Blomberg and I have an agreement. We're the same age, born just weeks apart in the same month, and I saw him hit the façade in old Yankee Stadium during batting practice, and he saw me get my single to center. We both need to stay alive to bear witness to each other's feat. Somehow, I don't think I can count on El Duque remembering my base hit.

Third Inning

In 2014, Major League Baseball instituted a video review system allowing umpires, stationed in a Manhattan studio, to review disputed calls when requested by a manager.

At once, this ended the days of fiery managers inciting their team and its fans onto victory with colorful, cap-throwing, dirt-kicking demonstrations on the field. The days of John McGraw, Leo Durocher, Billy Martin, Earl Weaver, and Bobby Cox drew to a close, and managers came to be replaced by rather nameless company men skilled on reading analytics tables.

But there is more to the story.

Almost at once, nearly half the close calls were overturned upon video review. After more than eight years of practice, the percentage of plays overturned remained near 50 percent.

And so, we can make a fair judgment that the same percentage might well be applied to all of baseball history. Half the time that managers argued close calls…they were right.

Think about the implication of that! With so many pennant races decided by just a few games, the entire course of baseball history might have changed! Did the Boston Red Sox really win the 1967 American League pennant by one game over Detroit and Minnesota? Surely all three franchises had decisions that would have been overturned if video replay was used. In one-run games, Minnesota was 39–42, Detroit was

20–19, and Boston was 27–28. Some of those games could have gone the other way.

The Red Sox '67 pennant—in fact, the "Impossible Dream" season—turned the fortunes of that franchise around to this day. From that magical year of Yastrzemki and Jim Lonborg, Red Sox Nation took off, the great rivalry with the Yankees would flourish, and the team would become one of the great financial success stories of the last half century. Red Sox Nation was a brilliant marketing plan.

One thing that really separates Boston from New York is that there is one pro team per sport: Red Sox, Patriots, Celtics, Bruins. The region finds unity in rooting for its sports teams. In New York, with two or more teams per sport, it's all just another reason for division.

Would it have all happened if they hadn't won the 1967 pennant? We will, of course, never know. But umpires getting it wrong on close plays half the time certainly gives one pause. The first umpire in the Hall of Fame, Bill Klem, claimed to have "never gotten one wrong." ("In my heart," he would add.) I suspect we might need a replay on that quote of his.

There is talk now of robot umpires calling balls and strikes. It's already being tried in the minor leagues. It could indeed reach the majors one day, and that makes me think that someday, someone will go to MLB with a way to save $90 million a year, simply by eliminating pitching staffs—with their salaries and benefits.

In 2000, I was asked to do PR for a new invention—an elite pitching machine called ProBatter that could be programed to throw different kinds of pitches to different locations at different speeds, even topping 100 mph, all with remarkable accuracy. It was developed by a fellow named, ironically, Greg Battersby. The pro version goes for about $25,000, but what is that compared to the $90 million for a pitching staff?

Could this one day be part of the game?

Before Major League Baseball expanded to 162 games, when the season was 154 games, a player needed 477 plate appearances (counting walks and HBP) to qualify for the batting title. That became 502 in 1961 (American

League) and 1962 (National League), but the formula, starting in 1957, was always 3.1 at bats per number of games on the schedule. Thus, 162 times 3.1 equals 502.

I always thought that was odd—how did 3.1 come to be? As it happened, when I worked in the Commissioner's Office, Harry Simmons was on the staff and was central to coming up with the rule. Talk about a firsthand opportunity to learn.

"You see," said Harry, "there was something wrong when Ted Williams was denied the batting championship in 1954 because he only had 386 at bats—short by 14 of the qualifying rule then of 400. But he had 136 walks and batted .345, losing the batting title to Bobby Avila's .341."

For 1957, the rule was changed to 3.1, which still exists today. Why 3.1? If you divide 400 at bats by 154 games, it comes out to 2.6, and the rule makers arbitrarily added an extra 0.5 to cover a walk every two games. Thus, 3.1.

I liked Harry, who had long written a feature for the monthly *Baseball Digest* called "So You Think You Know Baseball?" It was a test of baseball rules, and he would update it every 10 years or so by substituting current players for retired ones he had used. It became an annuity for him, even if each one only paid him about $20.

On one of his stops in his long baseball career, he worked for Charlie Finley, the eccentric Oakland A's owner. One day, Finley showed up at the Commissioner's Office, probably to contest a fine or some sort of discipline.

When Harry heard that his old boss was there, he said, "Oh, I have to go say hello!"

So, he walked to the reception area where receptionist Gloria Coleman was phoning Bowie Kuhn to let him know his favorite owner had arrived, when suddenly Finley stopped in his tracks and shouted, "Harry Simmons! My god, I'd heard you'd passed on!"

Apparently not.

A long-forgotten Ted Williams note was that he quit baseball after that 1954 season. Just walked away from the game at age 35. He was going through a divorce and his lawyer explained to him that most of the money he stood to make in 1955 (about $70,000) was going to go to his ex-wife! So, Williams, as only he could, said, "The hell with that," and quit!

He did not go to spring training. The Red Sox considered him retired. As author Leigh Montville recounts in his Williams biography, one day he was at Union Station in Baltimore waiting for a train, when an adult fan named Eddie Mifflin of Swarthmore, Pennsylvania, spotted him and said, "Ted! Ted! You can't quit! You only need 70 hits to reach 2,000. And in home runs you're not even in the top 10 yet!" On and on this fan went, long before there were sabrmaticians at every turn. Most people only knew stats from the back of Topps baseball cards and the occasional all-time charts that would appear in preseason magazines like the *Dell Baseball Annual*.

Williams liked goals and milestones and liked being in the same sentence with baseball immortals. So not only did he reconsider and play his first game on May 28, but he kept in touch with the fan as his lifetime stats accumulated. He now had a personal statistician, and he put in six more full seasons of play.

There is another fine Ted Williams biography out there, written by Ben Bradlee Jr., the son of the legendary *Washington Post* editor. I don't really know Ben Jr., but thanks to Facebook I have noted that he and I were born on the same day, same year. And one day I saw a televised Zoom interview with Governor Chris Sununu of New Hampshire, and he had behind him on a bookshelf, side by side, my *Pinstripe Empire* book and Ben's Ted Williams book, *The Kid*. I like a guy who arranges his bookshelf by birthdate of the author.

When Williams managed the Washington Senators/Texas Rangers for four years, it was heaven for the sportswriters of the day. They didn't relate to the hell that he could be for the sportswriters of his playing days. They would drop any story they were working on just to be in Ted's presence to hear whatever he was pontificating on at the time. It could be baseball, it could be fishing, it could be politics, but he was always opinionated, and all of his sentences seemed to end in exclamation points. I too would wander over just to eavesdrop and was fascinated by the man. He was a tough-guy version of John Wayne!

In his later years, he visited the Yogi Berra Museum on the campus of Montclair State University. I was on the museum's board of directors and doing PR for the museum, so I was there. Ted was in a wheelchair at this point, but no less boisterous—profane and opinionated as ever. It was actually a joy to see—a man unbound by any rules, basking in the attention. (He famously never wore a necktie.) It had to be a burden for him to travel, but Yogi had gone to his Hitters Hall of Fame in Florida, so this was sort of a home-and-home reciprical agreement.

I was in the lobby of the Otesaga Hotel in Cooperstown around that time when Williams, in his wheelchair, approached Dan Duquette, then the general manager of the Red Sox. Dan extended his hand and introduced himself.

"I know who you are," Ted bellowed, as he poked his index finger into Duquette's chest. "And let me tell you something—that kid you have at shortstop—Gar-SEE-uh something, however you say it [Nomar Garciaparra]—is the *best* player the Red Sox ever developed out of their farm system."

Since Williams and later Yastrzemski came out of that system, that was indeed high praise. But I came to learn that Ted was often over-the-top in

Ted Williams visits the Yogi Berra Museum, January 11, 2000. Also in the photo are Yogi, Ed Kranepool, and Bobby Thomson.

complimenting players, which was a nice trait in its own way. He signed a baseball for a 20-year-old rookie named Johnny Bench, in 1968, and wrote, "A Hall of Famer for sure."

He was right. But he wasn't right until Bench was elected 22 years later.

When news of Ted Williams' death broke in 2001, I phoned Bowie Kuhn, whom I had assisted with his memoir and kept informed of baseball news, because he wasn't doing this new internet thing.

When I told him that Willliams' son had arranged for his body to be beheaded and frozen (in two parts) at a cryogenics lab in Arizona, he was briefly speechless, and then gave a powerful "*Good grief!*" He couldn't add anything to that, but it did capture the shock most people felt.

I wasn't there for Ted Williams' first at bat in Fenway Park in 1955 after his "retirement" or his first at bat after Korean War duty, but I absolutely love the "first at bat" of a returning hero after they are traded away. It's one of the semi-spontaneous moments, predictable yet emotional, that has always touched my heart. You can't find it in any other sport because there is no "first at bat" in football, soccer, basketball, or hockey. It's a solitary moment that includes a public address introduction and the beauty of the standing ovation and outpouring of love. If you could put those all together in a single video, I would be on line to buy it.

One that comes to mind was the return of Tino Martinez to the Yankees. He had gone to St. Louis as a free agent after the 2001 season, having collected four world championship rings after succeeding Don Mattingly at first base. His grand slam in the 1998 World Series had Yankee Stadium rocking—and oh, that place could rock. It may have been its loudest moment.

So now he wore a Cardinals uniform. It was June 13, 2003, and the Cardinals were in Yankee Stadium to face Roger Clemens.

Tino, batting seventh as the DH, followed Edgar Renteria to bat in the second inning. Excitement was building—the fans wanted to show Tino the love.

But wait!

Renteria struck out swinging. And it was the 3,000th strikeout of Clemens' career! Oh no!

The announcement went up on the scoreboard, the game was stopped, and the ovation was for Clemens! Tino was robbed!

But Yankees fans know how to react. They knew they owed him one. Martinez came up again in the top of the fourth. No distraction this time, and the ovation came pouring out of the seats. "The multitide," was the term Ernest Thayer used in *Casey at the Bat*. Tino stepped out, waved his helmet, and acknowledged the 55,214 fans, who needed no prompting for this second chance of a welcome home. Clemens let the moment play out, and then "bade the game go on." (Thanks, Ernest.) It was one of those beautiful baseball moments.

You never had this with Ruth or Gehrig, DiMaggio or Rizzuto, Berra or Mantle, Murcer or Munson, Mattingly or Bernie Williams or Jeter. They never came back to Yankee Stadium as an opponent.

One can only imagine this small ritual playing out for them. The curtain call of a lifetime. Willie Mays had it when he returned to the Bay Area for the 1973 World Series. Albert Pujols when he returned to St. Louis. And only baseball offers it.

On the other side of the coin, imagine if Aaron Judge had opted to join the San Francisco Giants after the 2022 season. It was close to happening. The Giants were the Yankees' opponent for the 2023 home opener at Yankee Stadium. I would suggest that 50,000 fans booing the defending MVP would have been memorable, to say the least.

A different sort of moment came on Opening Day of 2010, when the Yankees from their world championship team of 2009 received their World Series rings.

By good fortune, Hideki Matsui, who was now with the Los Angeles Angels, was present as an Angel (his Yankees contract having expired) and was called out of the visitor's dugout for his ring. (He was MVP of the '09 Series.). So, this was more than just announcing him as "now batting;" it was summoning him from the dugout. That resulted in a fabulous ovation because the fans just loved Matsui for the way he carried himself, the way he approached the game, and the dignity he had on the field. His teammates loved him as well, especially Jeter, so it was a great moment for both the fans and the Yankees players when he came out of the Angels dugout for his ring. The Yankees players took turns embracing him, as odd as it was to see him in his Angels uniform. (This was recalled for me by the return of Freddie Freeman to Atlanta in June 2022, where Freeman, having moved on to the Dodgers as a free agent, received his ring on his first return home before a loving crowd.)

Matsui was certainly one of my favorite modern Yankees, and he seemed so genuinely touched when I met him at a press event at Mickey Mantle's Restaurant (for his Japanese language autobiography) and wore my Matsui T-shirt. He asked his father to take a picture of us.

My wife once brought home an English-language Asian newspaper that included an interview with Matsui. He talked about his admiration and appreciation for Yankee Stadium...but said that he was shocked to see players spitting tobacco or depositing gum onto the field. To him, it was a sign of disrespect.

Hideki Matsui did a press conference for his autobiography at Mickey Mantle's Restaurant, and he loved that I wore appropriate clothing to the event.

When Hideki was getting married, he drew a picture of his wife for the writers because he didn't want her photo to be published. He drew a stick figure like you make when you play hangman, complete with stick figure strands of hair.

The chewing tobacco issue has long lingered over baseball, no more so than in recent decades when it has been characterized with smoking tobacco as a health hazard. The baseball cards of Nellie Fox, Rocky Bridges, and Don Zimmer seemed to glamourize it. Joe Garagiola Sr. made it a central cause in his kit of causes, and once he took it up and spread the word to clubhouses, it greatly helped reduce its use.

Its reduction has not only made players healthier but has contributed to baseball fields looking better. There was a time when by September there were bare patches visible in the outfield; it was not a good look.

Groundskeeping technology has since improved, but the absence of outfielders spewing tobacco juice where they stand, or hitters spitting near the on-deck circle, has also made the fields look much better.

When Joe found a cause, he was always all-in and relentless. What a gift he was to baseball for his wisdom, his broadcasting work, his role in starting the Baseball Assistance Team (B.A.T.) to help baseball industry people in need, and his writing (*Baseball is a Funny Game*), which helped win over many new fans for the game.

For a number of years until the event was set aside, I was on the B.A.T. dinner committee, a great honor. We met monthly at the MLB offices, and I loved the company of the other baseball people. My personal highlight was in 2012, when the annual dinner honored the 50th anniversary of the New York Mets. I had a special request and Joe Grippo, the charity's director, honored it. I got to sit with Choo Choo Coleman, an original Met, a catcher whom Casey Stengel said was good at catching low pitches. In 1963 (their second season), he played 106 games without managing to hit a double or a triple. With Casey Stengel managing the original Mets, I couldn't help but notice them. They were awful, and Choo Choo was awful, but yet…it was hard to turn away. I loved his name, loved how he

It was an honor to sit with original Met Choo Choo Coleman at a B.A.T. (Baseball Assistance Team) dinner.

ran, loved the interviews with Ralph Kiner, and it was wonderful to be there with him a few years before he died. When the Mets retired Keith Hernandez's number 17 in 2022, in my own mind I knew it was really Choo Choo's number that was being retired.

Baseball Is a Funny Game, pubished in 1960, spent 13 weeks on the *New York Times* bestseller list. It was the fourth baseball book to make the list, starting with *The Babe Ruth Story* (1948), *Fear Strikes Out: The Jim Piersall Story* (1955), and Jim Brosnan's *The Long Season* (1960). I have been the keeper of the list since a long research project in cooperation with a Book Review editor at the *Times* in 2005. In recent years, the number of entries has dwindled. The all-time bestseller is George Will's *Men at Work*, which spent 35 weeks on the list in 1990.

(Despite my hard work on this, I never made the list. I missed by one ranking having my *Munson* book make it in 2009. I thought I deserved extra credit for all the work assembling the list, but hey, it was the *New York Times*; I couldn't cheat.) As of 2022, there have been 89 best-selling baseball books since the *Times* started its list in 1935. If you eliminate New York or Boston as themes, 47 books come off the list.

The Yankees had a player in the '80s named Rod Scurry, a good guy by all accounts, but someone who had serious alcohol and drug problems.

People are fallible, and this can happen in all professions. But, of course, when your picture is also on a bubble gum card, the spotlight is brighter.

I remember Scurry facing his alcoholism openly, and I'll never forget his quote in the newspapers: "I used to drink two six-packs a night; now I'm down to one."

Two six-packs a night? Who could stay awake through that? Who could afford that? Eighty-four cans of beer a week?

Poor Rod died at 36 in 1992, following an altercation with police who tried to quiet him after he complained about snakes crawling over him and biting him in his home. He became violent and died of a heart attack. Let us not speak ill of the dead.

But I can't get two six-packs a night out of my head.

We had a Yankees pitcher in the '70s who was a good friend of mine; an easygoing, generous person with a great smile.

I would hear, however, that when he was taken out of a game after a bad outing, he would absolutely destroy the clubhouse, inflicting serious damage to lockers, equipment, and personal items.

You never knew what monsters lay beneath the surface.

Substance abuse among the players seems to have subsided for now, at least until the next round of undetectable enhancements appear. We can easily see into a player's mind on this subject—*Yeah, I might get caught, I might get suspended, but this stuff is making me millions of dollars—I'm not sure if I can compete at this level without it!* And so it goes.

You might not think that the word *marijuana* appears in 1940s baseball, and like me, you might think it was limited to jazz musicians.

But when the Yankees lost the 1940 pennant to Detroit, interrupting what might have ultimately been eight pennants in a row (1936–43), manager Joe McCarthy gathered the Yankees beat writers in his office after the last game. What happened next was told to me by John Drebinger, the esteemed *New York Times* reporter.

"McCarthy was distraught. And he gathered his thoughts and traced it all back to a lost second game in Cleveland on September 11, when Babe Dahlgren, the first baseman, dropped a double play throw from Crosetti, allowing the Indians to rally to a victory. A win would have put the Yankees in first place. It was a miserable rainy day, and the fans were pelting the Yankees with fruit. McCarthy was in a foul mood.

"'If Dahlgren catches that ball, we win,' said McCarthy [according to Drebby]. 'And if Dahlgren wasn't a marijuana user, he would have caught the ball!'"

What a statement. Drebinger remembered it even though no one wrote about it. It wasn't intended to be quoted.

Dahlgren, Lou Gehrig's successor at first base, saw his career skid downhill. Ultimately, according to his son and grandson, he was blackballed out of the game. He had been the first baseman on the 1939 Yankees, one of the greatest teams in history. Now, he was hanging on with the lowly Braves, Cubs, Browns, Dodgers, and Pirates. The lingering suspicion apparently followed him.

His grandson, Matt, wrote a book about Babe called *Rumor in Town*, and while he was researching it, he came upon me and I told him the story. A light bulb went on. A family mystery seemed solved.

Matt assured me that his grandfather was simply not the sort to experiment with such a far-reaching idea. But the power of McCarthy was sufficient to derail Babe's career.

Drebinger was born around the time of Casey Stengel (1891). He joined the *Times* in 1923, covering the opening of Yankee Stadium and all World Series games from 1929 to 1963, writing the lead story on the games for all those years, all of them on Page 1. When I joined the Yankees in 1968, he was still on the scene, having been given a sweet job on our PR staff to be present at home games and to maintain a box score on Old Timers' Day. It may have been a reward of sorts for being such a loyalist for all those years when the closeness of writers to teams made them almost family. Seldom was heard a discouraging word.

Drebby was indeed a character, and when I was writing my first book on the Hall of Famers, he graciously lent me (without my asking) all his *Who's Who in Baseball* books back to the '20s. And oh, did he have stories, including his own story of a cross-country family trip by covered wagon.

He wore a hearing aid and could conveniently turn down the volume on it so he didn't have to suffer through the stories told by others if they didn't interest him.

One memory I have of him was a game in April 1970. President Nixon had expanded the unpopular Vietnam War by sending U.S. troops into Cambodia. This outraged a lot of people in the growing anti-war column, including George Vecsey, who was covering the Yankees for the *Times*—Drebby's old seat, so to speak.

During the national anthem that day, George did not plan on standing. This offended Drebby's sense of propriety, and while the anthem was being played, George moved to the press box lavatory to hide out. Bob Fishel had told him that John, having heard that George didn't stand, was looking for him and was going to swat him with a rolled-up newspaper. All newspapers were hefty weapons when rolled up in those days. That's no longer the case.

But we all moved on.

Drebinger's generation of writers would ultimately give way to a younger collection of scribes. A group of them were known as "Chipmunks" because they were more aggressive in their questioning and some thought they looked like overly eager chipmunks, based on Phil Pepe's pronounced overbite. *Newsday*, then an aggressive daily published in Long Island, was the first to tell baseball teams, *We will pay for our own travel, pay for our own meals, and write what the day brings; not to be confined by team boundaries.* Interestingly (was it the Long Island water?), most of the last surviving baseball writers of the early '60s in New York—Vecsey, Steve Jacobson, Joe Donnolly, and Joe Gergen—all worked at *Newsday*.

Dick Young of the *Daily News* emerged as the "star" of that next generation, and while he was hard-hitting and almost intimidating to a young publicist, he always took our calls and always heard us out. As he grew closer with management (and they to him), he moved from being a champion of liberty to a solid conservative in the owner's corner and had a hand in running Tom Seaver off the Mets when he sided with M. Donald Grant, the Mets' president. (I received the Dick Young Award in 1991 for long and meritorious service to baseball.)

But a seminal moment in journalism occurred in the mid-70s, before Young helped run Seaver out of town.

The *Washington Post* reporters Bob Woodward and Carl Bernstein had helped to show Nixon the door with their groundbreaking journalism that uncovered the Watergate scandals.

It is not a stretch to say that "Woodstein" became heroes to journalists throughout all sections of newspapers, and that included sports.

One such reporter was Murray Chass of the *Times*. Murray (followed by Moss Klein of the *Newark Star Ledger*) basically said, "Keep your press releases and daily press notes—we'll find our own news and report it as such."

This coincided with the emerging move toward free agency by the players, and the growing power of Marvin Miller and the Players Association. Chass, among others, gave Miller ample space to be heard in the paper and suddenly, readers were no longer reading notes about Bat Day being scheduled for Saturday. More serious stuff was being reported, and the style took hold. Covering sports was no longer just about scores. A new era, which we are still in a half-century later, had emerged.

A little "usage" note from me. One of my pet peeves is use of the term "the late" in writing about a person now deceased. Sometimes you will see a sentence like, "The late Hank Aaron broke Babe Ruth's career home record in 1974."

Wrong! He wasn't "the late" when he did it! Do we say the light bulb was invented by the late Thomas Edison? Or the late Abraham Lincoln issued the Emancipation Proclamation? You even see it in photo captions—"left to right are Tony Kubek, Bobby Richardson, and the late Moose Skowron." Hello? Moose is very much alive in the picture.

People, can we agree on usage here?

Billy Crystal is a terrific student of baseball, and when he produced and directed the acclaimed HBO film *61** (about the Maris-Mantle home run race of 1961), he hired my friend Andy Strasberg to be his "Maris consultant" and me to be his "Mantle consultant." He wanted to get everything perfect, and I was of course thrilled to be a part of that much honored project.

One of things my assignment entailed was reading the script, written by Hank Steinberg. I was to make any factual corrections in the attempt to get it perfect. Baseball fans would notice.

Early on, I noticed the character of Bob Cerv in a spring training scene. Cerv was an outfielder on the club and actually shared an apartment with Mantle and Maris in Queens during the '61 season. But he wasn't in spring training! He had rejoined the team in May, traded from the Angels, after the Yankees had lost him in the expansion draft following the 1960 season.

So, I attached a yellow sticky note to the page and pointed out the timing error with Cerv. (Cerv was played by the actor Chris Bauer; Mantle and Maris were played brilliantly by Thomas Jane and Barry Pepper.)

Well, a few weeks later, a revised script arrived from Ross Greenburg, Billy's co-producer and the head of HBO Sports. The script still had Cerv in spring training!

I was happy to serve as a consultant to Billy Crystal's film *61** (shown here at a screening with co-producer Ross Greenberg on the right).

So, I attached another sticky note, but the script wasn't changed. "We needed to establish the character," Billy explained to me. "That was the best place to do it."

I could live with that.

I took my daughter to the premiere and the cast party. I briefed her for the moment I would introduce her to Billy.

"Hello Deb, so nice to meet you," said Billy (whose own daughter played Maris' wife.) "How did you like the movie?"

Deb, an accomplished school play actress, didn't miss a beat.

"Well," she said, "when I saw Bob Cerv in spring training, I had trouble focusing on the rest of the film."

So, we got a good laugh, and a great memory of Billy came of it, which made the whole set up worth it.

I spent a good part of the cast party talking to the actor who played Ralph Houk. It was Bruce McGill, who has had a long and successful career in Hollywood, but who to me will always be D-Day, from National Lampoon's Animal House. We talked about how that movie never seems to make the cut in lists of greatest films of all time, and he agreed, not because he was in it, but because comedies are seldom taken seriously on such lists.

I was also a consultant on the ESPN miniseries *The Bronx is Burning*, based on a book by Jonathan Mahler. It was about the 1977 Yankees and other news events of the time like the Son of Sam murders. I was actually

I was a consultant to the ESPN miniseries *The Bronx Is Burning*, and I got to turn back the clock 30 years and play myself (left) in the scene depicting the signing of Reggie Jackson press conference. Daniel Sunjata played Reggie.

listed as a consulting producer in the credits (with Jimmy Breslin, Steve Jacobson, Fran Healy, and Graig Nettles), and they asked me if I wanted to play myself, 30 years younger, in the press conference scene when the Yankees announced the signing of Reggie Jackson.

They put me in a '70s style suit, and there I was at my seat at the dais in the Americana Hotel (now the Sheraton Centre), somehow pulling this off. I did have some lines at the podium, but they were cut.

John Turturro played Billy Martin, and I heard a lot of complaints about how his prosthetic ears were much too big—but that was accurate, and I have a picture of me and Billy and me and Turturro to prove it! I sent the photos to anyone who wrote to me about it.

Erik Jensen, who played Munson, really picked my brain for every nuance of Thurman's movements, speech, etc. We became friends and went to some Yankees games together.

I was on the set in Connecticut for a couple weeks while they filmed clubhouse and field scenes. To my surprise, the extra playing third base in the game action scenes was Jeffrey Maier, famous as the 13-year-old kid who reached over the wall in a 1996 playoff game at Yankee Stadium to grab the ball (which otherwise might have been caught) and give Derek Jeter a home run. This was a decade later and Jeffrey had gone on to play ball for his Wesleyan University college team. I also spoke with a quiet actor from the project who had a very small part and was sitting off to the side in the stands—but I recognized him as Alan Ruck, who was Ferris'

John Turturro as Billy Martin in *The Bronx Is Burning*. A lot of people thought his ears were too exaggerated.

But here is the real Billy with me at a press conference.

friend Cameron in *Ferris Bueller's Day Off*. (Ruck went on to play one of the Roy sons in the hit series *Succession*. That's the acting profession. If you're not seen as a star, you fill in with small, extra roles between jobs.)

A memorable scene for me was one in which Oliver Platt, playing George Steinbrenner, unexpectedly enters the clubhouse and screams, "BILLY!" Off on the side, I jumped at the familiar sound of that scream, and Platt told me when he saw me flinch he knew he had it right.

I had one other screen experience.

Long before distributors and the general public turned away from him following allegations of abuse, I had a chance to be an extra in a Woody Allen movie, and in three days, I learned a lot about the film business. It all feels tempered today by the allegations, but at the time, it was a remarkable experience.

When I worked at WPIX, it was necessary for me to read all the many broadcast industry trade publications, one of which was the famous *Variety*, which was the *Sporting News* of show business

As I was reading *Variety*, I came upon a very small ad that read, "Extras needed for new Woody Allen film." And it gave the contact information for the casting office. It was the fall of 1984.

Well, this was for me.

I wrote to the casting office, said I was not in SAG, the Screen Actors Guild, nor was I an actor, but I was a fan of his films and would love to do this. And I was hired!

The film was *The Purple Rose of Cairo*, one of his classic ones, and not only did I report for work for three days at $30 a day, but I was plucked out of line to be a stand-in for the actor who played the maitr'd at the "Copa" nightclub, so that they could set the lighting to my movements. It seemed I was the right height, and they didn't care that I wasn't in SAG.

That was the day I came to understand the importance of lighting directors, which came in handy when I married Lourdes, whose father was a lighting director in the Philippine film industry!

I learned that day the importance of the cinematographer, and in this case it was Oscar-winner Gordon Willis, who did eight Woody movies, and had also filmed the three *Godfather* movies and *All the President's Men*.

"My" scene was shot upstairs in a vacant Times Square building, the same location from which the legendary Camel cigarette ad blew smoke rings onto the street below.

I was outfitted in a tuxedo, as I was one of the extras in the nightclub, and there during my three days were the legendary Van Johnson (whose film career went back to the '40s,), Ed Herrmann, Danny Aiello, Jeff Daniels, Dianne Wiest, Milo O'Shea, Zoe Caldwell, and Karen Akers. Woody's girlfriend Mia Farrow also came by, although she wasn't in this scene. She brought her son, Moses, and I watched as Woody awkwardly tried to amuse the boy by taking off his glasses and pretending to drop them on the floor and stomp on them. In another Woody movie, I actually saw that scene repeated, with an actor playing young Woody as the victim.

I didn't communicate with Woody, but he did direct me, putting his hands on my shoulders and moving me around the way he wanted the real actor (Eugene Anthony) to move. Anthony tap danced in the scene; I restrained myself. (Neither of us went on to a long career in cinema.) I had never even been in a school play.

At one break during the shooting, an assistant brought Woody the poster art for his soon-to-be-released film, *Broadway Danny Rose*, for his approval. It was just a picture of an office door in a 1940s looking building that had the title painted on the glass. Woody initialed it, giving his approval, and said to his assistant, "Think they'll get this in Kansas?"

As for the scene itself, I was just supposed to sit at my seat at a table for four, pretending to eat my dinner. I was, regretfully, seated behind a potted palm and undetectable in the scene. I got to hear the assistant director yell "cut!" (Woody never raised his voice), and it was because I had turned around to watch the scene being shot instead of eating my pretend soup behind the potted palm.

So that was my Woody adventure, and all these years later, I am happy that I did it. And if you look up *Purple Rose of Cairo* in the IMDB.com directory of films, there I am in the credits as "restaurant patron."

Billy Martin, who outdid his natural talents during his 1950s run with the Yankees, wore the Yankees uniform like frat boys wear their fraternity jackets. He said he was the proudest Yankee and that may well have been true.

He was managing the Texas Rangers when they came to Yankee Stadium in early summer of 1975, and I received word that he wanted to see me in the Rangers clubhouse.

I had only met Billy a few times. The first time was when he came to spring training in Fort Lauderdale as a broadcaster for a Minneapolis radio station after the Twins had let him go as a manager. I helped get some Yankees lined up for him to interview.

One spring training, Bob Fishel agreed to go fishing with him and Texas owner Brad Corbett. This could not have been comfortable for Bob, who was definitely not the fishing type and probably wore a tie and sports jacket on the boat. (He once met Yankees president Michael Burke for breakfast in a suit and tie on a Fort Lauderdale beach.)

On that fishing outing, amazingly, Billy said to Bob—with his boss, Brad Corbett, right there!—"The one thing I'd really like to do, Bob, is manage the Yankees one day."

But that was Billy.

So, I went to the clubhouse as requested, and in the manager's small office, Billy asked me why he wasn't invited to Old Timers' Day.

I had the answer. Gabe Paul, our team president, had told me not to invite anyone who was managing or coaching other teams, so as not to create an issue for them taking time off.

Billy proceeded to almost beg for the invitation. It really meant a lot to him. So I told him I would revisit the matter with Gabe and impress on him how important it was to him. He was satisfied—nearly.

"And don't forget Charlie Silvera," he said, motioning toward his coach, who was a longtime Yankees bullpen catcher.

(Silvera earned five World Series rings from his time as Yogi Berra's backup—and got into one World Series game.)

I went to Gabe and told him about Billy's heartfelt request (and the request to include Silvera), but Gabe was adamant about not disrupting baseball with Old Timers' Day invitations. So there was no invitation for Billy and Charlie.

Fast-forward a few weeks.

Billy got fired by Texas and Mr. Steinbrenner dispatched Gabe to hunt him down in Colorado. (Oddly, Billy didn't seem anxious to be found.) With great reluctance, Gabe offered Billy the job, and it was agreed that he would be announced on—guess when?—Old Timers' Day. The incumbent manager, Bill Virdon, would be fired the night before.

I had a thousand things to do for Old Timers' Day, but I did need to connect with Billy about our announcement, about meeting the press, and about general procedures. When I saw him before the ceremonies, he winked at me and said, "I told you I'd be here."

One of the things I actually worried about was introducing Billy last— after DiMaggio!—and how that might play with Joe. But it was fine—a special exception. He did, however, roll his eyes when I told him the news.

(DiMaggio sort of tolerated Billy; they had that Italian heritage thing going, although Billy was part Portugese, and Joe just sort of tolerated all those people, like Mantle, who were a generation younger. Somehow, when Joe was dating Marilyn Monroe and doing pregame television shows for the Yankees, Billy got away with the audacity of hanging a nude *Playboy* centerfold of Marilyn in his locker, which he would proceed to imaginatively seduce when Joe walked by.)

Billy came to like me because of my knowledge of Yankees history and his time as a player and because I scored points with him by having the respect and friendship of Mantle and Ford. He sat with me on flights and asked me about each of the writers who covered us—he wanted to know their personal likes and dislikes. For instance, when I told him Red Foley (*Daily News*) smoked cigars, he came in the next day with a box of cigars for Red. Billy could be a good politician.

I once suggested to Whitey that I felt like Billy competed with him to be Mickey's best friend, and Whitey laughed and said, "Oh, absolutely."

I was never going to part of Billy's inner circle—the people who went out with him after games, drank heavily, and visited all the hot clubs. But I never pretended to want that, so we had no issues between us over postgame plans. I was going to be a total professional around him, and that seemed to work. (I knew he had punched out the traveling secretaries, Howard Fox in Minnesota and Burt Hawkins in Texas, so I was going to be especially cautious.)

When I think of Billy Martin today, I think that he may be the most famous baseball personality not in the Hall of Fame (excepting Pete Rose and the steroid users). The fact that George Steinbrenner arranged for him to be buried near Babe Ruth showed the indisputable affection the Boss had for Billy, despite firing him five times. There was certainly something magnetic about Billy's personality—people wanted to be in his inner circle, wanted to be liked by him—and then were ready with an absolute blanket of pity and sadness each time he was sacked. Who accomplishes this?! Billy was indeed a unique person, and he certainly knew how to work a room.

Part of the Billy–Casey Stengel legend is the story of Billy getting traded to Kansas City in 1957 and Casey not halting the trade and to "have his back." After all, Casey had managed him in the minors and with the Yankees, and they had been to so many World Series together. He was, as it says on his plaque in Monument Park, "Casey's Boy." For a long time after the trade, Billy would not speak to Casey.

To Casey, who was traded four times, it was pretty simple. It came down to "this is the profession he chose—people get traded or released or optioned every day. Tell him to grow up."

Part of the reason behind the 1957 trade was that the Yankees had Bobby Richardson ready to take over full-time at second base. And Billy went to Bobby that same day and said, "The job is yours—and you'll be great. Wear that uniform with pride."

I liked Bobby's baseball cards of 1957 (when Casey picked him for the All-Star team) and 1958, and by 1959 (when he hit .301), I decided he was going to be my favorite player.

Not long after that, *Sport* magazine posted a short notice about fan clubs, and I spotted one for Bobby run by Candy and Jimmy Lindstrom of New Jersey. So, I wrote to them, got a membership card, and I was in. No written exam.

Why Bobby? Everyone in my Maspeth, Queens, neighborhood had Mantle as "favorite," and I wanted my own guy. Soon I had a paper hanging in my room where I would keep track of his daily—and lifetime—statistics. Imagine updating lifetime statistics each day with an eraser and pencil.

Bobby came to know his fan club members. He took a genuine interest. In our periodic mailings would come a little religious tract, which my mother looked at with wonder. After all, we were a Jewish household, if not particularly religious. To Bobby, this reenforced his decision to be a baseball player—and to use it to help spread the gospel. To me, it wasn't going to change my religion (I was all in on Koufax when it came to that), but I did respect him for what he was doing. I thought it was admirable.

I wrote him a fan letter and still remember my thrill at receiving a postcard from him—"Dear Marty, Really appreciated your letter, Sincerely, Bobby Richardson." When I later answered Mantle's fan mail, I never forgot how important that response was on the receiving end.

Early in 1962, Candy and Jimmy announced a contest to pick the game in which Bobby would get his 100th hit of the season. To me, it was simple. I saw him as a 200-hit guy, even though no Yankee had done that since Rizzuto in 1950. So, I sent back my entry and picked the 81st game—the halfway point of the season.

Well, as it would happen, he got his hundredth hit in the 81st game. I nailed it. My prize was to meet Bobby at Yankee Stadium and to receive an autographed ball.

I didn't get a picture that day, but I did get the baseball, and I was thrilled that Bobby actually knew me. I guess he was briefed before our meet and greet (next to the stands), but he really did seem to know who I was and that I was in the fan club. And this was the first time I ever stood that close to a player in uniform. The pinstripe flannel uniform was almost as memorable as the guy wearing it!

Bobby retired after the 1966 season with five Gold Gloves and eight All-Star selections. I started my job in the PR department in 1968. I wrote to Bobby in South Carolina to tell him that the kid in his fan club was now working for the team.

To Bobby's great credit, we rekindled our friendship as adults. I was no longer the fan club kid; I was now a club employee. And I became his principal contact at the Yankees over my time there. I looked out for him. He would call me for advice on accepting an appearance or an award. When the rebuilt Yankee Stadium opened in 1976, I reached out to him for delivery of a benediction in the opening ceremonies. As we aged, the conversations became even more mature and freewheeling. As I bemoaned the fact that baseball had become homers, walks, and strikeouts in the 2010s, he would say, "Well, there would be no place for me today."

Actually, there might have been. He could hit to all fields and there would be no overshifts. And much as I ignore many SABR statistics, "exit velocity" makes some sense to me. Because if you hit the ball hard, using your forearms, you're going to get your hits. There are lots of players who

Two who wore No. 1: Bobby Murcer (left) and Bobby Richardson.

can hit the ball at high velocity between infielders. The old line to someone batting for the first time—"swing hard, in case you make contact"—is quite true. It's unnoticed for the most part, but strong forearms (like Bill Virdon's and Joe Girardi's, who were always flexing them), can get the job done, even if you're not hitting them over the fence. Scouts often look at the forearms of a prospect to help them make a judgment on potential, particularly after the 1980s, when it became standard on a baseball player, steroid use or not. Most players worked with weights then.

(Monte Irvin told me power hitters see their strength fading when their best shots no longer clear the fence. Singles hitters could just go on forever.)

Bobby and I talked about pitcher Jordan Montgomery, who came from Bobby's hometown of Sumter. Bobby knew Jordan's grandfather. And in Jordan's Yankees debut I did a little play-by-play over the telephone for the first inning as Bobby sat on his porch and listened.

The signed baseball from 1962? I had him sign it on two other occasions, once when he drove with his son to have lunch with me in Atlanta in 1992, and again a decade later when we were both speakers at a program in lower Manhattan.

To Bobby's credit, he could follow biblical teachings and maintain his religious beliefs while still forming friendships in the Yankee clubhouse without casting aspersions on anyone's lifestyle. Mantle, certainly not as clean living as Richardson was, especially loved Bobby, and had Bobby visit him in his final days to make his peace with the lord. Bobby was a eulogist at Mickey's ESPN-televised funeral in Dallas. He served that role for a number of teammates.

We developed a little ritual over the years. I started to call him the day after the World Series ended each year to congratulate him on his record of 12 RBIs in a Series still standing. That record is remarkable in that he only had 26 RBIs in the regular season, and the home run to left field in Yankee Stadium (a grand slam, no less) was something he accomplished only that once. He hit it off Clem Labine, an old Brooklyn Dodgers foe who was now pitching for Pittsburgh. He was a singles hitter, and he was as amazed as anyone by the outburst of run production that day batting seventh in the lineup. He had six RBIs in that grand slam game, and that record for one game stood alone for 49 years until it was tied by Hideki Matsui in 2009.

As this is being written, his record of 12 in a series has stood for 62 years. He knows when his phone rings the day after the Series ends, it's me, and we're going to "toast" the record lasting another year.

He won the MVP award in that World Series and remains the only player on a losing team to ever win it since it was first presented in 1955 to Johnny Podres. The award was a Corvette—not really a Bobby kind of car, since he had a growing family to transport and they couldn't all fit. So, he traded it in for a more practical car, but the Corvette itself continued to have life. As it moved from owner to owner, it was always known to be "Bobby's car" and he would get notified of its new home from time to time. It took on a life of its own in that sense.

How did he win MVP instead of Bill Mazeroski, whose homer in the last of the ninth gave the Pirates the win?

Fishel explained it to me, and I explained it to Bobby, who did not know this. In those days, all the writers covering the Series voted on the award, which was given by *Sport* magazine, and supervised by the magazine's editor, Ed Fitzgerald.

The writers, however, had to vote in the eighth inning, because then they had to descend down to the clubhouse of the winning team. So, the outcome could not be affected or changed by whatever happened in the ninth inning.

That's not the procedure anymore; it's now decided by a "committee" of writers and officials, a more manageable number of people, who don't have to seal the ballot after eight innings.

There was one other notable thing about Bobby's 1960 selection. For the first 11 years of the award, he was the only position player to receive it. All the others were pitchers. And in the first 15 years of the award, it was only Bobby and Frank Robinson.

He also holds the record for most consecutive World Series games played—30, between 1960–64. This record, of course, requires that your team be in the Series, but it's the Cal Ripken record for World Series, which is pretty cool.

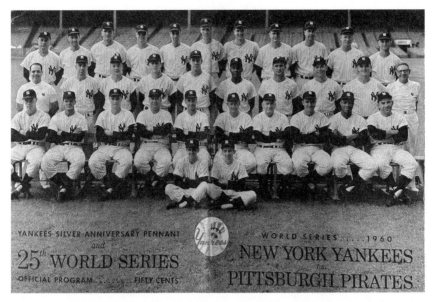

The 1960 Yankees World Series program, with the hint of a missing space in the front row for the absent Bobby Richardson, who organized the photo shoot.

One of the funniest stories Bobby ever told me was that he was the team's player representative in 1960 (usually the most responsible guy on the team), and one of his tasks that year was to organize a team photo for use on the World Series program cover. It was to spread across the whole

They didn't miss the photo, but Lefty Gomez and Babe Ruth (center) arrived late for the 1932 team picture and only managed to throw on a jersey and hustle into the group. No visible belt or uniform pants. Where could they have been?

back and front covers, with everyone in long-sleeve sweatshirts (a look that I loved). Bobby spent days posting notices and reminding everyone of the photo shoot—a "must be there!" moment, given the importance of its use.

Come the day of the shoot, Bobby forgot and missed the photo. There is even the suggestion of his being missing by a small space in row one. "It was really embarrassing," he admitted.

That could be the counter argument to his being in the front row in the Yankees 1955 photo. At 19, he played 11 games for the Yankees that year and had four singles, spending most of the season at Denver. He wasn't part of the World Series roster. But he was there the day they shot the team photo, and Rizzuto pulled him along to sit between him and coach Frankie Crosetti in row one.

"That was embarrassing in a different way," he said. "I didn't really belong."

On the subject of records, in case you haven't noticed, not many records get broken anymore. Why? Well, when Major League Baseball was 20 years old, it wasn't hard to have the "best ever" in 20 seasons. The theory still worked for 40 or 50 years. But now with MLB considered to be some 150 years old, it's not easy to be the best ever in 150 seasons. So, we've pretty much settled into a period now where we see a lot of "best since," or "record since expansion," or qualifiers like that. "Only the fourth player to…" is another example.

In the early '60s we had Roger Maris breaking Babe Ruth's home run record, then Whitey Ford breaking Ruth's consecutive shutout innings record in the World Series, then Maury Wills breaking Ty Cobb's stolen base record, and it was exciting that these things were still possible. Later on, Hank Aaron and Pete Rose took down lifetime Ruth and Cobb records in homers and hits. Those were exciting times, for sure. So, it's nothing more than pure math that is depriving us of that now.

Imagine trying to set a new record when the game passes its second century. Good luck. It will be more likely you will see announcements of "becoming only the 14th player in team history to…."

The steroid-induced home run records are obviously tainted. Will someone break Nolan Ryan's single season strikeout mark or his record of seven no-hitters? It's unlikely now with starting pitchers getting only 33 or 34 starts and lasting only six or seven innings. Rickey Henderson's stolen base records? Unlikely, given the way the game is played today. But it was sure fun while we had it.

Most people in baseball in the '50s to the '80s would agree that Bob Lemon was as likable a fellow as was in the game. Everyone loved Lem (who told me to call him Lemon so he could call me Apple, the frequent mispronunciation of my name.)

I always wondered why managing jobs hadn't come along earlier for Lem, who certainly proved to be a fine manager, taking the 1978 Yankees to a world championship. Mostly he let the players play, he didn't overmanage, and he certainly kept things calm in the Bronx Zoo era, after Billy Martin had stirred things up so turbulently. He said he never took the game home with him.

"I'd usually leave it at a tavern on the way home," he said.

Not many pitchers become managers, largely because their focus on pitching kept their eyes off other parts of the game. Lemon, though, had started as an outfielder before becoming a member of that brilliant Cleveland pitching staff of Bob Feller–Mike Garcia–Lemon–Early Wynn–Art Houtteman who won 93 of Cleveland's 111 victories in 1954 and went to the World Series. (Lem was 23–7.)

I once took my father to a sportswriters dinner at Shea Stadium, where Lem sat with George Steinbrenner at the head table. I wanted to introduce my father to them, and they both stood as we approached (Lem called him the Big Apple, a real macintosh), told him what a fine son he had, and asked him about himself and his interest in baseball. Even Mr. Steinbrenner complimented me to him. It was a special moment with my dad, made so by the graciousness of these two prominent figures at the head table.

My father said, "George Steinbrenner seems like such a nice man! What is all this stuff in the papers about hin being such a tough boss?"

Just 10 days after Lem celebrated the 1978 World Series win, he was notified that his 26-year-old son Jerry had been killed in an auto accident in Arizona.

The worst possible news that a parent could receive.

Knowing he could not get to Arizona until the following day, Lem called Joe Garagiola Sr., who lived in Phoenix, tearfully explained the news to him, and asked that Joe go to the hospital and stay with his deceased son until he could arrive, even as he was transferred to the morgue. Joe and Lem were never teammates, they were just part of the baseball community, and the act of calling on Joe (who, of course, went right to the hospital) spoke to the brotherhood of the profession.

Lem tried to manage the team in 1979, but his mind was elsewhere. Tommy John told writers he thought he was always, understandably, distracted. In June, Mr. Steinbrenner let him go, but always made sure he was on the payroll and taken care of until his own death in 2000.

I saw recently that Vito Valentinetti died at age 92. Vito was a workhorse batting practice pitcher for the Yankees and the Mets in the '70s, a really nice man who had pitched for five big league teams in the 1950s. Throwing BP was a side job for him. His "day job" was working at the Bronx County Courthouse just up the street from Yankee Stadium, which was always visible beyond the bleachers in telecasts. He was the court's purchasing agent.

Vito, a high school teammate of Whitey Ford's in Queens, would invite Fritz Peterson and me to sit in on trials in the courthouse on the mornings of night games. Fritz and I would trek up the hill and would be enthralled by the entertainment value of the trials. This was before court programs on TV became so popular. These were sometimes murder trials, like on *Perry Mason*. That was certainly an odd place to find the two of us.

Vito's fellow batting practice pitcher was the very charismatic Tony Ferraro, a former minor league player and college coach, a sometime actor and model who was one of those fellows who befriends everyone he meets. No one really knew how Tony earned a living—certainly not by throwing

BP or by acting, but he was welcome and loved everywhere. He used to take me to clothing wholesalers and fix me up with good deals, and the next thing you knew he had a part in *The Natural*, and the next thing he had a piece of a restaurant. He had a rubber arm and threw BP almost daily. Ballplayers loved him. Ron Darling and Art Shamsky of the Mets became especially close friends.

In 2007 Shamsky was a manager in the Israel Baseball League, an attempt at pro baseball in the Middle East which, sadly, only lasted one summer. (Blomberg and Ken Holtzman were also managers in the six-team league, although Holtzman quit midseason and made sure he got paid in full). I did the league's public relations, which resulted in my first trip ever to Israel. Dan Duquette was in charge of player procurement, and the rosters were loaded with Dominican players he knew about from his time as general manager of the Red Sox. My big PR coup was having one of the teams draft Sandy Koufax (then 72) with its last pick. A sure way to get attention although, of course, Sandy never played.

The league's commissioner was Daniel Kurtzer, a great baseball fan who happened to be U.S. Ambassador to Israel and to Egypt under Presidents Clinton and George W. Bush. A smart guy who became a good friend.

Shamsky suggested to Kurtzer that he'd like to bring Ferraro along to serve as his pitching coach for the Modi'in Miracle. (Sham had been on the 1969 Miracle Mets.) Don't look for it on a map, because I learned the Israeli road maps are intentionally deceptive, to confuse would-be terrorists.

So, there was Tony, and in short order, he worked his way up from coach to assistant commissioner, the No. 2 man in the whole operation.

When Tony died in 2009, many of us were shocked to learn he was 82. He was still in remarkable shape and was still throwing BP in Israel two years earlier!

A final word on the Israel Baseball League. It could have worked, but I believe they rushed into their season. I think they needed a full year to build awareness, conduct clinics, and get fans curious and engaged. As it was, there was really only one usable field in Israel (although they somehow created two others, including one with a light pole in right field). The main field (at least) needed a big-time scoreboard, which would have made them appear professional. Instead, the scoreboard looked like a hand-me-down from the Bad News Bears. We had one game shown on ESPN, but it wasn't a good representation. NBC News did a feature story on us. They completed the full season (Blomberg's team beat Shamsky's team for the championship, although Ronnie never learned the names of his players, and had his coach Eric Holtz handle that.) The league drew "crowds" that could sometimes be counted on two hands. (Holtz went on to manage the Israel team in the 2020 Olympics in Japan, which we all thought was an outgrowth of what we had begun in 2007 with the IBL.)

The guy flipping burgers at the concession stand didn't wear a shirt, and his sweat made its way into the burgers.

A film about that season called *Holy Land Hardball* was produced, and I appear in it briefly, explaining our efforts to get the Israeli media to cover our games. The reporter asked, "How did that go?" and I could only smile and say, "Not so good."

My greatest regret was that despite making sure we had an official scorer and a box score at every game (no easy feat), I couldn't get *Baseball America* to include our final stats in its 2008 Almanac. It would have meant "we were" and "we existed." It included other international leagues.

And hey, I did get to Israel, did get to see Tel Aviv and Jerusalem, and did get to a Mediterranean beach. I almost got to eat an Israel burger (without sweat) from McDonalds, but on a trip back to our hotel we stopped and Blomberg got out and brought back six Big Macs for the van…and ate them all himself.

Israel fielded a team in the qualifying round of the World Baseball Classic in 2012 in Jupiter, Florida. You needed at least one Jewish grandparent to qualify for the team, and I was again asked to again do public relations. Brad Ausmus was manager and Gabe Kapler, a player-coach. The team included Kevin Youkilis, Shawn Green, Danny Valencia, Jason Marquis, Joc Pederson, and Craig Breslow, all players with major league experience (and a Jewish grandparent). The team lost to Spain 9–7 in 10 innings, so it missed qualifying for the WBC tournament, but made it in 2017, losing to Japan after winning four out of five to get to that point in the Tokyo Dome.

I was all set to handle PR for the USA team in 2013 (Joe Torre was manager, Joe Garagiola Jr. was general manager), but there were limits to the number of people who formed "staff," and I was replaced at the last minute by a massage therapist. In the end, maybe that was a good metaphor for public relations.

Shamsky lived just a few blocks from me in mid-Manhattan and despite our Mets and Yankees DNA (he is actually from St. Louis), we became good friends and frequent lunch companions. Together Sham and I would regularly review the state of baseball, and he, like most retired players, could barely recognize the way the game had evolved. And although he was one of the few Miracle Mets of 1969 to reside in New York (Ed Kranepool and Bud Harrelson were others), he was amazed at how distant they seemed to be kept from Citi Field, which seemed to celebrate the

With Ron Blomberg and Art Shamsky in Israel for the Israel Baseball League in 2007, the first pro league in the Middle East.

Brooklyn Dodgers more than it did Mets history. (That began to change when the Mets' PR man Jay Horwitz created an alumni department and when Steve Cohen bought the club from the Wilpons.) Still, there was no 1969 representation when the Mets dedicated a Tom Seaver statue in 2022 outside Citi Field.

The thing I like to tell people about Sham is that "he was a .300 hitter on the '69 Mets, batted cleanup in the first ever World Series game at Shea Stadium, once hit four consecutive home runs…but he's just a normal human like you and me!" Which is true.

My other close friend from the National League side of town was Rusty Staub. Rusty was a unique man-of-all-seasons. Aside from his near-Hall-of-Fame career (he was seventh all-time in games played when he retired in 1985), he was a gourmet chef and wine connoisseur, owned two notable Manhattan restaurants, was deeply involved in charities (including his own foundation and a special fund for police and firefighter widows and children, for which he was the right man at the right time after 9/11), and was a special ambassador for the game of baseball.

I wanted to do a book with Rusty—he had a story unlike anyone else in the game. And he had a lot to say; very interesting observations. We hatched the idea driving back to the city after going together to sportswriter Jack Lang's funeral in Long Island in 2007.

But we couldn't find a publisher. Rusty had a firm price in mind, or he wouldn't do it (even though it would all go to his foundation). And no one was interested in the book at any price.

We even had lunch with an editor from a major publishing house who admitted to being an enormous Rusty fan. He said it was the honor of his lifetime to have lunch with Rusty. But eventually, he passed on the book.

Rusty was among the most popular players at every stop he made—Houston, Montreal (where he learned to speak French), New York, Detroit, and Texas. But no takers.

Finally, one editor confided in me that if Rusty were to reveal that he was gay, "It would be the difference between getting on *Good Morning America* or on *Cold Pizza* on ESPN."

Since he was a lifelong bachelor, suspicions followed him around. It goes with the territory.

So, I had to ask him before I prepared an outline. (Not an easy ask.)

"Nope," he said, without any disdain for the question, "but I've always heard the whispers and I know how they started." And he proceeded to tell me about some Montreal teammates who drew the assumption when he didn't join them in pursuit of Expos hostesses when he played there.

"It was my workplace," he said. "You don't do that at your workplace."

In that, he was decades ahead of his time.

Another film in which I briefly appeared was called *Up for Grabs*, and it detailed the dispute by two claimants over ownership of Barry Bonds' record-breaking 73rd home run ball. A young filmmaker named Mike Wranovics produced it and made a nice comedy out of it. Lelands was the company handling the auction, and I appear in the film as the publicist talking about it. It gave me a chance to reunite with a terrific guy, Sal Durante, who had caught Roger Maris' 61st home run at Yankee Stadium in 1961. I liked Sal and loved his story. He was a teenager who was there with his girlfriend, and he fought off others in the right field stands to catch the ball—and the $5,000 prize that went with it.

He used the money to marry his girlfriend, drove a school bus for a living, and was as regular a New York kinda guy as central casting might have produced, right down to the cigarette pack in his rolled-up white T-shirt sleeve.

In 1976, when Graig Nettles became the first Yankee since Maris to win a home run title (both wore No. 9), I called Sal and invited him to throw out the first pitch at our final home game of the regular season. (Nettles had a substantial lead and wasn't going to be caught.) Furthermore, I had Sal throw it out from the very location where he sat and caught Maris' homer. It was a nice stunt, except I forgot to get security to move with Sal, and he had trouble getting to that seat, trying all the time to explain to ushers what he was doing. But we got it done—I had Nettles run out to right field to receive the toss, and we all (Sal, Graig, and me) felt good about pulling this off.

One more thing about Roger's home run record. It remained the American League (many would say major league) record for 61 years, until No. 99, Aaron Judge, broke No. 9's mark 61 years later by hitting 62. As Judge approached 60, I found myself hoping he might finish with 61, thereby maintaining Maris's standing as the champion, albeit tied. But with the record of 60 (Ruth), 61 (Maris), and 62 (Judge), all held by Yankees right-fielders, it seemed that Roger's name would long stay in the conversation anyway. And a Seton Hall Sports Poll conducted in October 2022 found that 56 percent of sports fans across the nation found Barry Bonds' 2001 mark of 73 to be flawed and recognized Judge as the new record holder. (Only 21 percent recognized Bonds.)

It was always thought to be a record interpreted in the minds of fans anyway, and this was the first quantified proof.

Another oddity that grew from this: if indeed fans largely discounted Bonds' total (and therefore the totals of presumed steroid users Mark McGwire and Sammy Sosa), then the clean National League record holder would be Judge's teammate Giancarlo Stanton, who hit 59 for Miami in 2017, the year before he was traded to the Yankees.

Of course, we care less about league records since interleague play began in 1997.

Fourth Inning

If I couldn't run around with Billy Martin, I certainly couldn't have kept up with Mike "King" Kelly, baseball's first matinee idol. After my first book, *Baseball's Best* (biographies of all the Hall of Famers), I was so intrigued by his story that I vowed to do a full-blown biography of him one day, and for the centennial of his passing in 1995, I did. It was called *Slide, Kelly, Slide.*

"Kel" played from 1878 to 1893, achieving his greatest fame with Chicago and Boston. His sale to Boston in 1887 made him the "$15,000 Beauty," with the sale price including the right to use his image on team promotional advertising. That was probably a first, or at least the first time a player was paid for that. He was a better player in Chicago (two batting titles), but a bigger star in Boston, where he wasn't under the shadow of Cap Anson. It didn't really matter much how he played there. As he drank too much, gained weight, and got famous, he became the beloved hero of the city. He probably never paid for a drink, although he joined the Elks Lodge because it was the only place you could get a drink on a Sunday.

So popular was he, especially with the Boston Irish, that they presented him with a house! And while it probably was well mortgaged, it was a lovely house at 507 Main Street in the southern suburb of Hingham, where a ferry service could get him to the city. Upon arriving, sometimes with a pet monkey on his shoulder, he would occasionally be carried, sultan-like, to the ballpark. (His house still stands and is beautifully maintained. I spoke there one year at the invitation of the Hingham Historical Society.)

The cultural impact of Kelly on the public was enormous, long before there was national media to draw attention to athletes. Probably only heavyweight champion John L. Sullivan (also of Boston) was better known.

The song "Slide, Kelly, Slide" was performed on the vaudeville stage (sometimes by Kel himself) before it became the first pop hit record in America after Thomas Edison invented the phonograph. Before "Slide, Kelly, Slide," all the cylinders that played on the Edison were patriotic, classical, opera, or religious.

A painting of him sliding into second hung in pretty much every pub in the city, replacing one of Custer's Last Stand.

He "authored" the games' first autobiography, *Play Ball: Stories from the Diamond Field*. While it was likely ghostwritten by the uncredited Boston writer Jack Drohan, he clearly participated with the contents and discussed his childhood in Paterson, New Jersey, where he would awaken early, take a boat to Manhattan, buy up New York newspapers, and return to Paterson, where he would sell them for a penny profit. He was not without ambition.

But where he really made a cultural mark was with autographing! Before Kelly, people knew it was nice to own a Lincoln or a Washington or a Grant signature, but the idea of spotting a celebrity in the street and running up for an autograph actually began with Kel. Kids knew his route to the ballpark and had their pencils ready.

Because they were in pencil, few of those autographs, if any, exist today. There are a few contracts signed in ink.

When I was doing the book, I called autograph expert Charles Hamilton in New York to authenticate all of this. Hamilton himself answered the phone and when I told him my tale of Kelly, he agreed that he would have been the first, and that they would have been in pencil. He thanked me for educating him about Mike Kelly.

Kelly died in 1894, at age 36 (he caught pneumonia traveling by boat to Boston for an election day stage performance), and his funeral attracted

The grave of Mike "King" Kelly at Mount Hope cemetery in Mattapan, Massachusetts.

thousands, lining the street for seven miles to his final burial place in the Elks Lodge plot at Mount Hope Cemetery in Mattapan.

I hoped the city of Boston would recognize the centennial of his death in 1994, which would help my book sales. Bad news: Boston had just elected its first Italian mayor after always reliably electing Irish ones. Thomas Menino proved to be a beloved mayor…but he had no interest in the centennial.

So I visited Kel's gravesite on the centennial and left a miniature bottle of whiskey from my flight. It felt right.

I loved doing the Kelly book—I loved the challenge of the research when there were no living people to interview. I made a brief attempt to see if there were any descendants, but good luck to me looking for descendants of Michael Joseph Kelly in Boston. Most obituaries from the time did not list any children, but one said he had a son. Could we even trust such a mention? One could picture someone at the city desk preparing the obit and calling out, "Did he have children?" and someone shouting back, "Yeah, I think he had a son." And so it made its way into that one newspaper. We rely on news accounts for history, and they usually get it right, but there will always be cases of "yeah, I think so" floating around, and suddenly, someone is writing a biography a hundred years later and this happens. Proceed with caution is all I can say.

One book that people always suggested to me was to work with Yankee Stadium public address announcer Bob Sheppard on a memoir.

Really?

After you get past "First lineup you announced?" (Mantle's first game), and "Favorite names to pronounce?" there wasn't much left.

Bob never really knew the players and actually spent a lot of time between batters catching up with the Book Review section of the *New York Times*. He was a charming, well-educated man who taught public speaking at St. John's University, but there really wasn't a book there, certainly not about the Yankees. He played baseball and football at St. John's from 1928 to '32 but was reluctant to reveal his age, despite the obvious invitation to do the math.

The background on his Yankees job, however, is of some interest. Early on, before there was an electronic public address system, the announcements were done on the field by a man with a megaphone. At Yankee Stadium, that was Jack Lenz, who was there Opening Day in 1923, and who was considered a fixture at the ballpark, notable for his girth as well as his announcements. Players teased him. The idea of using a megaphone actually continued to 1974 at Wrigley Field with Pat Pieper, who started in 1916, the third year of that charming ballpark, which was then called Weeghman Park. George Levy was Lenz's backup and successor at Yankee Stadium. For days when huge crowds were expected, they both worked, their megaphones reaching the bleachers and the upper and lower decks.

In the '40s, Yankees PA announcer Fred Sharp sat next to the visitor's dugout and had his own system, with speakers set up around the stadium. As we know from Lou Gehrig Appreciation Day in 1939 ("today...day... day, I consider myself...self...self..."), there were attempts at a PA system, even if temporary. A state-of-the-art public address system was installed in 1946, along with lights, a better scoreboard, a public restaurant, a press dining room, and a better clubhouse.

When Sheppard began, the job was not very challenging. The PA announcer would give the starting lineups and then announce pinch-hitters, pinch-runners, and relief pitchers. Even that was an outgrowth of the early days, when, armed with a megaphone, the PA people would give the starting batteries, not full lineups, and be pretty much done for the day, save for the occasional substitutions. So, you might have Jack Lenz, out behind home plate, saying, "The battery for the White Sox: Lyons and Grube, and for the Yankees: Ruffing and Dickey." He would turn toward right field and then left field and repeat his announcement. And then, his work completed, he could go off and eat a few hot dogs before any substitutes entered.

When a PA system was installed, the assignment didn't change. In fact, immediately preceding the hiring of Bob Sheppard in 1951, the Yankees public relations director Red Patterson would just have a second microphone at his seat and would make the occasional announcements. (His prime microphone was to make press box announcements, like the day's attendance.)

In the late '60s and early '70s, we made Bob Sheppard better known to the fans, including him in the Yankee Yearbook and having the broadcasters refer to him by name. And we gave him a few promotional announcements to read, such as, "The full-color, 1972 New York Yankees Yearbook is available now at souvenir stands for fifty cents." I think Bob resented this added duty, but he was quite good at correcting any grammatical errors we had in our copy. And as time evolved, we had him announce each batter every time he came to the plate. That really cut into Bob's time with the Book Review section. By the time Paul Olden succeeded him, teams were making 14 pitching changes per game, and the job became one of high concentration. No time for side reading.

Early in the 2000s, I suggested to the Hall of Fame that they record Bob reciting each member's name in a hushed tone, to be played softly and continuously in the plaque room in Cooperstown. "No. 6...Stan Musial..." They liked the idea, but it was a little too late. Bob's ability to do the recording had faded.

Sheppard lived to be nearly 100 and died the same week as George Steinbrenner. His recorded announcement of Derek Jeter's turn at bat continued as long as Jeter played. When Derek wrapped up at Fenway

Park, the Red Sox offered to use the Sheppard recording in his final game, but Derek rejected it as something belonging only to Yankee Stadium.

I went to Fenway for Derek Jeter's final game. Whether as a fan or a Yankees employee, I always loved the trips to that wonderful old ballpark of the Olde Towne Team. It was my wife who observed that the fans (as seen on TV) aren't engrossed in their phones; they actually pay attention—at least during the first half of the game.

Jeter was the DH for the Yankees that day; he wanted his final game at shortstop to be at home, and he happened to drive in a game-winning run with a single in his final at bat. He was always a man who could rise to the occasion.

My son secured two bleacher seats at Fenway early in the year, which we hoped might be his final regular season game.

That last game at Fenway was very emotional. First of all, Fenway turned into a Yankees crowd that afternoon. Red Sox fans, for whom the game was meaningless, sold or gifted their tickets to Yankees fans. Only a few Boston fans were on hand, many of them just appreciating the history

On ESPN's *Outside the Lines* with Bob Ley, the day of Derek Jeter's last game. One squirt left.

of the day. After all, Ted Williams and Carl Yastrzemski had played their final games there—as had Mickey Mantle.

That morning, I appeared on ESPN's *Outside the Lines* with Bob Ley. I went on camera holding a bottle of "Derek Jeter's Driven," an aftershave spray that everyone who had attended a Turn2 Foundation dinner (Jeter's charity) a couple years earlier had received. Remarkably, my bottle contained just one remaining squirt. It was a miracle.

Brian and I walked from his Back Bay apartment to Fenway and the crowd, largely dressed in Yankees blue, grew bigger and bigger as we approached. The pregame ceremonies were well done, and when Derek got an infield single his second time up, Joe Girardi motioned to him with a palms-up gesture: *That it? Pinch-runner?*

Jeter nodded and Brian McCann went in to pinch run. Jeter shook hands with the first baseman and stopped at the pitcher's mound. Clay Buchholz had been warming up in the bullpen during the pregame festivities and Jeter had the presence of mind to realize that he hadn't shaken hands with him. So, he paused and said, "It's been an honor to compete against you."

Jeter just got everything right. That was his upbringing and that was his style.

The Yankees fans emptied out soon after. The Yankees were not going to the postseason, and disappointing as that might have been, it meant everyone knew when Jeter's finale would be. It would not be overshadowed by an elimination game in the postseason. It was actually perfect, and remarkably, those final games of the regular season were the only ones he ever played in his whole career that didn't matter. (Those, apart from games after a playoff berth had been clinched, but even those had some home field advantage going for them.)

A few remarkable statistics stand out for me. Jeter was third all-time in postseason home runs and ninth on the all-time Yankees list in home runs—despite never being considered a real home run hitter. And his 3,465 hits ranked sixth all time, with only Pete Rose, Ty Cobb, Hank Aaron, Stan Musial, and Tris Speaker ahead of him.

He played 158 postseason games, essentially another full season against only elite teams, and batted .308 with 200 hits.

It was a gift to watch Jeter day in and day out. It was my honor to witness his entire career and what it meant to the sport.

Mickey Mantle's final time at bat, also at Fenway Park, was less dramatic than Jeter's, to say the least. He was batting only .237 in 1968, having seen his lifetime .300 mark drop to .298 during the season, a statistic pointed out to us by statistician Bill Kane of our office, who kept track of these things. Mick called dropping under .300 his greatest regret.

In September of '68, things really hit rock bottom. He was swinging for the fences on every at-bat, but he could be pitched to now, and the power was all but gone. Famously, Denny McLain grooved one for him in Detroit on September 19, and that resulting home run allowed him to pass Jimmie Foxx on the all-time list for third place. He hit another one, No. 536, the next day. It would be his last one.

Then he went 0-for-19.

He didn't announce his retirement until the following spring, so no one really knew that the weekend the Fenway game would be his farewell.

He went 0-for-3 on Friday night in a 12–2 loss in what was his 2,400th game.

On Saturday, he batted in the first inning, cracking his bat while popping up to short left field. Shortstop Rico Petrocelli pedaled back for the catch. And with that, Mick took himself out of the game, had the clubhouse man call a taxi, and went to Logan Airport for a flight home to Dallas. He was done. He would not even be present for the team's final game of the season the next day.

There was a little more to the story.

All season long, while I was handling Mickey's fan mail, the Yankees batboy Elliott Ashley had promised me a cracked bat. It could have been anyone's. But Elliott had gone to Boston for the final games, and retrieved the Mantle bat. On Monday, he came to my small office near the Yankees clubhouse and handed it to me. He remembered, and it was just my good luck that it was a Mantle bat.

I was never much of a collector, despite my surroundings. I was with Mick at his locker a few weeks earlier when he tossed a used pair of baseball spikes into the trash can 10 feet away, donned a new pair, and said, "This will be my last pair." I should have retrieved those discarded spikes, right? And I should have noted that he was essentially telling me that he was quitting, right? But I had no idea how long a pair of baseball cleats lasted.

I put that cracked Mantle bat in a case and held onto it for more than 25 years. And then it paid for my son's first year of college. Thanks, Mick, and thanks Elliott.

And as for not being much of a collector, well, Mick used to give me his gift certificates from doing television interviews. I'd redeem them, but kept whatever they produced for years, like a pair of shoes from Thom McAn.

At Mantle's locker, trying to look like I belong as much as he did.

I'm asked from time to time who I think the best manager in Yankees history was. And despite all the world championships won by Miller Huggins, Joe McCarthy, and Casey Stengel, my vote goes to Joe Torre.

I told this to Joe once and explained it, and he said, "Would you mind sending me a letter that says that?" I was surprised by the request but of course happy to do it.

You see, Joe gets the nod because, unlike the others, he had to defeat 13 other teams in his league to get to the Series; his predecessors had to beat seven. He had to win three postseason rounds. His predecessors went right to the World Series.

Unlike Huggins, McCarthy, and Stengel, he had to manage an international, multicultural roster, speaking many languages, covering many races. His players were on multiyear contracts and many made more

Joe Torre with me at the Tribeca Film Festival premiere of the Yogi Berra documentary *It Ain't Over*, 2022. Joe may be the most likeable person in the game over the last half century.

than the manager did. His every move was analyzed on sports talk radio and cable TV shows. His obligations to do pre- and postgame interviews were intense, and he had to deal with microphones in his face where every word mattered. And, oh yes, he had a very demanding boss who was famous for firing managers who didn't produce.

Miller, Joe, and Casey, for all their success, had it relatively easy.

The source for my coming up with the name Fred Sharp as a 1940s PA announcer was my special friend Tom Villante, one of the lesser-known titans of baseball.

Tom was a Yankees batboy during World War II, and McCarthy had him in mind as a future second baseman. He worked out regularly with Frank Crosetti during those batboy years. The Yankees helped pay for his college, but after he graduated, McCarthy was gone, Stengel had arrived, and Billy Martin was his guy for second base. So, Tom went into advertising and wound up producing Brooklyn Dodgers television and radio, since he headed the Schaefer Beer account ("the one beer to have when you're having more than one") and it was the team's principal sponsor.

So, he was there with Red Barber when Vin Scully broke in, became friends with the great Dodgers players (Jackie Robinson was among those at his wedding), and moved to Los Angeles with the team, since Schaefer still had broadcast rights. (No Schaefer was sold in California, so the company sublet the advertising, but Tom was still the producer.)

When he eventually went back to New York, still employed by BBDO advertising (and perhaps the model for a character on *Mad Men*), he went on to organize baseball's 1969 Centennial Celebration in Washington and its Greatest Players Ever promotion. Then he became the head of broadcasting and marketing for Major League Baseball ("Baseball Fever: Catch It").

He had so many little side accomplishments, like producing *Yogi at the Movies* and *Lasorda at Large* for commercial syndication, and, employing another skill, giving me the title for my *Pinstripe Empire* book. (He gave me about seven titles to choose from in one hour.)

Tom Villante wasn't just the Brooklyn Dodgers' broadcast producer, he was a genuine friend to those "Boys of Summer," and here he is at his wedding with Jackie Robinson and Ralph Branca in attendance.

In his nineties, he is still a fount of information, such as the Fred Sharp memory, and of course as the last survivor of the Joe McCarthy dugout, his recollections of those years are invaluable. Who else could draw me a sketch of what the old Yankees clubhouse looked like before the 1946

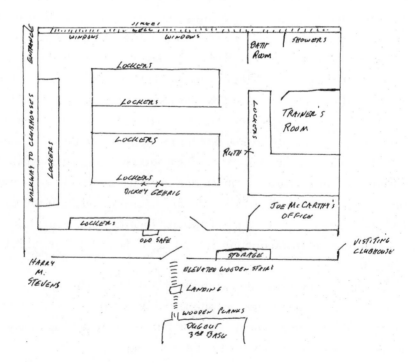

rennovation of Yankee Stadium? And he still drives into Manhattan from Westchester to meet me for hot dogs at Papaya King, or I'll meet him for hot dogs at Walter's in Mamaroneck. Late in his life, I got him hooked on watching *Jeopardy.*

There were two life lessons he imparted to me: never cross the street between two parked cars (one might suddenly be backing up), and always put all your "stuff" in one pile, instead of creating separate folders. You will always find what you're looking for with one pile. Thanks, Tom.

Bill Shannon, the longtime, incomparable official scorer in New York, set out to compile a biographical encyclopedia of all New York sports, from the well-known pro teams to six-day bicycle racing. Bill was a master historian and his determination of who belonged in that encyclopedia was laudable; no one was better qualified. But Bill would not include anyone whose date of birth was unavailable—like Sheppard, and like John Sterling. He was stubborn on that.

Tragically, Bill died in a fire at his home in 2010. Jordan Sprechman (a successor official scorer) and I took it upon ourselves to preserve the Shannon Encyclopedia (which had never been digitally formatted; Bill was a typewriter guy to the end). We brought the complete work to the New-York Historic Society where it resides on their website for researchers.

Bill also created the concept of a New York Sports Museum and Hall of Fame, and I was on the board of directors. It was an idea that should have worked, but he died before we could see it to fruition, and it was his baby and we couldn't continue without him.

I always thought of myself as having two "grandfathers" in the game. Because Bob Fishel hired me, mentored me, and was somewhat of a father figure to me, I thought of Bill Veeck, who first hired Fishel, and Red Patterson, whom Bob succeeded at the Yankees, as my baseball grandfathers. They both liked that reference a lot.

Arthur "Red" Patterson, born in 1909, went to NYU and then covered baseball for the *New York Herald-Tribune*. He traveled with the Yankees and was with the team when Lou Gehrig's playing streak ended in Detroit.

After World War II, he was hired by his former colleague Ford Frick, then the National League president, to join the "National League Service Bureau" as a publicist. Teams and leagues were just beginning to hire PR people—or even beginning to think of PR.

Public relations was still a relatively new profession; certainly a 20th century one. I once took a three-day course in it from Edward Bernays, one of the founders of the profession, a man who had suggested the March of Dimes to Franklin Roosevelt and had John D. Rockefeller handing out pennies to little children. Bernays taught us, "Graphs, charts, surveys, statistics, details—the press loves that. Always incorporate it!" He also told us of his memories of the William McKinley assassination, when everyone hung black crepe over the doors as a sign of mourning.

"That's just PR" is a quick throwaway line to dismiss a public statement, and sometimes I wonder who is coming up with "this stuff" when I see statements really off the mark. A recent example was a response during the anguish the nation went through during the 2020 George Floyd killing and its aftermath, when it suddenly emerged that "defund the police" was a good PR slogan.

I am not suggesting that I have inside dossiers on whether it was a good idea or not—but I can tell you as a PR professional that "rethink the police" would have been far more accepted. It was a statement that didn't immediately polarize so many people. It was thought-provoking with plenty of room for good ideas from all sides, including the police.

Larry MacPhail was part of a triumvirate that purchased the Yankees in 1945 (with Dan Topping and Del Webb), and MacPhail, a showman at heart, hired Red Patterson the following year to become the team's first official PR director. Prior to someone having the title, it was usually the team's road secretary (especially Mark Roth), who would answer questions from the newspapermen. ("How come Babe's not in the lineup?")

Red staged a grand event in 1947—Babe Ruth Day, the one in which Babe Ruth (looking quite ill, his hair all gray, wearing his camel-hair coat)

The first Yankees yearbook (then called a sketchbook), created by Red Patterson in 1950.

delivered his "remember the kids" speech. And then Ruth was the focus of attention in 1948 when he wore a uniform for the last time (black hair), and was captured from the rear in the Pulitzer Prize–winning photograph by Nat Fein. The 1947 event came to be considered the continuation of the 1939 Lou Gehrig Appreciation Day ceremony ("...luckiest man"), and soon they bore numbers...the fourth annual, the fifth annual...going back to '39, but skipping 1940–46. And so Old Timers' Day was in place as an annual tradition, thanks to Red.

Red also published the team's first yearbook, called a sketchbook, and they quickly became collector's items. (I see one today on eBay for $350.) His greatest legacy though was the birth of the "tape measure home run." It was a long home run hit by Mantle in 1953 that left Griffith Stadium in Washington. Red left the press box and returned to tell people he had found the ball and walked off the distance—no tape measure—counting the feet by his footsteps. He returned to the press box to announce that it traveled 565 feet.

It turned out he never left the park, and the 14-year-old boy who found the ball came into the park, had an usher take him to the Yankees clubhouse, and apparently Red met him there and gave him $100 for the ball. This part was uncovered by Jane Leavy in *The Last Boy*, her Mantle biography, but I didn't know that when I knew Red. No one did.

I asked Red once if he still had the shoes he wore that day to pace it off. "They would be Hall-of-Fame worthy," I said. Well, not only did he not have the shoes (at least I learned they were a size 13½), he admitted the 565 feet was an estimate. But he didn't correct the belief that he had left the park to walk it off. Oh well, it is what publicity men did back then. Red had a story, but few facts.

In 1954, Red had a dispute with George Weiss over free tickets he was leaving for the elevator operator at the Yankee offices at 745 Fifth Avenue (now the Bergdorf Goodman building). He thought he had earned the right to pass out some freebies now and then. Weiss didn't buy it, or so the story went, and Red quit, immediately joining the Brooklyn Dodgers at Ebbets Field. They had a midseason vacancy, and I suspect Red had the job—assistant general manager—in hand when he quit the Yankees.

And that left the position open in a year in which the Yankees were not going to the World Series.

Bob Fishel was a respected baseball figure by then, but he was unemployed, with his team, the St. Louis Browns, having moved to Baltimore without him. So, Weiss hired him, thinking that since so many of the reporters covering the team were Jewish, it would be good to have a Jewish PR man. (Weiss was not himself Jewish.)

Had Weiss asked, he would have learned that Fishel was a nonobservant Jew, never took a day off for a holiday, and was agnostic when it came to religion.

Patterson went on to move to Los Angeles with the Dodgers, and when Buzzie Bavasi moved from the Dodgers to the Angels, he hired Red as team president in 1975. (He was actually hired by club owner Gene Autry, but Bavasi changed it to assistant to the owner.) Red died in 1992 at 83.

Fishel's first baseball boss was Bill Veeck (pronounced, he proudly reminded people, like *wreck*), who owned the Browns. Bob had an advertising background in Cleveland, had done work for the baseball team through his ad agency, and Veeck, having previously owned Cleveland, knew him. Now, he owned the St. Louis Browns and reached out to Fishel to come work with him.

Although liberal in his political thought, Bob was quite a conservative person in his behavior. Never married, he became a fine connoisseur of restaurants and Broadway shows, and no one ever sent out more birthday and Christmas cards than Bob did. His Christmas card list had more than 1,200 people on it, and he signed and addressed all of them himself. And he was admired and loved back by all of them. I once suggested to him that he could have been a league president or commissioner—he was certainly smart enough—but he confessed that he couldn't see himself presiding over meetings with all those millionaire barons who owned teams.

So, although he was by nature conservative, he fell under Veeck's charm. Bill called him "Roberto" and would always ask me how Roberto was doing. Veeck is perhaps most famous for signing Eddie Gaedel, a midget, to pinch hit (and presumably draw a walk) in an actual game. It's no longer politically correct to use the term *midget*—it's now little person—but it's hard to separate Veeck, Gaedel, and midget because that was what went down that day and the language that was used.

It was August 19, 1951. Gaedel, 26, had popped out of a birthday cake earlier in the day (the American League's 50th birthday). Now in the second game of a doubleheader (attendance 18,369, biggest of the season), Eddie did indeed walk, and he's included there in Baseball-Reference.com just like everyone else. It shows him as 3'7" and lists no weight.

"Roberto signed him in the back seat of his Packard," Veeck told me, something that Fishel didn't seem anxious to report. "They later credited me with being party to a rule against midgets, but actually the rule was that you couldn't sign anyone without reporting it to the league office."

After he sold the Browns and the team moved to Baltimore, Veeck was out of baseball. He reemerged in 1959 and purchased the White Sox (in a pennant-winning season) but ran out of money after just three years. In 1975 he accumulated enough partners—and cash—to buy the White Sox again. (His father had been president of the Cubs and Bill had planted the ivy in Wrigley Field. His heart was really with the Cubs.) That purchase was a year before free agency, and he was in no position to compete for those expensive free agents.

I visited with Bill every time the Yankees were in Chicago. He'd ask about Roberto, and I'd ask him some old baseball questions. (One I remember—what happened to the dirt path from home plate to the pitcher's mound? He said, "Probably Phil Wrigley got rid of it, he always cared about aesthetics.") His office was hardly the office of a club owner. The door was always open, and the place reeked from beer and cigarette smoke. He'd light a new cigarette by stroking a match across his wooden leg, which he'd keep propped up on his desk. (He had lost the leg in World War II.)

Like Patterson, he liked when I'd call him my grandfather, and I suspect that if he'd hung around for a few more years, he might have made me an offer to work for him. And that might have been more fun than I ever had. I know longtime baseball executive Roland Hemond, who worked for six teams over 65 years, said his years working with Bill were the most fun years of his career.

Fishel went to work for the Yankees and pretty much shelved the flamboyance that Veeck taught him. It just wasn't that kind of place. But after Veeck installed a fireworks-emitting scoreboard at Comiskey Park in 1960, designed to go off when a Sox player homered (which wasn't often), Fishel countered his old boss by putting sparklers in the Yankees dugout and suggesting the Yankees players set them off when a Yankee homered (which was often). Casey Stengel, who knew how to have a good time, okayed it, and when Clete Boyer homered, the players paraded through the dugout with the sparklers. It was a wonderful moment for Fishel, sort of winking at Veeck, and a fine moment for Stengel, whom Veeck couldn't stand. In fact, Veeck hated everything about the Yankees success, but was nice to tolerate me, as I had little to do with it.

Bill Veeck's plaque in the Baseball Hall of Fame.

BILL VEECK

OWNER OF INDIANS, BROWNS AND WHITE SOX. CREATED HEIGHTENED FAN INTEREST AT EVERY STOP WITH INGENIOUS PROMOTIONAL SCHEMES, FAN PARTICIPATION, EXPLODING SCOREBOARD, OUTRAGEOUS DOOR PRIZES, NAMES ON UNIFORMS. SET M.L. ATTENDANCE RECORD WITH PENNANT-WINNER AT CLEVELAND IN 1948; WON AGAIN WITH 'GO-GO' SOX IN 1959. SIGNED A.L.'S FIRST BLACK PLAYER, LARRY DOBY IN 1947 AND OLDEST ROOKIE, 42 YEAR OLD SATCHEL PAIGE IN 1948.
A CHAMPION OF THE LITTLE GUY.

In 1991, Veeck was elected to the Baseball Hall of Fame, five years after his passing. At the time, I was assisting the Hall with writing the plaques, something I did with love.

Veeck's plaque would be a bit of a problem. He was most famous for Eddie Gaedel, but that was not the sort of thing that gets you in the Hall. In fact, it was the sort of thing that keeps you out. Still, I felt it needed to be mentioned…somehow.

And then it came to me. He was also a populist owner, playing to the common man. And so, recognizing that the word *midget* was falling into disuse, I composed a sentence meant to be the last line on his plaque.

When you visit the Hall of Fame today, look for that last line. It was my favorite of my 21 years of contributing: A CHAMPION OF THE LITTLE GUY

More on Bob Fishel. For his 65th birthday in 1979, I organized a party at Gallagher's Steak House, which was attended by an A-list of baseball people—Mantle, Ford, Red Smith, Dave Anderson, and Dick Young among them. Even Hall of Famer Hank Greenberg was there. Everyone chipped in for a special gift—a 1958 Yankees World Series ring. Back in those days, front office people didn't get rings (the 1969 Mets changed that and even gave rings to beat writers who had been with them from the start). The 1958 World Series had been Bob's favorite, the Yankees coming back from a 3–1 deficit to beat the Milwaukee Braves and avenge their Series loss to the same Braves in '57. It was a wonderful gathering, and George Steinbrenner approved the ring idea, which was needed.

Back in 1970, which was my first spring training, the Yankees and the White Sox played a couple of exhibition games in Venezuela. Fishel went on the trip, and I stayed back in Fort Lauderdale, minding the store.

The oddity of the trip was that the games were meant to honor native son Luis Aparicio—but Aparicio had been traded to Boston after the games were booked! So, what happened? The Red Sox loaned Luis back to the White Sox for the games, and Luis, dressed in his old Chicago uniform, played for his old team. Hard to believe stuff like this could happen, but it did!

Anyway, back to Venezuela. The series concluded and everyone headed for the airport in Caracas, but suddenly "tax officials" from the government arrived to say that both teams owed thousands more in taxes on the games. This was, of course, a complete farce; all the arrangements had long been set; payments had been made. The government officials demanded that each team leave behind a representative until the matter could be solved. For the White Sox, it was traveling secretary Don Unferth, and for the Yankees, it was Bob. They were not imprisoned, but they were "detained" while the charter planes departed. Lee MacPhail, sensing the potential gravity of the situation, gave Bob a blank check. For Lee to do this was a recognition that the matter was indeed serious. (I once waited two years for him to authorize a $1,000 raise to my salary.)

Unferth and Fishel did indeed leave behind payments under duress and returned the next day. It was, briefly, quite frightening.

Bob had dinner plans in Fort Lauderdale the day that Fritz Peterson and Mike Kekich's exchange of wives story broke. Those were primitive days for celebrity gossip media. Today we would have had to employ a team of people working phone banks to handle the inquiries and media requests, while dealing with Twitter, Tik Tok, Instagram, and Facebook, among others. But those were the days of six TV stations in New York, three networks, two wire services, and local newspapers. There wasn't much else, and Bob felt okay about going to dinner and leaving me in the office, where calls would come through the hotel switchboard.

Before he left, we put together a brief statement from "management," saying this was a personal matter between the parties, but the Yankees "certainly don't condone such behavior," or something like that. And I dutifully read the statement to media callers and a few irate fans who managed to crack the code and reach our office.

Mike and Fritz, two lefthanded starters who wore No. 18 and No. 19, were, with their wives, very close friends. How close, I guess we didn't understand. But they were also zany enough to pull this off and think that the world would find it acceptable.

They agreed to trade lives, not just wives—exchanging children, pets, cars and homes, and the children part would be the most difficult. In June, when the Yankees traded Kekich to Cleveland, I felt his sadness at leaving his kids behind.

Mike's arrangement with Marilyn "Chip" Peterson didn't last the month and he wanted to call it all off. But Fritz's relationship with Susan Kekich did take hold, and they spent a half-century together, although Fritz developed Alzheimer's disease in the mid-2010s.

Some fallout proceeded in small ways. We called off Family Day, where the kids played against their dads, which was heartbreaking for many of the players and their wives. Also, we had always put marital information

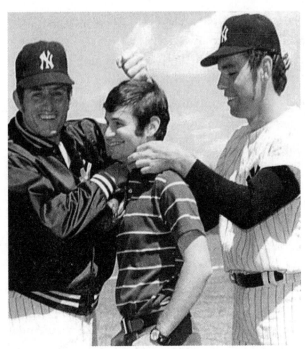

Before their infamous family/life "swap," Fritz Peterson and Mike Kekich were great friends and practical jokers, who took turns bopping me on the head in this spring training photo.

in the team roster—*M* for married, *S* for single. We dropped that, lacking an appropriate letter for the Petersons and the Kekichs.

Fritz and Mike were never again close friends, but they did have a relationship of sorts, and one lent the other money when it was needed years later. When I would be asked about "PR crises" that I had to deal with, I used to name that first, but with the passage of generations, their names would draw a blank look from people and I had to use it more cautiously. It didn't provide an automatic reaction.

Bob Fishel was very loyal. The Yankees offices in the '50s and early '60s were in the Squibb Building—745 Fifth Avenue. They were settled there when Larry MacPhail and Dan Topping owned the team and they wanted to be closer to the 21 Club, Toots Shor's, and the Plaza Hotel. Squibb was known for Squibb Dental Cream, among other products, and even after they went out of business, Bob would drop into drugstores around the American League to see if they had any remainder Squibb Dental Cream, which he had come to favor.

Bob's conservative style found him mostly dressed in suits or sports jackets, but that came in handy for him, as he liked to carry the last 10 Yankee press guides in his coat pocket for reference. This was possible when they were pocket size and 32 pages. Toward the late '70s, that exercise got out of hand when a Midwest PR director redid the format so that none could fit in a coat pocket. Since then, they have only mushroomed in size, held to a nearly 500-page count only by the employment of type small enough to require a magnifying glass.

Fishel brought old-school mannerisms and behavior to the office. He parted his hair in the middle. If Michael Burke or Lee MacPhail wanted to see him late in the afternoon, Bob would pull out an electric shaver from his desk and give himself a quick touch-up, donning his jacket as he headed upstairs. I noticed he reduced the practice when George Steinbrenner and Gabe Paul came on the scene. Many people thought he eventually quit because of George Steinbrenner's dictatorial style, but he confided that he really quit over working for Gabe Paul, whom

My mentor and predecessor as Yankees PR director, Bob Fishel. Here he is on the phone with Lee MacPhail explaining what he sees on a video replay which, by my expression, clearly went against the Yankees.

he didn't trust, having followed him for three decades from within the baseball community. Paul, in turn, had largely taken Fishel off road trips, sending me instead. Bob would stay home in his East 53rd Street bachelor apartment, fully dressed and sitting in a "hard back chair," keeping box score.

And so, he resigned after the 1973 season, his 20th with the Yankees, joining Lee MacPhail in exiting to the American League office and leaving open the position for me. His parting gift? We gave him a Yankees jersey with No. 20, a Horace Clarke jersey. He said he couldn't have received a nicer present.

Bob by then had become a true citizen of the game, and his moving to a league office was perfect. His idea of perfection was for every team to sell out its home opener and send everyone home happy with a victory.

Bob worked at the American League until his last day and died of an asthma attack in the back seat of a New York taxi in 1988. He was 74. I helped to organize a memorial service for him at Yankee Stadium, even though he hadn't worked for the Yankees for 15 years. George Steinbrenner, who liked Bob, approved it. It was outdoors, on the field, with his many friends and colleagues seated behind the Yankees dugout. The eulogists were wonderful, including Bob's boss, Dr. Bobby Brown, the American League president and former Yankees third baseman, along with Bill Guilfoile, me, Lee MacPhail, and the Orioles' longtime PR man, Bob Brown (so, two Bob Browns). Bob thus became the only person besides Babe Ruth (who lay in state inside the Gate 4 rotunda in 1948) to be memorialized at Yankee Stadium, not counting moments of silence, or Paul Simon playing "Mrs. Robinson" in memory of Joe DiMaggio.

And each year until they died, MacPhail, former Yankees vice president Howard Berk, and I would toast Bob on his May 15 birthday, choosing a special restaurant and inviting a guest who had a special relationship with Bob. One year we invited the actor Robert Joy, who played Bob Fishel in the 61* film.

I mentioned Lee MacPhail earlier and waiting two years for a thousand-dollar raise. And Lee could be frugal! One year, Bob Fishel had eye surgery for a detached retina at Columbia Presbyterian Hospital. Lee and I decided to visit him at lunchtime, and I drove. After our visit, exiting the parking lot, the attendant told us the fee was 80 cents. Without hesitating, Lee reached into his pocket and handed me 40 cents. His share. (His second marriage was to an heiress of the Dayton-Hudson Department store fortune. They threw an annual party for baseball people at their luxurious apartment at Fifth Avenue and 61st Street.)

But I really liked Lee, a gentleman, and the son of the former one-third owner of the team. Everyone felt he was a genuinely nice man. I wound up helping Lee with his memoir, *My Nine Innings*.

I once asked him why he wasn't a limited partner in the group that joined with George Steinbrenner to buy the team in 1973. After all, team ownership was in the MacPhail bloodline.

"I wasn't asked," he said. "I would have loved to be part of that."

Instead, he left after one year to become president of the American League, and he took Fishel with him as his PR counsel.

Lee presided over several strange events during his years of baseball administration. While working for Commissioner William "Spike" Eckert at MLB headquarters, he was the one who drew "New York Mets" out of a hat, which is how Tom Seaver wound up a Met. (Tom's draft status has been the source of a dispute.) When I once asked if he still had that hat (thinking about a Cooperstown contribution), he admitted, "There was no hat; it was probably an ashtray or a cup."

Then came the famous coin toss of 1978, when, in his office, home field advantage for a possible American League playoff game needed to be determined. Al Rosen, then the president of the Yankees, went to the league office in New York, while the affable Dick O'Connell, general manager of the Red Sox, was on speakerphone.

Rosen called heads as Lee did the toss. It came up tails. What came to be called the "Bucky F. Dent Game" would be played in Fenway.

As Bill Madden recounted in his biography of George Steinbrenner, Rosen used a car phone to call the Boss while driving back to Yankee Stadium.

"Sorry to report, but we lost the coin toss. The game will be in Boston if it's necessary."

"WHAT?! YOU LOST THE COIN TOSS? WHAT DID YOU CALL?"

Rosen reported that he called heads.

"HEADS?! YOU CALLED HEADS? EVERYBODY KNOWS IT COMES UP TAILS 70 PERCENT OF THE TIME. YOU FUCKING MORON! I'VE GOT THE DUMBEST FUCKING PEOPLE IN BASEBALL WORKING FOR ME!"

Lee's third celebrated decision was in the so-called 1983 "Pine Tar Game" in which he overruled the umpires who had determined that the pine tar on George Brett's bat was too high. Choosing common sense over the rule book, he ruled that the Kansas City Royals would have to return to Yankee Stadium to complete the game from the point it was halted, this time with Brett's home run approved. Obviously, too much pine tar would, if anything, keep a baseball from going a long distance.

The Yankees considered the makeup inning a farce and played it like that, with Ron Guidry in the outfield and left-hand throwing Don Mattingly at second. The Royals prevailed. Bob Fishel was a hero of sorts by anticipating a protest from Billy Martin, who claimed that the Royals runners—in the original game—had left their bases too soon (and that new umpires couldn't possibly rule on that). Fishel got the original umpires to provide sworn affidavits saying the runners did not leave early.

Mr. Steinbrenner issued a veiled threat on MacPhail's safety, and charged his PR man, Ken Nigro, with helping to facilitate fans going to court over their tickets for the original game not being honored in the conclusion of the game. At a sportswriters banquet soon after, at which all the past Yankees PR men were honored, the Boss refused to attend because of Nigro's inclusion.

When I joined the Yankees in 1968, it had been four years since Mel Allen was fired. He was the "Voice of the Yankees" since they started radio broadcasts in 1939 (missing 1940–41 and 1943–45) and you either hated or loved Mel based on whether you hated or loved the Yankees.

The question I was most asked in those early years with the Yankees was, "Why was Mel Allen fired?" I, of course, wondered the same, as he was the man who taught me baseball.

The Yankees table at the 1976 expansion draft to stock Toronto and Seattle. Left to right: Cedric Tallis, Pat Nugent (back turned), George Steinbrenner, Gabe Paul, the author.

People really did care. As I came to realize over the years, and especially in the years I was producing the Yankees telecasts, the announcers are discussed as much as the games, perhaps more.

"Did you see the game last night?"

"I did…but I can't stand (*fill in the blank with an announcer's name*)."

Although I worked with people who were directly involved with Mel's departure, they were, perhaps understandably, unwilling to ever share the full answer with me. The Yankees let unfounded rumors fly among the public, never offering a reason that may have let Mel make a more dignified exit. In fact, they never told Mel why he was being let go.

So, I came to know the older, sadder Mel Allen. "I wear my heart on my sleeve," he would say to me, somehow hoping against hope that the Yankees might have him back one day.

Finally, I had to draw my own conclusions. There was a business reason (which could have been a public reason). Ballantine Beer, so associated with Mel and the Yankees for so many years, was winding down its business and, with that, its association with the team. To find a replacement beer sponsor would be difficult if Mel were still calling the games. New ownership—CBS—understood broadcasting better than anyone, and this reason held some weight.

But beyond that, I think Yankees people were just getting tired of Mel. It was personal, not professional. They would cross the street if they saw him coming. The long-winded stories he would tell on the air—about DiMaggio or Tommy Henrich or Joe McCarthy—he might tell again and again at a casual lunch. It could be maddening.

He lost his voice doing the 1963 World Series and Vin Scully had to finish the game alone. Then NBC replaced him with Phil Rizzuto for the '64 Series. That wasn't a good sign. And so he was let go, but the good news was that he was reborn for a new generation as the voice of *This Week in Baseball*, a terrific syndicated show that perfectly fit with baseball's efforts to better market itself starting in the 1970s. And he came back to the Yankees on their cable broadcasts, even masterfully doing play-by-play for Dave Righetti's 1983 no-hitter.

Mel's voice was very much "in my head." I remember him explaining, without being patronizing, how the home plate umpire would signal a strike by raising his right arm. Before that, I never "got" that subtlety of the game.

In 1976 WPIX produced a half-hour special on the team's return to the new Yankee Stadium. They wanted Mel to narrate it and asked me to write the script. With Mel's voice in my head (and of course a knowledge of the footage they were working with), I wrote the whole thing in one take, beginning to end. It took me about a half hour.

Eventually, as the years passed, people stopped asking me, "Why was Mel Allen fired?"

It was never lost on me that my junior high school yearbook in Spring Valley said "Mel Allen Stepaside" next to my picture. Even in my early teens I aspired to be a Yankees broadcaster. This of course was not to be, but becoming the executive producer of their telecasts and writing a script for Mel was pretty darn close.

∂ ∂ ∂

The Mel question was succeeded by another frequently asked question: "What's it like to work for George Steinbrenner?" We had a page in our annual media guide called "Frequently Asked Questions," like how many plate appearances are necessary to win the batting title or how you calculate earned run average. I used to think I would slip that Steinbrenner question in there one year and see if anyone noticed.

The answer was complex but made simpler for me when the hit TV show *Seinfeld* incorporated a Steinbrenner character. In a second, I could say, "It's just like the TV show." And in many ways, it was.

The further irony of this answer was that even before that, a lot of people thought the George Costanza character was based on me! Costanza's job at the Yankees was assistant to the traveling secretary, a job that didn't actually exist. My job with the Yankees had been assistant public relations director until I was promoted to director. Close.

It's true that there is a lot of Costanza in me, although I didn't sleep on Yankees bed linen, nor under my desk.

People had apparently been telling Jason Alexander about me (my friend Art Toretzky was in a poker game with him), because when I met Jason backstage after a Broadway performance he later did, his face lit up into a big smile and he said, "I understand you're Costanza!" My wife was with me, had bought into the comparison, and loved that moment. She liked telling people she was married to George Costanza. We had a nice talk, and he did ask about some of my responsibilities and about working for George Steinbrenner. I told him about a really tough personal day I had once gone through, but how that night at 11 PM, alone in a new apartment, there was a Seinfeld rerun on Channel 11, and everything suddenly seemed like it was going to be okay.

"I hear stories like that a lot from people," he said.

I was only 24 when George Steinbrenner, 42, and his group bought the Yankees. I thought it was a great thing, because he sounded like a guy who really wanted to win. Under CBS ownership, the team had lost that fire.

Our ground crew guys were pretty astute baseball fans, and I used to sit outside with them at lunchtime and hear their gripes about the team. Nick Priore, the assistant clubhouse man, felt the same way. So did Bill Kane, our statistician and later traveling secretary. These guys all knew their stuff and hated the CBS years.

Fishel wasn't so sure. He had been so loyal to the CBS people, and suddenly, they were leaving. He felt vulnerable, especially when Mr. Steinbrenner came to town bringing the former Cleveland publicist Marsh Samuel in tow. The gentlemanly Samuel had worked for the White Sox, Cleveland, and the Browns football team, and had done non-sports work for Mr. Steinbrenner in Cleveland. (He eventually became vice president, marketing and public relations for the Yankees, a few months after I left in 1977.) He was credited with creating baseball's first press guide.

So, Bob was a little nervous about his job, but at 24, I didn't feel vulnerable, not being a department head. I thought, *Why would they replace me?*

It wasn't long before George Steinbrenner took control full throttle, despite famously saying, "I'll leave the running of the team to the baseball people; I'll stick to building ships." But he was, in fairness, a very smart guy and certainly had leadership qualities in abundance. I suppose it was inevitable that he took full control.

Bob had elevated me to a higher position earlier on, following the Dodgers' move of elevating Fred Claire to a more senior position under Red Patterson. Everyone in baseball considered the Dodgers to be the model front office.

But now Bob was departing. And I got a call from the Boss (which Mr. Steinbrenner was already being called).

"Would you be ready to step into that job and head our public relations?" he asked.

The culture of baseball had been that PR directors had mostly been more senior people, often former sportswriters like Red Patterson was, who had been around the team for a long time. But Mr. Steinbrenner did not realize that was the culture, or if he did, he wasn't bothered by it.

Because I had started at 19, I think I would always be "the kid" if CBS had continued to own the club. The purchase by the Steinbrenner group removed that. I was already one of the senior employees.

"I'm ready," I said. "I've been learning from Bob Fishel for six years. He's the best. I couldn't have had a better mentor."

And just like that, I was the team's third PR director, after Patterson and Fishel. I was so proud of that, although the honor would become watered down after I left, with seemingly a new guy every year or two in the role. It changed as often as managers for a long time. One year Harvey Greene, a successor, celebrated the Yankees having two spring trainings in a row with the same PR guy and same manager, Lou Piniella.

Working for Mr. Steinbrenner was challenging for me. The ones who fared best gave it right back to him when he yelled at them. That was never going to be me. I took it and told him I'd do better. But I was developing a hacking cough and a skin rash in the process. As Brian Cashman once said, "George doesn't get enough credit for being the reason human resources departments were created!"

Others left; I stayed. My seniority was rising. The job was easier in 1974–75, our Shea Stadium years, because Mr. Steinbrenner had been suspended by Commissioner Kuhn for making illegal contributions to the 1972 Nixon campaign and making his ship-building employees lie about it. Having him suspended found me reporting to team president Gabe Paul, which was no walk in the park either, but at least it didn't come with hacking coughs and skin rashes.

The angry calls from the Boss were numerous. Sometimes, just "get down here." Occasionally there would be, "Now I'm not going to put you out in the street over this, but next time, I might."

Out in the street was quite literal, it turned out. Once he fired a PR guy who had a company car. All the department heads did. He wouldn't let him drive the company car home, so he was literally out in the street until his wife came to pick him up, holding his W.B. Mason box with his personal possessions.

We had red phones installed on our desks, only for incoming calls from him. If you were on another call, you dropped it—you dropped whatever you were doing—and leapt for the phone. There was no second ring. He had no patience for second rings.

We had several meetings in his office each day, although when the team went on the road, he usually went to Tampa to work at American Ship Building, his other business. Our schedules, then, were lined up with the AmShip people. We each looked forward to either the team being on the road or the team being at home. It depended on who you asked.

When Steinbrenner was in Cleveland or Tampa, he could not watch or listen to Yankees games. Not only was there no internet or cable TV, but not all the games were televised. So, he did the next best thing. He had me call him from whatever press box I was in and do a play-by-play on the payphone, exclusively for him. (The home team people did not like this very much, and Bill Veeck once took the receiver out of my hands and hung up on him.) I tried to keep it light, but I knew I couldn't keep it light if the Yankees were losing. He was angry and he'd bark at me about why the manager was doing such-and-such. It was tough to fill the silence between pitches and between innings.

I recall the expansion draft to stock Toronto and Seattle after the 1976 season. I sat by him at the Yankees table at the Plaza Hotel, with Gabe Paul taking charge of who the Yankees would protect and who might be left vulnerable to being selected.

Gabe wanted to protect Ron Guidry. Mr. Steinbrenner wanted to protect reliever Grant Jackson. He didn't think Guidry seemed like much of a battler.

"You have to listen to your scouts," said Gabe. "They all say Guidry can be a front-line pitcher." He had only relieved in seven games in 1976 and was a pinch-runner in the World Series.

"Well, protect Guidry then," said the Boss. "But remember, Gabe; this is on you, this is on your head."

It was a good example of the George–Gabe compromises between two generations and how they played out. As Guidry's star rapidly rose, I don't ever recall credit going to Gabe Paul from that moment in time.

Even when I left the Yankees and was producing the telecasts (working for WPIX), I would get calls at home from Steinbrenner, complaining about something the announcers had said, perhaps that the Mets had won their fifth game in a row.

When Joe Garagiola Jr., our in-house lawyer, and I resigned together in 1977, we did it in person. He cleared his throat, and adjusted the knot in his tie, surprised that we would be doing this, and said, "Just remember, once you leave me, you can't ever come back. It's just a rule I have."

As it happened, he twice reached out to offer me positions to return. One offer, over breakfast at the Carlyle Hotel, was to be the team's minor league and scouting director. It was a job for which I was ill equipped, and I told him that. He did ask me to think about it. (He once called to ask me if I thought the Yankees should pick up Carlos May from the White Sox. I asked him if he knew that Carlos had lost a thumb in an Army accident. He didn't know that, but we got Carlos anyway and he helped us win the 1976 pennant.)

Another time was after one of my successors got into an argument with a sportswriter and may have hit or shoved him. There was some talk of a lawsuit. I got a call during spring training from Arthur Richman, a senior advisor and longtime friend, and he said, "Mr. Steinbrenner would like you to come back and be PR director again. He trusts you and greatly admired the job you did for him."

That was news to me, although he had always been friendly when we'd meet and occasionally sought my opinion on potential hires I might have known.

And although this was flattering, and in a sense put an exclamation point on my time there, I turned it down. From all reports, people were still coughing and itching. I couldn't go back to that.

The current generation of club PR directors should know that it was me who saved the practice of traveling with the team. The complexity of the business having grown enormously, I suppose it would have happened anyway, but in 1976, I was to be on a flight to Dallas, where, that night, a series with the Texas Rangers was to begin. The team had gone the night before, but Mr. Steinbrenner wanted me in the office for a morning meeting.

The meeting started late and went on and on. I may have been fidgeting, but I had mentioned my one o'clock flight when our discussions started. Now, as 11:30 was approaching, the Boss looked at his watch and asked, "What time is your flight?"

"One o'clock," I said.

"How about you send Morabito on the flight, and you can get a later flight and relieve him?" he suggested. Mickey Morabito was my assistant.

Now, I could have said, "I can take the later flight; it's not critical that I be there for first pitch." But of course, if I said that, he would have thought, *Maybe it's not critical you be there at all!* So, I decided to go along with this ridiculous idea of Morabito, with no overnight bag, traveling four hours to Dallas to handle the first three innings, and I could be there with a later flight to succeed him mid-game. And he could get a flight home that same night to save the cost of a night in the hotel.

And that's exactly what happened. And if I hadn't thought quickly, that might have been the end of PR men traveling with their teams.

Today, with the benefit of seeing Mr. Steinbrenner mellow over time along with all his accomplishments as the longest tenured Yankee owner, I have a kinder view than I did in my twenties. I tell people, "The media loved him (Murray Chass and Red Smith excepted), because he was always great copy—a larger-than-life New York character." The fans came to love him because he did whatever it took to put a winning team on the field. The players loved him because he paid so well and surrounded them with great teammates. Other owners loved him because they would fill their stadiums when the Yankees came to town. (Although they also blamed him for driving salaries up.) So for the 40 or 50 of us in the front office who found him hard to work for…who cared about us? We were, as demonstrated many times, replaceable. He redefined what being an owner meant—he was an activist who always put the team first. He got involved in roster moves. He poured his profits into the team. Aided by the growth of the industry as a whole with its marketing and broadcasting, he saw the franchise's value go from $8.5 million in 1973 to *billions* today, without even including the value of the team's holding in the YES Network.

He was a genuinely charitable person and put many young people through college. I never heard him utter anything racist or discriminatory. And, of course, he gave me the promotion to PR director at 24.

When I visited him for the last time in Tampa during that fantasy camp experience I had, I sat with him in his office at Steinbrenner Field. He was a shell of the bombastic general he had once been, and I did more talking than he did.

"You've done amazing things with this team," I said. "But I hope you remember those early days kindly, because they meant a lot to me."

He said, "You were a big part of it. We got this business on the right track. I'll never forget it."

Maybe he had forgotten how he had flung the 1976 Yearbook at me and told me to redo it because a lot of the photos showed the players with long hair. I hope so.

That was a cough and itch day.

Fifth Inning

After the Mel Allen and George Steinbrenner questions, it came to pass that my most asked question became, "What do you think of the new Yankee Stadium?"

Most who asked did not care for the new stadium, which opened in 2009 with a world championship. "Too much advertising," they would say. "It's like a shopping mall that happens to have a ball field instead of a carousel!"

The questioners usually proclaim their love for the old stadium across the street (1976–2008), and it is true; that place could really rock when the stands were full. Older fans still claim allegiance to the original stadium (1923–1973), forgetting the lack of escalators, the obstructed views, the narrow seats, and the lack of concession choices.

My answer to the "mall" charge is, "Yes, that may be true, but when you just watch the game and look at the field, it's still Yankee Stadium. You can feel the history there as though Ruth–Gehrig–DiMaggio–Mantle–Murcer–Munson–Mattingly–Jeter were still playing. I think they did a great job preserving the feel of the historic old ballpark, while adding more comfort than ever before."

One thing I particularly liked was that you could circle the stands without finding the bleachers blocked off, keeping those true fans penned in. I liked that there was open access to the whole park for bleacher fans. I discovered this when they played their very first exhibition game there in 2009, testing the place, so to speak. I was really pleased to be able to wander the whole circumference and explore it all. And the Yankee Museum, which could easily have become more commercial space, is a special presence beautifully curated.

I didn't sit in the regular seats much in the original stadium once I started working there. In the current stadium, I go often with friends. But I always seem to sit in a row where the Bronx Beer Olympics is taking place, with people getting up 10 or 12 times a game for another serving, never mind the cost. They stop saying "excuse me" after about six trips, according to my real-time research. How sports created a "keep buying" culture, whereas theaters didn't, remains a tribute to concessionaire extraordinaire, the Englishman Harry M. Stevens, who serviced both the Polo Grounds and Hilltop Park more than 120 years ago. Some credit him with the invention of the hot dog. His historic company was sold to Aramark in 1994.

As for all the advertising in ballparks, people claim to hate it, the crass commercialism of it all—but when you look at photos of old ballparks, your eye is attracted to the advertising, which sets the timeframe of the photo better than anything.

Two decades ago, Milwaukee and Detroit introduced advertising panels behind home plate, to be seen on every pitch from the centerfield camera. People were appalled. Now, every park has it, and who cares? We adapted.

After the All-Star game of 2021, umpires had to don "FTX" stickers on their uniform jerseys. After finding out what FTX meant, (the official cryptocurrency of Major League Baseball), I thought, *This might be the most valuable advertising space in America! How many hours of primetime television does that FTX sticker appear on camera?*

So, after Mel Allen, George Steinbrenner, and the new Yankee Stadium, I suppose the next "most asked question" might be, "What in the world is FTX, and how many Bitcoins does a Yankee Yearbook cost?"

My landing the Mantle fan mail job that got me started with the Yankees was the simple action of sending a letter from my dorm room to Fishel (whose name and image I knew from Yankee Yearbooks), looking for a summer job. Frankly, I didn't expect a response—this was the New York Yankees. I thought it would be like writing the White House looking for a summer job.

But two things made it happen. The first was that Pete Sheehy, the much-admired Yankees clubhouse man, had wheeled in a dozen or so boxes of unanswered Mantle fan mail. This was 1967. Mick was no longer taking fan mail home with him to make sure it was answered. The mail was basically all the same—"Dear Mickey, you are my favorite player, please send me an autographed baseball."

He was done answering the fan mail.

The other thing, which never really occurred to me, was that college kids were not looking for careers—or a summer job—in baseball. My generation had grown discontent with ordinary American institutions like baseball. What sports attention they had was being drawn to the physicality of the NFL, the coolness of the NBA, or the personality cult of Muhammad Ali. Baseball was not only stuck in its old ways, but in recent years it had failed to grow the game. In the mid '60s, Tom Seaver, Reggie Jackson, and Johnny Bench had come along, but not many others. The game hadn't yet learned how to market itself well and was losing appeal to young fans.

So Fishel had no other letters sitting on his desk looking for a summer job. He called me to come in for an interview (I was back in college in Oneonta, New York, 19 miles from Cooperstown) and followed the interview by offering me the fan mail job at $100 a week. He told me it was better than $400 a month because of the occasional occurrence of more than four weeks in a month.

After two summers in the PR office, Bob's assistant director, Bill Guilfoile, accepted the head PR job with the Pittsburgh Pirates. And Fishel called me in college and offered the full-time position to me.

But it had to be immediate—and I still had a semester to go. I thought long and hard about it and found four professors to allow me to take independent study courses to get my needed 12 credits and to graduate on time. With that in place, I said yes.

Guilfoile, meanwhile, had offered me the opportunity to go with him to Pittsburgh as his assistant there, and even offered more money, but the lure of the Yankees and the thought of leaving home influenced me to stay where I was.

I had loved working with Bill. One project I did with him in 1969 was press guide–related. I was so pleased he asked me to assist on it.

We created a page showing the top 20 Yankees lifetime leaders in a variety of hitting and pitching categories. This had not been compiled before and was harder than you would think. For instance, if a player had a split season with two teams, it was not always easy to get his Yankees-only totals, which would be the only ones that mattered in our charts. (The annual Sporting News and Reach/Spalding Guides did not always break apart the season totals. And, by the way, our office-bound copies of those books all had Ed Barrow's name embossed on the covers. Barrow had been the Yankees general manager from 1920 to 1945.)

But we knew that a company called Information Concepts was recalculating baseball statistics using early mainframe computers for a project called *The Baseball Encyclopedia*, to be published in 1969 by Macmillan. (It would become one of the most beloved baseball books ever published.) Bill and I made contact with the statisticians there and told them our needs. They were fully cooperative, and we got our top 20 charts into the 1970 press guide. The charts are still there a half-century later (I look at pages 340–341 with pride and memories of Bill each season), although Frank Crosetti's 98 home runs for 20th place was long ago obliterated.

Bill went on to become a beloved member of the Pittsburgh baseball community. He had a special moment in Pittsburgh before he left a decade later to become the public relations director at the Hall of Fame. He had worked with Mantle for nine years in New York (they sometimes went fishing together) and now was working with the great Roberto Clemente in Pittsburgh.

The final day of the 1972 season arrived, and with Clemente sitting at 2,999 hits, he was considering not playing, so that the buildup to his 3,000th would last all winter, for whatever value that might be. He told

Guilfoile what he was thinking and Bill, cautious to a fault, suggested he play. "You never know what can happen over the winter," he said, hardly thinking of what actually did.

So, Roberto played and got a double off Jon Matlack of the Mets for his 3,000th hit. It would, of course, prove to be his last, as he died tragically in a New Year's Eve plane crash flying a relief mission to earthquake-stricken Nicaragua.

In his later years, Bill developed Alzheimer's disease and moved to a nursing home. His son told me that despite the loss of memory, obliterating all of his baseball years, he never lost the same wonderful personality that he'd always had and that everyone loved.

Anyway, I joined the Yankees as a full-time employee, and literally days later, I was on a plane for beautiful Fort Lauderdale for spring training, where I could assist Bob with media and help get photography done for the Yankee Yearbook. I was all in.

Another member of our PR department was our statistician Bill "Killer" Kane. Bill eventually became the Yankees' traveling secretary and got his nickname from Sandy Alomar, our second baseman at the time. Our manager was Bill Virdon, and the two Bills would sit together in the front of the bus. Calling out "Bill!" led to Alomar taking matters into his

In Bradenton, Florida, 1973—the Pirates' spring training camp, with Pittsburgh's PR chief Bill Guilfoile, who preceded me as Bob Fishel's assistant.

own hands, knowing a nickname was needed. (Killer Kane never actually killed anyone.)

Kane, a St. Bonaventure grad, was hired as Mel Allen's statistician. It was 1961, quite a year to break in, with Mantle and Maris racing to hit 60 homers and calculations needed daily on how they were pacing against Ruth's record.

Mel was very tough on Bill. One day (and this was a bad mistake), Bill had the wrong pitcher starting for Minnesota. Three or four innings went by before Bill realized his error. So, he slipped Mel a small note in the booth: "It's not Kralick pitching for the Twins; it's Dick Stigman. Sorry." Both were 6'2" lefties.

Mel did what I suppose any of us would do…he proceeded to repeatedly pound Kane over the head with his scorebook. That was a tough day for Killer.

Bill had polio as a child, and it left him with one leg much thinner than the other. He walked with a limp. But sitting on a bar stool, no one had reason to notice. One day, in a darkened hotel bar, he was sitting with Whitey Ford. A man came in, spotted Whitey, and presumed that Kane was Mantle. In a dark room, one could make the mistake; they had a similar look.

So the fan came over and began telling "Mantle" (Kane) what a hero he had been to him, how he had admired him for so many years. Whitey was listening and smiling. Then the fan said, "And my god, Mickey, the injuries you've had, the way you play despite those bad legs, your courage…"

So Killer had to interrupt.

"You don't know the half of it," he said. And he pulled up his pants leg to show that withered leg about six inches in circumference.

The fan nearly fainted. He gulped, said his goodbyes, and exited the bar. Surely he told all of his baseball friends of his Mantle encounter…for the rest of his life. And Whitey's esteem for Kane soared. It was his kind of joke.

When Bill became traveling secretary, it meant his job was micromanaged by the Boss. It was a tough enough job as it was, with a traveling party of 50 having special requests, and the need for precision with buses, planes, hotels, doling out meal money, handling ticket requests, and certifying the ticket count on road games with the home team so that a check for 20 percent could be drawn. (This is no longer the way it is done.) There was last-second transportation for optioned players or traded players, and even an occasional trip to the local magistrate to quietly handle an incident involving a player from the night before.

Before the flight to Boston in 1978 for the "Bucky F. Dent" playoff game, Kane had a tense conversation with the Boss that began with Mr. Steinbrenner saying "Newark? No good. I want that plane moved to LaGuardia!" Bill: "You can't move a plane from Newark to LaGuardia. It can't be done. And we've been flying out of Newark all year; they know how to handle us; it's actually much better for us."

Mr. Steinbrenner: "No good. I want the plane at LaGuardia."

A shouting match followed, and Bill quit ("You can fly the f—— plane to LaGuardia yourself!") right there before the playoff game. Jerry Murphy, a former batboy now working in the ticket office, was summoned and told he would be taking the team to Boston.

Jerry wisely resisted and Kane was persuaded back but eventually put in charge of the liquor supply for the luxury suites, which was, to put it gently, not a good idea. (Murphy then became traveling secretary.) Killer

In the Fort Lauderdale press box with Bill Kane.

died in 2013, but he left behind an unpublished manuscript of his Yankees years done in collaboration with sportswriter Maury Allen, which I have. To those who worked with him, Killer was a legend.

Bruce Henry was a beloved Yankees traveling secretary with a great sense of humor, complimented by the required sense of precision the position demands. If he said the bus was leaving for the airport at 11:15 PM, it meant you better be on that bus at 11:14, or you risked having to pay for a taxi—or worse, your own flight—to the next city.

I remember a fairly new player was exiting the clubhouse one day and screaming, "Hold the bus, hold the bus!" as Bruce stood at the door. And Bruce shouted back, "We don't hold the bus for Mickey Mantle, we sure aren't holding it for you!"

When I first began traveling with the team, we had a mixture of commercial and charter flights, with the latter only reluctantly used when there was simply no commercial connection available.

Sharing commercial flights with regular passengers was never fun; a few passengers would figure out who we were (especially when Yogi was with us), but most would grudgingly resent that there were no first-class tickets available and that they might be held up for a few minutes while the players boarded. It was a much better situation all around when all the flights were chartered. The manager, the coaches, and the front office people sat in first class or the first few rows of coach, while the players happily sat near the back, playing cards, enjoying their beer, smoking, and generally complaining about management. I never felt comfortable in first class, knowing Stottlemyre, Murcer, White, and Munson were in coach, but the players didn't want to be sitting with the manager and front office people, so it worked out. And I got to sit with Yogi or Billy or Lemon, which was always fun.

I remember one flight where the first-class flight attendant wanted to write down everyone's name so she could be more personally friendly with us, and Yogi responded to her request by answering "Lawrence," which she used the whole flight.

Charter flights also frequently allowed the team bus to go right to the plane without the players having to go through the terminal, which was a wonderful time and security savings.

Yet another member of the PR department when I got there was 5'1" Jackie Farrell, a confidant of Babe Ruth's and the head of our speaker's bureau. Jackie, born in 1896, was one of the few people Babe called by name, rather than "kid." He was a wonderful goodwill ambassador for the team, making hundreds of speeches each year to the Knights of Columbus, B'nai B'rith, Cub Scout groups, and many more. When I began making such speeches, the older people in the group would say, "Where's Jackie Farrell?"

I shared an office with Jackie; our desks were back-to-back. Every memo or letter he ever received seemed to be sitting on this desk. He smoked continuously, but before smoking became such an annoyance, I didn't mind.

Jackie was starting to lose it, just a bit, in the '70s. (He died in 1979.) Over and over again he'd fumble through his mail and stop at a letter from Sally Rand, a famous stripper/fan dancer from the '40s. They were apparently friends. He would read the letter as though he'd never seen it before, and then he'd toss it my way and say, "Get a load of this!" So, I became very familiar with Sally Rand's letter.

In his past was an opportunity to be Frank Sinatra's manager in the 1940s. They were both Jersey boys, and Frank liked him. Jackie was writing for the *Daily News*, mostly boxing, and Frank asked him to manage him. Jackie was happy covering boxing and turned him down. What a mistake.

In 1968, Frank came to Yankee Stadium to film some scenes for his movie *The Detective*, which co-starred Lee Remick. (Bob Fishel went to dinner with the beautiful Ms. Remick!)

Anyway, when Jackie learned that Frank would be shooting there, he said, "I gotta go out there and say hello."

The Yankees secretaries were very excited by this but afraid that Jackie might be embarrassed. Frank might not remember him. Nobody wanted to see Jackie embarrassed.

Jackie wandered down near the Yankees dugout and shouted, "Hey, Frank!" We all held our breath.

Sinatra, near home plate, turned and yelled, "Jackie!" He headed for the dugout to give Jackie a great embrace. We were all very relieved.

My first summer with the Yankees was a summer of wonderment. If you opened the door outside of our basement-level PR office, you would see a sign on the wall leading to the clubhouse: No Women Beyond This Point. And that would be adhered to until the matter finally landed in court and women journalists were at last admitted—but that came in the remodeled stadium, which opened in 1976.

I wandered onto the field at lunchtime to discover that the outfield was not smooth like a carpet, but uneven like a golf course, with small hills and valleys and imperfections. I had always thought it was perfectly flat, as it is now.

Outfield prospect Steve Whitaker asked me to play pepper with him one day, which was a thrill. And the first Yankees besides Mantle to learn my name were Ruben Amaro and Rocky Colavito, who joined us that summer of '68. I think Rocky mistook me for someone whose name he needed to know.

Mel Stottlemyre arranged with Spalding to get me a glove—a Johnny Callison model, which I used until 2015, when I finally had him sign it for me and retired it.

I was once walking up Fifth Avenue in New York with Whitey Ford. We had been together at an event in Bryant Park, and he had a meeting in Rockefeller Center. So, I walked with him, about eight blocks.

At one point I said, "I'm a little surprised that no one has recognized you! We're on Fifth Avenue in New York City in the middle of the afternoon, and you didn't get one greeting!"

"That's because I'm with you," he answered. "If I was with Mickey, everyone would recognize me!"

On that same walk, I asked him if he had ever been to the Yankees offices at 745 Fifth Avenue, across the street from the Plaza Hotel.

"A few times," he said. "I'd go there to pay my fines in cash rather than have them deducted from my paycheck, which Joanie would have seen."

One year, when I had my own PR agency, I arranged a lucrative appearance for Whitey in Miami. He was going to give me a commission for it, which was appropriate. I think he got something like $20,000 to meet fans and sign autographs.

Some weeks later, when I was visiting my father near Fort Lauderdale, I called Whitey to get a restaurant recommendation. (He and Joanie wintered in that onetime spring training home of the Yankees.)

"Oh, you're here?" he asked. "Let me come over and give you your commission."

"You can just mail it, that's fine, Whitey," but he insisted on driving over. Wynmoor Village was near Pompano Race Track (and near the Cheetah II strip club), so he knew the general directions. And sure enough, an hour later, he drove past the security gate and to a parking spot in front of my dad's condo. (My mother had died in 1994.) All the other cars there were beige or grey Toyotas or Nissans. It was a retirement community in Florida. Those were the official cars.

His was a Cadillac. Everyone noticed.

He came in and hit it off nicely with my dad, who was 13 years older. Then he proceeded to pay me—in cash—explaining how he had done the math to determine the commission in a manner so confusing I stopped following him and said to myself, *Whatever this comes out to be, I'll be fine with it.*

And so, I took a photo of my dad and Whitey, which he later signed, "To Irv, I'll meet you at Cheetahs for a drink."

Whitey Ford came to visit and we took a photo with my father. I'm not sure anyone at Wynmoor Village had seen a Cadillac in many years.

They didn't call him Slick for nothing.

We kept in close touch. He'd stop by my 57th Street apartment for a breather on occasion when he had multiple appointments in Manhattan. Once he gave me a bit of parenting advice that I took to heart and never forgot.

I did PR for a book he did with Phil Pepe in which he picked his all-time Yankees team. This was 2001, and he picked Jeter at short.

"How are you going to explain this to Rizzuto?" I asked.

"Are you kidding? Phil's seen this kid play; he knows how great he is. He'd agree."

We were going to do a press conference to reveal his choices and introduce the book—on September 12, 2001…the day after 9/11. There was no press conference, of course, and so I sheepishly had to spend part of my day on that awful Tuesday alerting people that there would be no press conference Wednesday, and feeling so embarrassed that I even had to make those inconsequential calls.

I once told Whitey the story of his last complete game, which came on April 25, 1967, against the White Sox. I was still in college but could get Yankees games on my car radio, and I sat in my car for the whole two and a half hours as he beat Chicago 11–2. I was so thrilled that he still had a dominating complete game in him.

"I remember that game," he told me. "None of those pitches were legal."

He was joking, of course, but I remember when he was a spring training instructor and we would set up a yearbook photo with him and a group of rookie pitchers. As we got everyone set and the camera ready, he would spit on the ball and show them how to throw a spitball. And that's why we always had laughter in those photos.

Whitey's final years were spent with increasing forgetfulness. The team would get him to Old Timers' Day somehow, and he'd wear a No. 16 jersey and a Yankees cap but would otherwise seem confused and disoriented. He was approaching 90. He didn't know any of the current players. When they announced his name, he had to be guided up the dugout steps so that he could wave to the crowd. He seemed uncertain of what was going on.

But as he reached the field, standing on familiar baseball dirt, hearing the familiar roar of the crowd, suddenly, he was taken back in time. He broke into that great Whitey Ford smile, waved, and acknowledged the cheers. I thought I could detect a tear, as though he had indeed been transported back to a special place in his life.

But the tear was mine.

When Whitey and Mickey were elected together to the Hall of Fame in 1974, we decided to make their election the theme of Old Timers' Day and let them pick the guest list. Or at least to augment the list—we wanted to have the usual suspects there, especially those who didn't require airfare.

So the list began to unfold with just about every rascal they had played with or against…Bo Belinsky, Hawk Harrelson, Mickey McDermott, George Brunet, Don Zimmer, Dick Stuart, Billy Loes, Jimmy Piersall, and so on. It would be an Old Timers' Day with more laughter than ever before.

When they were ready to go to Cooperstown, they chartered a bus for friends and family and packed it with beer, and the tales of that four-hour bus ride were told for many years afterward by those aboard.

The following year, whereas I usually selected the gift for the day, this time Gabe Paul had a friend who promised to deliver high-end crystal ashtrays with the Yankees logo smoked into the base. I had to admit they were nice and did look like a high-end gift, although in keeping with our budget, they were about $75 each—a lot for an ashtray.

They were also handsomely packed in blue felt and into custom designed boxes with the Yankees pinstripe design.

But Whitey decided they were bad gifts. And so, he playfully tossed his ashtray into the large trash bin in the middle of the clubhouse. Mantle, of course, followed and did the same. Then Ellie Howard. Then Rizzuto and Raschi and Reynolds and Lopat…and eventually, pretty much all of them. I don't know how many survived, but I did see one on eBay for $500. I suspect the seller had no idea how few there were.

Or perhaps the porter who emptied the garbage that afternoon is living off those ashtrays to this day.

A lot of players—indeed, a lot of Americans—regularly smoked before health reports demonstrated the link to cancer. Laws began to pass banning smoking in restaurants. It was all about health.

I remember when we had the veteran outfielder on the Yankees, Johnny Callison, who smoked a lot. One day he found himself on first base and the batter hit a triple. His worst nightmare. Everyone was laughing in the Yankee dugout as Calllison chugged to second, third, and barely to home. He just didn't have the lungs for a 270-foot dash at full speed. But he made it.

Author Dan Schlossberg was one of the early ones to speak out against smoking in ballparks. I thought, *They will never mandate this; it's impossible. There aren't enough cops to enforce it, and you can't ask ushers to do it.*

Eventually the Yankees and the Mets sealed off "no smoking" sections, and they worked! It spread throughout baseball. And eventually, when Mayor Michael Bloomberg began pushing through tougher anti-smoking laws, they spread to Yankee and Shea Stadiums, and they took hold! Today, the New York parks are smoke free, which is something I never would have imagined.

When I wrote my Yankees history book *Pinstripe Empire*, I found two friends who were in the bleachers on Lou Gehrig Appreciation Day in 1939. One, Broadway producer Irv Welzer, described his day there well. "You could barely see," he remembered. "Cigarette and cigar smoke had formed a cloud over the bleachers. The ceremony was between games of a double-header, so there was already two to three hours of smoke in the air. I wish I could tell you that I saw the ceremonies, but mostly I just heard them."

At Old Timers' Day in 1973, I had the thrill of not only meeting Satchel Paige (and acquiring the Monarchs uniform for him) but also sitting with him at the private dinner that night at Toots Shor's.

Satchel was invited as a recently chosen Hall of Famer. I couldn't wait to meet him. (He earned his nickname by always starting road trips with an empty satchel, which he would fill with gifts as the trip unfolded. At least, that was the story.)

I had read and enjoyed his autobiography, *Maybe I'll Pitch Forever*. He and Josh Gibson were, frankly, the only Negro League players whose names I really knew. As others were elected to the Hall of Fame—Oscar Charlston, Judy Johnson, Cool Papa Bell, and others, I came to know them.

Everyone, though, knew Satchel's name, and by some good fortune, my first baseball cards were two St. Louis Browns from 1953—Paige and shortstop Billy Hunter.

At dinner (I sat with Bill Kane), Satchel told what I came to learn were his usual stories, including how Cool Papa Bell was so fast, he could turn off the light and get into bed before the room got dark. A good one.

There were so many more questions I should have asked that night, but he was fairly quiet, not especially outgoing, so I didn't feel as though questions were welcome. But still, it was an amazing night just to be in his presence.

We all learned more about the Negro Leagues as the years went by, and Bowie Kuhn (who said he was somewhat influenced by the publication of Robert Peterson's book *Only the Ball Was White*) gets credit for easing the Negro Leagues into public knowledge. Until Paige went into the Hall of Fame, at Kuhn's directive, the Negro Leagues were out there like a cloud, few among white fans really understanding them.

But I did learn more from Monte Irvin, the former Negro Leagues and New York Giants star with whom I worked during two years I was at Major League Baseball. Monte became a great friend, and since he shared a birthday with my wife, I would always look forward to his calling on February 25 to wish her a happy birthday. (You read that correctly.) He made sure my kids had all the necessary equipment for Little League. And he always reminded me to wear a hat in cold weather.

We'd go to lunch often, and he would regale me with stories. He would laugh and tell me how sometimes the teams would employ local ringers. "In one town, we knew of a great player who was in the local prison," he recalled. "Someone had a connection to the warden, and we would make arrangements to borrow the player for our game that day—so long as we returned him afterward. And we always did."

Monte insisted that the talent level was major league–worthy, despite poor fields and inferior equipment, despite sleeping on buses and eating less-than-nutritious meals.

He was a very modest man, never one to boast of his abilities or his records. But one day I asked him, "At your peak, who would you compare yourself to from today's game—Willie Stargell? George Foster? Jim Rice? Mike Schmidt?"

He didn't hestitate.

"Oh, DiMaggio," he said, as though, among his peers, the answer was obvious.

He said his peak was pre–World War II, around the time DiMaggio had his 56-game hitting streak. And he was certain of his claim. This from a man not giving to boasts or brags.

And to this day, I think about how America was deprived of another DiMaggio talent, thanks to the nonsense that was segregated baseball.

Monte lived to be almost 97 (it must have been the hat), passing away in 2016. With his passing, the last living Negro League star who would graciously give time to all historians looking for more information on the leagues and its players left us. On our last phone conversation, he said, "Might as well go for 100!" but he fell short. He was fine right to the end. He was probably the greatest schoolboy athlete to come out of New Jersey, and he was third in MVP voting in 1951 when he hit .312 with 121 RBIs for the world-champion Giants. He stole home in that World Series. He fought in World War II and had some of his greatest days playing in Mexico or Cuba or the Dominican Republic— stats that are lost to history and aren't included in the incorporation of the Negro Leagues as a "major league," as determined in 2021. In the years of the Negro Leagues, many of the players spent half their year in the Caribbean. They thought of it as just as important as their Negro League season.

A favorite story he liked to tell was of the Dominican dictator Rafael Trujillo calling him over during a game and offering him bonus money if he would hit a home run right there, right with this time at bat.

Monte returned to the batter's box. Roy Campanella was the catcher.

"Campy, want to make some money?" said Monte. "Trujillo is going to give me $250 if I homer here. Call for a high fastball and I'll give you half."

He did, and Monte hit it out. He and Campy shared big smiles as he crossed the plate, Campy's hidden behind his mask

And maybe that's why it's better not to include stats from winter ball after all.

Monte's favorite baseball movie was not *The Bingo Long Traveling All-Stars & Motor Kings*, a funny film with James Earl Jones, Richard Pryor, and Billy Dee Williams. "They had a great subject and a chance to tell a wonderful story, but they chose to make the Negro Leagues seem clownish," he said. "It was a lost opportunity. I hope they do something more authentic one day. I wish they could do for the Negro Leagues what *A League of Their Own* did for women's baseball."

Picking a favorite baseball movie is a good question to get baseball fans engaged. Older folks often say *Pride of the Yankees*, the 1942 Lou Gehrig biopic that starred Gary Cooper and Teresa Wright as Eleanor Gehrig. Teresa lived until 2005 and even did a movie with Matt Damon. I had a chance to know her and even drove her back to New York from the Yogi Berra Museum one day. Late in life, she embraced the film as having been a classic and even became a Yankees fan.

But, she said, "I didn't look at it as anything more than my acting assignment for a few months, and then it was on to the next picture. The lasting importance of the film didn't hit me at the time. Remember, you do scenes out of order, you concentrate on hitting your mark and remembering your lines, and then you're done. It never occurred to me people would be talking about the film more than a half-century later. It was a job, I did it, and I was off to do the next project. I was doing two or three a year in the '40s."

So much for getting special insight on *Pride of the Yankees*, although I used to phone the real Eleanor Gehrig (who lived until 1986) to tell her, "I saw your movie last night on Million Dollar Movie, and you were as pretty as ever! You never age!" She loved that. And I loved making arrangements for her and Claire Ruth to visit Yankee Stadium, although they preferred not to sit with each other. They had issues. But they knew their place as placeholders for Babe and Lou and loved the crowd's cheers for "them."

Ask younger people their favorite baseball movie and you get votes for *Bull Durham, Field of Dreams, The Natural,* and *The Bad News Bears.* Mine is *Eight Men Out,* which happened to be Yogi's favorite, believing it captured 1919 realism to a tee. Yogi was quite the moviegoer, and his choice mattered to me.

If I was keeping count over the years, I would say *Bull Durham* has the most votes among those I've asked.

"Ask any player who spent time in the minors back in the day, and without hesitation most of them will say *Bull Durham,*" said my friend Peter Bavasi, the first general manager of the Toronto Blue Jays and later president in Cleveland.

"I lived in that minor league world for six years," he adds, noting that the screenwriter, Ron Shelton, played minor league ball. "Back then, there was nothing more minor than playing or working in the minor leagues. We were all scuffling to make a living on $600 a month (paid only during the season) but down there we made hundreds of good baseball friends, shared a thousand great true-life baseball stories, and had a million laughs."

Another friend, Robert Wuhl, the actor who played a coach in the film ("…candlesticks always make a nice gift"), says, "First of all, it's told from a woman's point of view, which is rare. And it's not about whether the team wins or loses, it's about characters who go through a journey…and about the inequity of life. The player who has the brains but not the talent to succeed versus the one who does have the talent but not the brains. But the two main characters find each other."

The 2021 Yankees–White Sox game on Iowa's "Field of Dreams" seemed to enthrall the nation's baseball fans, played as it was before 8,000 bleacher fans with corn stalks beyond the outfield and the teams in vintage uniforms. The event brought about numerous recollections and replays of the final dialogue in the movie when Ray Kinsella (Kevin Costner) says, "Dad…you wanna have a catch?" And the young version of his father, John Kinsella (played by Dwier Brown), says, "I'd like that." The way Costner's voice breaks as he delivers his line…the first time he has acknowledged that the man in uniform is his father, and the way Brown responds knowingly, even though it was unspoken, was cinematic genius. And yes, I choke up every time I see it. I even did just now as I was typing this.

It didn't make me think of playing catch with my dad. We didn't do that, and he grew up in Brooklyn without being much of a baseball fan. But he did take me to my first game at Ebbets Field sometime in 1955. I marvel at people today who have ticket stubs and remember every detail about their first game. I remember nothing, except that we sat behind the backstop, protected by the screen, and I was fascinated and amused all day by No. 39, the Dodgers catcher Roy Campanella, who was on the roly-poly side and thus interesting to my seven-year-old self. This would have been slightly before I could say I was a fan, which came with the 1955 World Series.

It's odd that I remember where I sat, but I always remember my point of view at every movie, show, concert or sports event I've ever been to. I might not remember the movie's plot or who won the game, but for some reason I remember where I sat.

Despite this odd memory trait, I must confess, I never was able to wink, snap my fingers, crack my knuckles, blow a bubble, or whistle a tune. I can't drive a stick shift, and I've never eaten rice pudding, macaroni and cheese, or oatmeal. I can't drink hot beverages or soup until they cool down. I can, however, still throw strikes for the top of a pitching mound (at about 55 mph) and can name all the presidents in order, but that was because a chart with all of them, purchased by my mother from *Women's Day* magazine, hung over my bed for years. (I have to slow down after Eisenhower, which is where the chart ended.)

I hate to admit this, but while I like to think of myself as an eyes-wide, aware New Yorker, I tend to be a sucker for smooth talkers with big ideas who seem on the surface to be big achievers. I've been taken by more than one over the years.

One such memory involves a fellow who visited us at our Flushing offices by Shea Stadium in 1974. Polaroid had just come out with its breakthrough SX-70 instant camera, which did away with negatives and had a picture in your hands in seconds. Very cool.

So, this fellow came in and said he would like to create a "photo day" at Shea, where fans would line up in the aisles, facing the field, and when they reached the front, they could pose with a waiting Yankees player or coach, get their shot, have it handed to them, and be gone. If we made the players sit there for an hour, we could do many thousands of photos, and the fans would love it.

The promoter—we'll call him Bill—would provide all the cameras, all the film, and a team of photographers and ushers at each aisle to keep the line moving and hand the fan his photo. It was heavy on logistics, but his presentation was well thought out. The burden was on us to convince the players to cooperate, assisted by our manager Bill Virdon in explaining it to the team. It was one of the few closed-door clubhouse meetings I was ever present for, and I had to address the team and give them the instructions.

Then came the big day, and guess what—it worked like a charm! "Bill" was right; he organized it perfectly and even less-than-cooperative players like Alex Johnson happily participated.

While "Bill" was strong on organization, he apparently had some other weaknesses. Four days after the promotion, the *Daily News* ran a story about his being found dead in the trunk of a car at a LaGuardia Airport parking lot. Details were sketchy, but the description sounded like he had been fooling around with the wife of a mob figure, and the hit men left a signature known to address that. There was nothing in there about his Yankees promotion.

Barry Landers (our promotion director) and I took the article to Gabe Paul.

"Holy shit," said Gabe. "Did we pay him yet?"

You could always count on Gabe getting to the heart of the matter. Turns out we paid him the first half of his fee, but not the second.

"Well, that's the silver lining to the story," he said.

Gabe did have a reputation of being cheap. "Do it cheap, but first class" he used to tell me in catering press conferences. One tale we used to tell among ourselves was his role in the 1940 suicide of Cincinnati Reds catcher Willard Hershberger (a former Yankees farmhand), who was found dead in his Boston hotel room at the Copley Plaza. Gabe was the team's traveling secretary.

There followed Gabe's apocryphal phone call to Reds team owner Powell Crosley, which we assumed went like this:

"Powell? Gabe Paul. Listen, I have good news and bad news.

"The bad news is Hershberger; he's dead. Slit his throat in the bathtub. It's a mess. And we need to call up another catcher.

"The good news is that I recovered the balance of his meal money in his pants pocket. I'll bring it home."

Americans love their coffee, and I usually have a cup with breakfast, but I find it so annoying when people obsess over it. "More coffee? More coffee? More coffee, more coffee," say the servers at restaurants. I couldn't believe it when Jerry Seinfeld created a cable show called *Comedians in Cars Getting Coffee*, with endless beauty shots of coffee being poured. I thought this was exactly the thing Jerry could be counted on to take a stand against! I thought he would be with me on this! "People! What is this thing we have about coffee?"

The biggest coffee drinker during my time with the Yankees was our pitcher Pat Dobson, who would have a cup between innings—or nine cups during a game, if he went the distance.

Pete Rose is easy to like; he has a winning personality, and he has the confidence and swagger that goes with being one of the elite athletes of the 20th century.

But he's Pete. Joe Garagiola Jr. and I once took him out to Bern's Steak House in Tampa because we had some business to discuss with him. We were going to spend big bucks to meet him (and his wife) in the classiest place in town.

When he arrived (not with his wife, but with teammate Doug Flynn), he confessed he had never heard of the place, and was more of a fast-food guy.

The waiter brought out the wine list.

"Just bring out a slab of beef," said Pete. "We're on our way to the dog track."

Twenty minutes later, they were fed and gone. That was Pete.

Now he's on people's minds as the most famous guy not in the Hall of Fame. He was placed on baseball's ineligible list in 1989, which made him ineligible for Hall of Fame consideration. Even if he is one day taken off that list, his time to be voted in by the writers has long passed, and I don't think any veterans committee would vote him in.

But Pete thrives as a dispenser of Pete Rose memorabilia and lives in the perfect town for him, Las Vegas. A majority of fans seems to think he should be, at long last, elected.

The problem with this is that those people don't consider the full story; they just like Pete Rose. He bet on baseball while he was still an active player (the last player-manager). And if he had bet on the Reds to win every day, I suppose a forgiveness argument could be found in that. But he didn't bet every day. He was selective. And what about those days he didn't bet? What was going on with that?

You could make an argument that he might have been delivering a message to his bookmaker to "bet against the Reds," and in so doing, wiping out any debts he had accumulated in return for the "tip." An understanding.

Did this happen? We don't know for sure, but the possibility of it happening is exactly what baseball must avoid. The games can't appear suspicious. Pete knew that; it's posted on clubhouse walls under "no gambling" and he was in clubhouses for more than 25 years. It wasn't exactly in small print.

Baseball's embrace of legalized gambling in the 2020s is disturbing to me but used by Rose supporters as a reason to forgive. I can see their point. I'm surprised baseball ever wandered down that path, but the sponsorship revenue was too tempting, and the commissioner is first and foremost charged with generating revenue. Can naming rights to a ballpark be far behind? Perhaps a ballpark that once displayed those No BETTING signs?

Next to TV rights and ticket sales, it could become the third-largest piece of revenue in the pie. But the day could also arrive when fans can bet on every at-bat with their smartphones. (Or field goal attempts in football and foul shots in basketball.) They would need to be quick, but imagine when a home team player strikes out and thousands of fans cheer because that's what they bet. It will be a bad optic for the game, for sure. And people will surely think—whether true or not—that the player told his struggling brother-in-law to bet on a strikeout on that at bat. That's when it really gets ugly.

Then there is the case of the steroid users. Here I'm not as certain of my position as I am with Rose.

As my late friend Bob Creamer, the great *Sports Illustrated* journalist, said, "I'd rather they didn't do it, but they were trying to play better, make more money, and help their team win. They weren't trying to lose or harm the team."

And he was right. So, I suspect that one day, this thinking will slide into the thinking of the veterans committees, and they will be selected. They were, after all, the best players of their era, even if steroid use cost people who didn't use them their jobs—and kept clean minor leaguers from reaching the majors. And kept players like Bernie Williams, who we assume played clean, from having greater Hall of Fame consideration because he "only" hit 30 home runs in his best season.

In February 2000, a season after the remarkable Mark McGwire–Sammy Sosa race to break Roger Maris' record, the Major League Baseball Players Association held a home run hitting contest at Cashman Field in Las Vegas to raise money for the association's charitable arm, the Players Trust for Children. It was called the "Big League Challenge," and I was asked to be on the scene to interview the players, the transcription of which would appear on their individual pages within the Players Association website. I was told not to bother McGwire, as he didn't want to do any interviews, even this one.

I was on the field for a group photo for a few professional photographers. I took one too. And there they were—McGwire, Barry Bonds, Jose Canseco, Shawn Green, Nomar Garciaparra, Chipper Jones, Rafael Palmeiro, Mike Piazza, Alex Rodriguez, Jason Giambi, Manny Ramirez, and Andruw Jones. Sosa missed the event and the photo, diagnosed with the flu and confined to his room. (Canseco beat Palmeiro in the finals.)

I wonder what these guys talked about during their private times together.

Not all of them were named, or suspected, of being steroid users. And I'm not saying others were suspected, but I remember looking on with amazement in the early '90s as certain players appeared with muscles that looked like they were doing World Wrestling Entertainment in the off season. Willie Randolph and I recently ran down some names we both suspected in the late '80s and chuckled at the ones we had in common.

I did all my interviews and, of course, didn't ask anything about steroid use. I was on assignment from the Players Association. As the next season unfolded, Bonds would shatter the record book by hitting 73 with an .863 slugging percentage. My interview with Barry, as we sat on a small couch

Recording an interview with the generally reluctant Barry Bonds.

in the middle of the clubhouse, was actually quite nice. I had been friends with his father, Bobby, who had been a Yankee in 1975, and I met Barry as an 11-year-old that year, since players sometimes brought their kids to the clubhouse. I told Barry that I thought Bobby was the best all-around athlete I had ever met, although later on, I thought Dave Winfield was his equal.

My best interview of the weekend was Alex Rodriguez, and when I see his proficiency at the microphone today, I flash back to how good he was at 24.

During his year of suspension from the Yankees for steroid use, I was in a souvenir store by Yankee Stadium and saw that they were still selling Rodriguez jerseys, No. 13 with his name on the back. I was curious how briskly they were selling and asked the salesman as much.

"They're our best seller after Jeter," he said. "You know how many people are named Rodriguez in the Bronx?"

A-Rod was born in Washington Heights in Upper Manhattan. This fascinated me, because that was where the Yankees were born. They were called the Highlanders by some when they arrived in 1903, playing at Hilltop Park, where New York–Presbyterian Hospital now sits above the 168th Street subway station. (The station requires an elevator to reach street level—hence, "hilltop.")

I was present in 1993 when a bronze home plate was dedicated in the courtyard of the hospital, on the original spot of the base, to mark the 90th anniversary of the opening of the wooden ballpark. Red Hoff, 102, a Highlander pitcher in 1911–12, was there. At the 1903 opening, Wee Willie Keeler, the right fielder, had to stand on wooden planks, as most of the area was mud. The boulders that had populated the right field area had only been removed by dynamite weeks before. Excavating and leveling the land cost more than the franchise rights did.

Most of the photographs of action at Hilltop Park (many taken by the great early baseball photographer Charles Conlon) show three attached apartment buildings over the outfield wall. Those buildings are still there, and I worked with WPIX to do a feature on the buildings in 2021, asking residents if they knew the history of what their windows overlooked. We found one couple who did! The woman's mother had lived there starting in the 1930s, and although Hilltop Park was long gone, she did know the history and passed it on to her daughter. It's called luck when you are doing a report like this and happen to stumble into just the right couple.

I tried to determine if A-Rod had been born in New York–Presbyterian (which was called Columbia–Presbyterian when he was born in 1975), but he had no idea, and historians at the hospital had no record. "There were a lot of hospitals in Washington Heights in the '70s," one told me. "And even if he was born here, we couldn't tell you due to HIPAA [patient privacy] laws."

So, I couldn't know for sure, but it would have been a very cool fact.

On the matter of Jose Canseco, he may have been a terrific and colorful ballplayer, but whereas some players just "get" baseball, Jose was a little slow in fully understanding its nuances.

There was, for instance, the time he encountered his athletic trainer, Barry Weinberg (a former Yankees assistant trainer), in the Oakland clubhouse after a Saturday victory. "That was fun," he mentioned to Barry. "Who do we play tomorrow?"

I'm not aware of any time that the opponent was different on a Sunday than a Saturday. Apparently, Jose hadn't picked up on that.

There was a time in baseball when "baseball clowns" could make a good living touring the country and performing, mostly at minor league parks. The early ones were former players with a good sense of theater and humor—Al Schacht, Nick Altrock, and later Max Patkin, all variously known as the "Clown Prince of Baseball." It helped to have loose limbs or a big nose.

Schacht was a little before my time, but I do remember him performing at Yankees Old Timers' games, which I guess Red Patterson and Bob Fishel thought was a good addition to the festivities.

Patkin, seemingly without bones in his Jello-like body, was terrific at pantomiming the first baseman from the coach's box and working up the crowd. He had regular annual stops throughout the nation's minor league system, but George Steinbrenner always liked him and brought him to Yankee Stadium. He was entertaining, but for a New York audience, it was pretty hokey.

I remember Max after the games, sitting with the players in the clubhouse lounge, drinking his post-game beer as though he was one of guys, like a coach. I suppose most of the players had seen him perform his routines in the minors.

The clowns had a good thing going and a full summer schedule. Their main competition was none other than the great Bob Feller, who developed a business pitching to locals at minor league venues. He'd throw to fans and was still winging them in there into his late seventies. Even at 90, he took the mound in Cooperstown for a pitching exhibition. And he had a pilot's license and would pilot himself from one town to the next.

When we invited Feller to Old Timers' Day, it would cost him two or three appearances, and Fishel would make it up to him by allowing him to cash a check in our ticket office, making sure the check was never deposited. They had an understanding, which I carried on when I succeeded Fishel.

When Feller phoned you, he wanted no doubt as to who was on the line. "This is Hall of Famer Bob Feller," he would say. It got attention.

The clown princes of baseball were eventually replaced by lovable mascots. No team could be without a mascot, and the furry creatures could be at every game, work the crowds for photo opportunities, appear at the local mall, and generally be considered part of the team. Mr. Met was among the first of these, and he has had enduring appeal, but the first to really break through were the San Diego Chicken (originally a promotional opportunity for a local radio station, developed by Ted Giannoulas) and the Phillie Phanatic, for which Dave Raymond, inside the costume, developed routines that made him stand apart as simply the best of them all.

The Yankees had a mascot, very briefly, named Dandy. (Get it? Yankee Doodle Dandy?) It was a most unlikely Yankees thing to do. This was the team with no names on the uniforms, no beards, no long hair—not even cardboard fans during the pandemic season of 2020.

But Dandy did appear on occasion between 1979 and 1981. Some people thought he looked like Munson. He had a Yosemite Sam mustache and a pinstriped furry body the shape of a pear. It was, frankly, a disaster. Not only did the fans not appreciate it, but he was said to have been beaten up in the upper deck one day and never seen again. It was for the best.

For me, the handwriting was eventually on the wall for the Yankees production portion of my job at WPIX—the games were migrating to cable and we wouldn't be producing them ourselves anymore; SportsChannel would. They had 100 games and we had 40, even though much of New York City was not yet wired for cable. So, an offer out of nowhere to go to Atlanta for the 1996 Olympics was well timed.

Billy Payne, a football player at Georgia who went on to become an attorney, had led the Olympic bid effort for the city, which somewhat remarkably was awarded the games on its first attempt. It was said that Payne told the International Olympic Committee (IOC) that the average daily temperature in Atlanta in the summer was 77 (including the overnight hours). It was also said that some of the IOC members thought they were voting for Atlantic City with its casino hotels. And many IOC members, potentates and sultans as they were, mostly cared about hotel quality.

Anyway, I was recruited by a search firm and was told that the higher-ups in Atlanta were impressed that I had stood up to George Steinbrenner. I have no idea where they would have gotten that idea.

My work in Atlanta was "hit the ground running" even as I had to learn Olympic-speak and master the American south and Georgia style. "I surely don't" was an answer I had to get used to if I'd ask someone if they happened to know something.

And then there were all the steps that went into building a world-class Olympic Games.

Early on, a number of design companies submitted entries for consideration of an Olympic mascot. That should have been a fun project.

Billy Payne had made it clear that he would personally choose the mascot. No focus groups, no sponsor input, no staff input. Only one other employee would be in the room.

On a Sunday morning, one of my colleagues laid out sketches of the potential mascots for Billy to choose. He walked around the room, pointed, and said, "That one."

The mascot was called Izzy, as from "What is it?" and it was a blue blob that didn't seem to have much charm. When we formally introduced it at closing ceremonies in Barcelona in 1992, you could feel the embarrassment from the assembled stadium crowd and the pall cast over our large contingent from Atlanta. We knew we had a problem, and things didn't get better when we got home. The mascot was poorly received everywhere.

Sometimes you just have to listen to public opinion and acknowledge it. But I thought we had a solution.

The mascot had been created to "morph" into different forms—like a golfer for Olympic golf, or a swimmer for swimming, or a track star for track and field.

I went to Billy and said, "Let's face it, it's not going over well. How about we just pick one of the other ones and say, 'It's still Izzy, but he has morphed into this.'"

Billy was not amused. And he never yielded on the subject. The mascot remained Izzy and remained an object of ridicule. It was universally hated.

I was back in New York by the time the actual '96 Games came around, having completed my work on helping organize the PR operation, publish a quarterly magazine, work with Dick Clark Productions on a spectacular musical event to herald the arrival of the Olympic flag at the opening of the Georgia Dome, and set in place a weekly "Olympic Report" on local radio. I made good friends and learned Olympic-speak. My two weeks in Barcelona for the '92 Games were sensational and I learned a lot. We all did—and we came home wondering, *How are we ever going to duplicate that?!*

But by mid-1993 I was gone, happy to return to New York. Civil rights icon Andrew Young, a co-chairman of the Olympic Committee, and Shirley Franklin, the future Mayor of Atlanta, helped steer me through the process of extricating myself.

Civil Rights leader, former UN Ambassador, former Atlanta mayor, and Atlanta Olympics co-chair Andrew Young.

The Atlanta Olympics is best remembered for the pipe bomb that went off at Centennial Olympic Park, wounding 111 and killing two, and for the carnival-like street commerce that defied all efforts to control the use of the Olympic marks. Vendors set up along Peachtree Street selling all sorts of cheap souvenirs.

I did learn a lot about the politics and culture of the Olympics (and of Atlanta) but never did learn—nor did I feel comfortable—with something called the "Olympic Movement." I still have no idea what that means, but it feels creepy.

Sixth Inning

I never worked in the minor leagues, but I have enormous respect for those who have. That is really baseball for the love of it. And while it has seldom been a step to major league front office employment, it also breeds hard working dedicated officials who provide terrific grassroots, affordable entertainment for portions of America outside reasonable driving distance of major league markets.

If a family wants to plan an outing, without care for who the players are or what the outcome is, this is America's destination. Minor league operators have found a way to keep it fun and entertaining from first pitch ceremony to postgame fireworks. They share ideas that work and have made the minor league experience an affordable family experience.

The major leagues, long ago, used to operate on shoestring budgets, so it's possible to get a taste of how things must have been in olden times by seeing a minor league operation today.

For instance, when the major leagues switched out of the "dead ball era" and into a lively ball...do you think the owners really threw out the dead balls? Of course not! It would have been costly; a waste of money. Rather, they must surely have slowly eased in the new lively balls, making the seasons in the early 1920s transitional seasons. For Babe Ruth to have suddenly hit 54 home runs and the rest of the American League 315 combined (with no full team besides the Yankees over 50) tells me that the dead ball didn't stop Ruth, but it was clearly still in use. So, saving money on new baseballs was surely something that owners felt they needed to do, and no one would especially notice.

Jacob Ruppert, now in his sixth year owning the Yankees, could be the exception. He had money to spend (Prohibition hadn't yet kicked in to kill off his brewery business). Maybe he did throw out all the dead balls, leaving the Yankees the lone team playing at home with a lively ball. After all, why did he buy Babe Ruth if not for the lure of the home run! (Only 20 of his 54 home runs in 1920 were hit on the road.)

The camaraderie of the minor leagues is something major league players always cherish, long before direct deposits of millions of dollars hit their checking accounts.

We tend to think in generalities about the minors: *Oh, those long bus rides*. But Yankees announcer John Flaherty, a former catcher, talked about it on a broadcast and said, "We preferred those bus rides to air travel. You'd get on the bus, settle in, tell stories, make friends, play cards, and adjust to the long trip. With air travel, you had to wake up extra early, make connecting flights (seldom are direct flights available between minor league cities), have the tension that airports bring, and arrive anything but rested."

I believe one thing missing from most baseball broadcasts is the work involved in asking players about pre–major league relationships they have with the day's opponent. Those guys know each other more than you think—sometimes back to travel ball in Little League days. Most major leaguers played against some of their opponents on a given day—and might have great stories—from college or minor league days. It would be worth exploring, but it takes effort.

Because I went to college in Oneonta, a lot of people thought I must have worked for the Oneonta Yankees (New York–Penn League) before jumping to the Yanks. Actually, because it was a summer league, I never even went to a game at Damashke Field, although I became good friends with the team's owner Sam Nader, a former mayor of Oneonta. In 2012, when he was in his nineties, he made the 19-mile journey to Cooperstown (where I was speaking), just to say hello to an old friend. That really meant a lot to me. He lived to be 101.

Bill and Millie Gladstone were Larchmont neighbors, and Bill was a world-class collector of valuable baseball art as well as Brooklyn Dodgers memorabilia. Some of his art was on loan to major art museums. Bill was the head of the Arthur Young accounting firm and helped steer its merger with Ernst & Whinney, becoming co-chief executive of the new Ernst & Young. He was on the board of directors of the Baseball Hall of Fame, and with his wife, a former teacher, owned the Pittsfield Mets, playing in historic Wahconah Park in Massachusetts. When the Mets moved that team to Brooklyn as the Cyclones, he chose to stay in Pittsfield, establishing a new working agreement with the Houston Astros, and then moving the team to Troy, New York as the Tri-City Valley Cats. He had Jose Altuve, J.D. Martinez, Dallas Keuchel, George Springer, and other prospects on the way up, and he and Millie cared for these young prospects—and the ones you haven't heard of—like family. He lived and died with the wins and losses and would be despondent for hours after a tough loss. We went to a game with him in which the ValleyCats lost in the ninth when a game-ending grounder hit the base and jumped over the first baseman. Three runs scored and the Cats lost. Dinner plans were cancelled.

He spent his summers in Troy, and when he died at 88 from Covid in 2020, the local newspaper read, "Beloved Valley Cats Owner Dies," noting that Millie had passed away two years earlier. My family loved them, and they were great to my children. There were a lot of minor league owners like them who weren't in it to get rich.

I had further experience at this level when my PR company took on an account with the independent Atlantic League in 2015. Rick White, the commissioner, with whom I had worked at MLB, hired us for this exciting project, with the major leagues turning to the Atlantic League from time to time to experiment with new rules. We generated a lot of publicity for one game in particular—at the ballpark of the Long Island Ducks—when it was just three balls for a walk and two strikes for a strikeout. The league experimented with a lot of "pace of play" rules, and let's face it, you can hardly meet anyone in baseball—an employee, a journalist, or a fan—who doesn't decry the length of games today. Even a lot of players do, although the games seem to move a lot faster when you're out there playing.

One modest suggestion from me: ban Velcro from batting gloves. That would save a lot of time. The game-delay practice of stepping out of the batter's box and adjusting the Velcro straps goes back at least to Thurman Munson, I think. But it probably preceded him.

Waving batters to first base for an intentional walk without throwing the four pitches saves about 90 seconds a month, if that. It was a silly rule that didn't speed up games, although some would argue that throwing the four pitches is silly too.

As rules were tinkered with and the look and speed of the game evolved, doubleheaders became scarce, largely because separate admissions were required for revenue stream purposes. So they became rare, usually scheduled only to make up for rainouts.

When I worked for the Yankees, we hated doubleheaders. Not only because of the long workday, but because a huge percentage of doubleheaders resulted in splits. So, you'd spend all those hours at the ballpark and wind up right where you started. There would be about a half-hour between games—a rush for the players to change uniforms and grab some unhealthy snack.

But for a couple of years, Ralph Houk made second games a lot of fun. We had veteran players on the bench who would get rare starts in those games, and they had a blast getting some playing time and performing well as a unit, as they had in the old days when they were regulars. So there were Pete Ward, Johnny Callison, Ron Hansen, Bernie Allen, Hal Lanier, Felipe Alou, Ron Swoboda, and others—good guys all—rising to the occasion and reliving their days of regular play. It was great fun sending in the "B" team, and they made the most of it.

Marv Goldklang not only owned a piece of the Yankees but interests in five minor and independent league teams, including Hudson Valley. His ownership group included actor Bill Murray and Mike Veeck, son of Bill.

Goldklang was also a friend and neighbor to the world-class collector Barry Halper, a gregarious guy who looked a little bit like Babe Ruth.

At Barry's funeral in 2005, Marv talked about how they met. "I was having a catch on my front lawn with my son, and the sound of the ball hitting the gloves got the attention of my new neighbor, Barry Halper. At once, Barry came running out of his house with his own glove to join in. It was the start of a beautiful friendship."

Barry and I became friends through baseball, and one year we talked about doing an annual "hot stove league dinner" with the two of us and the *Daily News* baseball columnist Bill Madden. Madden had written the first column about Barry's amazing collection, so friendships were formed. And those dinners continue to this day, with Barry's son Jason (who played a season of minor league ball when Barry, with Goldklang, was also a limited partner of the Yankees).

One year, our hot stove trio was to meet at Nino's on First Avenue. It was a stormy night and I encouraged Barry to hire a car service from his home in Livingston, New Jersey. But he insisted he would be fine.

We were to meet at six. Bill and I arrived on time, but by 6:30, still no Barry. We started to worry. At 6:50, still no Barry. We were now facing three dilemmas in this era before cellphones: First, should we call Barry's wife, Sharon? It would surely alarm her. We decided not to. Second, as it was already 6:50, should we overlook our concern and order dinner? Was that impolite if Barry had driven off the road into a ditch? But third, and perhaps most important, who was going to pay? Barry, by agreement, was to pay the first 10 years. This was already year 18, but I kept telling him we were only up to seven, and he kept paying. (He used to say, "Seven, really? Seems like more.")

Finally, around 7:00, he walked through the door. We were so relieved— on many levels. *What happened?*

Turns out, he did hire a car service. And he fell asleep in the back seat. The driver parked right in front of the restaurant at 6:00 but didn't want to wake him! He was asleep right in front of the entrance all this time. And so, we dined and celebrated the season, and he paid. After all, we had years to go before we reached 10.

Barry's remarkable collection—including rare vintage uniforms on display on a dry cleaner's circulating ceiling rack that he installed in his home—eventually went for many millions at a Sotheby's auction, with the more valuable items purchased by MLB for display at the Hall of Fame. Billy Crystal bought a Mantle glove.

Some time later it began to appear that not all the items were as authentic as Barry believed them to be. It wasn't as though he was pulling a fast one on anyone—he believed them to be real when he acquired them. He was a sucker for a good story, and authentication hadn't really taken hold yet.

So, after his death, items being "from the Halper Collection" lost some clout, even though more than 90 percent of it was good. And he was a great and generous friend.

His wife, Sharon, an internationally trained gourmet chef, used to host dinner parties in their home for players Barry would invite. Joe DiMaggio was a regular who even slept over on occasion. She saved photos, menus, recipes, and thank-you letters, and as she was dying of cancer, she created a very limited-edition hardcover book with all of those memories, which was produced in 2016, just weeks before she departed.

The first book I ever had published was the reason I first met Barry. The book was called *Baseball's Best: The Hall of Fame Gallery* and it was published in 1977. It had biographies of all the Hall of Famers to that point, and while biographies of Ruth and Cobb and Mantle and DiMaggio were readily available, this was the first to give lengthy profiles of the umpires, the executives, the 19th century players, and the early Negro League inductees. The Associated Press used it for years for obituary research, and President Reagan used it for "overnight briefing material" prior to a White House gathering of Hall of Famers.

In the biography of 19th century home run champion Roger Connor, I made mention of a weathervane in the shape of a baseball bat atop his old home in Waterbury, Connecticut.

This was the sort of thing that fired Barry up. He drove to Waterbury's older sections and searched atop all the houses looking for the weathervane. He figured no one would have thrown it out. (Connor died in 1931.)

He found it! He rang the bell, made an offer for the weathervane, and made arrangements to have it moved and installed at his home in Livingston, New Jersey.

Babe Ruth's camel hair coat, part of the Barry Halper collection.

And then he found me and invited me to visit to see the weathervane, and, while I was there, to try on Ty Cobb's uniform jersey and Babe Ruth's famous camel hair overcoat.

A friendship was formed.

When *Baseball's Best* was being developed, when books were typewritten, my publisher sent me page galleys along with the manuscript, to be proofread. The carton, which was sent to me at Yankee Stadium, had to have weighed 70 pounds.

It was sitting at the security desk with my name on it and when I tried to lift it, I knew we had a problem. It was not only heavy but also unbalanced. So, I was contemplating going down to the clubhouse to borrow a hand truck—the sort of thing they used to move fully loaded bat bags with.

As I was pondering this, who comes out of the elevator on his way to the parking lot but Thurman Munson.

I seized the moment. "Thurm, give me a hand here? Can you help me carry this box to my car?"

I use "help" in the figurative sense.

He said "sure," and I don't know if he expected it to weigh 70 pounds, but here I was with our All-Star catcher, happily walking ahead of him to lead him to my Toyota. *That* was All-Star service.

The Toyota, by the way, had been the Yankees' bullpen car, and I had purchased it from the ad agency, to take possession after the 1976 season. After Chris Chambliss homered to win the AL pennant and thousands stormed the field for souvenirs, Sparky Lyle stayed in the bullpen to protect my car, knowing that I had bought it. The stadium was chaos that day. What a beautiful gesture of friendship that was by Sparky.

When I succeeded Don Carney as executive producer of Yankees games on WPIX (he was also the director), I was only the third person to hold that position since the station started doing Yankees baseball in 1951. (Jack Murphy was the first.) It was similar to my being the third Yankees public relations director—I was filling big shoes.

The job of being executive producer is first and foremost a business job. Hire the announcers (with team approval), hire production trucks for road games, coordinate staffing with our engineering department, and work to reschedule rainout telecasts. We also worked a bit with our counterparts at the Mets station to avoid too many conflicts in the days before all games were telecast. It's hard to imagine today that we did some road telecasts with only four cameras and two tape machines. Today's local Yankees telecasts employ 16 cameras.

There was also billing visiting clubs (or rather their stations) for a shared use of our feed, arranging for satellite time with Hughes Sports Network to transmit our games, and conferring with our director, the gifted John Moore, on daily plans to try and add something special to the telecast. Oh, and explaining to Pat Harper, who was standing by to do our 10 o'clock news, why the game was going into extra innings. She was not a fan of extra innings.

There was no doubt I had a lot to learn about the technical side of broadcasting games, but we had an amazing team of engineers on the scene, including some who'd been involved since the black-and-white rabbit-ear days of the 1950s. This was, after all, the station that first used instant replay, going back to a 1959 near no-hitter by Ralph Terry that they were able to call up at Mel Allen's on-air urging. (A new invention called videotape was being saved by then for use on the post-game show; this was the first insertion during a game itself, if not exactly instant.)

In my office, I hung a photograph of the Hall of Fame plaque of Alexander Cartwright, considered the man who codified baseball rules, including nine innings in a game.

Under the photo I added my own caption: WPIX SALUTES ALEXANDER CARTWRIGHT, WHO CREATED THE CONCEPT OF 18 COMMERCIAL BREAKS. Today, those breaks translate into more than $1 million in advertising money per game.

Make no mistake, we knew those commercials were paying all of our salaries. There was no disrespect for them. That Bud was for us.

I used to have nightmares about whether I remembered to order a truck for every road game. (Fortunately, I never missed.) For home games, there was no truck; a control room was built inside the stadium.

One additional problem that I anticipated had been going on since baseball on the radio began in 1921. The player wives would be watching or listening at home, and when their husbands came home, they would tell them the awful thing that the announcer had said about them. Both in my time in Yankees PR and my time as executive producer, that never ended. And it was seldom what was really said that was repeated. The wives just wanted to hear good stuff, and when they thought it wasn't delivered, they remembered things differently. With the advent of tapes, I was at least able to play back what was really said (if indeed I had the time) and report back to the player. I wouldn't dare report back to the wife.

An early challenge came when I got a phone call from our announcer Bill White, saying he needed to see me the next day. My immediate reaction was the right one: *Oh no; they didn't offer you the National League presidency, did they?*

I had it right. It had been on my mind as they searched for a successor to Fay Vincent, who had moved up to commissioner after the death of Bart Giamatti. It was a domino effect. Ever since Al Campanis of the Dodgers had gone on ABC's *Nightline* with Ted Koppel and said that Black players lacked the "necessities" to become owners, managers, or front-office executives (ending Al's career), pressure was on MLB to right that wrong with a high-profile hire. And if I was doing the search for a league president, I would have come up with Bill White as a candidate too, Campanis or not.

Bill and I had a deep friendship since he had become a Yankees announcer in 1971. I worked with him in his early days, listening to tapes and critiquing his work. He also hired a voice coach at his own expense. He wanted to master the craft, and I believe he did. When that bass voice said, "Deep to left…!" on the Bucky Dent home run swing at Fenway in1978, you knew you were hearing it from a voice with authority.

At first some of his mistakes were remarkable—he kept getting right field and left field mixed up; he said "Cominsky" instead of "Comiskey," and he even called the Washington Senators the Redskins. Phil Rizzuto, with whom he worked so well, would simply call him a "National League huckleberry" when he'd say Redskins.

But he got better and eventually, the fans loved his work with Rizzuto and missed him when he took the National League presidency. I remained friends with Bill long after his retirement from baseball, visiting him at his home along the Delaware River, and he would flatter me by telling people that I one, helped him become a better broadcaster and two, was his only remaining friend from baseball besides Sandy Koufax, Bob Gibson, and his National League office colleague Katy Feeney. I was in the same sentence as Koufax and Gibson!

Setting up a yearbook photo with Bill White, Phil Rizzuto, and (back to camera) Frank Messer.

In the 2010s, I began filling him in on what was going on in baseball, because he had stopped watching, hated the game's politics, and really didn't care. I just thought there were things he should know, especially with the rule changes they were putting in for the pandemic.

Naturally we released Bill from his contract with WPIX and to his misery, he went to the National League, wearing a suit and tie every day and dealing with all those millionaire owners. He was at once the highest ranking African American sports official in history. The history wasn't lost on him—it was one of the reasons he knew he had to take the job.

Now I had to fill his position with the Yankees. He strongly recommended that we bring back Frank Messer. Both he and Rizzuto were very loyal to Frank, but for some reason, Mr. Steinbrenner had lost enthusiasm for Frank and told us we had to let him go. He had final approval over the announcers. So, no Frank, who was a fine and decent man and a really proficient announcer who gave the Yankees 18 great seasons, most of it in primetime in the nation's biggest market.

Announcers in general are vastly unappreciated for delivering hundreds of unscripted hours of primetime television and radio with barely a misstep. This is not easy. In general, in unfiltered conversation, we all say things we wish we hadn't. Occasionally an announcer will cross a line with something offensive, and it can result in dismissal. The pressure to never cross that line is enormous. You need not only inherent intelligence, but you need to be up to date on sensitive cultural and political issues. Frank

Messer was a master of always doing as close to a perfect broadcast as one can do.

White was especially good at squeezing Rizzuto's wrist until his circulation stopped when he anticipated that Phil was going in a politically incorrect direction.

Phil was, of course, from another generation, and these things happen. He used to call "cheap" home runs that barely made it over the wall a "Chinese home run." Where that expression originated, I do not know, but it was part of Phil's repertoire.

One day I received a phone call from a woman who identified herself as Chinese. She couldn't have been more polite or sweeter, but she pointed out that the use of the term was troubling to her and her friends because it suggested "inferior" (which it did).

I mentioned it to Phil, and he never used it again. He recognized that the woman was indeed correct.

After conducting about a dozen interviews for White's successor, including some who came to New York at their own expense to meet with me, I got a call from Matt Merola, Tom Seaver's agent, expressing interest on Tom's behalf.

I admit I was always a Seaver fan. He may have been a Met, but to me he was like Christy Mathewson reborn. I loved that I was able to watch and appreciate one of the all-time great baseball players, playing in our era.

I had written two books with Tom—*Baseball's Greatest Players* (a children's book) and *Great Moments in Baseball* (in which I wrote about the historic games and Tom added his expert viewpoint and opinion to the narrative). We got along fine, and can you imagine a better slice of baseball heaven than sitting in his backyard in Greenwich, Connecticut, on a sunny afternoon, talking baseball for five hours, while his wife, Nancy, kept our lemonade glasses filled? Those afternoons were forever memories.

I had also liked Tom's work for NBC on postseason games, where he demonstrated a professionalism and an appeal despite little previous experience.

If there is a 'best day ever" category, how about working on a book with Tom Seaver in his Connecticut backyard?

My boss, Lev Pope, loved the star quality he would bring. And of course, we needed George Steinbrenner's okay too. We held our collective breaths. And he gave the approval.

And so, he was hired, and we also added George Grande, an ESPN veteran and a genuinely good person, as a third voice, thinking we needed a real "pro" in the booth aside Rizzuto and Seaver.

Not that Rizzuto wasn't a "pro"—he had been broadcasting Yankees baseball since 1957, could read commercial copy perfectly, and was brilliant at setting up game situations. But he never took himself seriously, and that of course, was part of his appeal. Fans loved his style.

I got to see him in action when he did a daily CBS Radio Network show, which he could do from any city we were in just by going to the local CBS-affiliated station, recording his 60-second copy (which Herb Goren wrote and faxed to the station ahead of time), and departing. He used to have his cab wait for him in front of the building, and he'd be in and out in less than 10 minutes, depending on how fast the elevators were running.

Then there were his low-budget commercials for the Money Store, a lending institution that bought a lot of air time in off hours. They paid him more than his Yankees job!

"Scooter," I would say. "Tell me what happens if you don't pay back your loan from the Money Store…"

"Holy cow, you don't want to know that," he'd reply, laughing. The suggestion was that some guys from Jersey City would look you up to collect payment.

Phil was really underpaid for his Yankees work, but of course, he loved still being part of the game—the fan adulation, the perks it brought, and staying relevant. Finally, though, after we signed Seaver, he spoke up about this salary and that fell on me. Our friendship grew strained. And Seaver, off to the side, was urging him on! Thanks, Tom.

My hands were tied. Lev Pope wouldn't budge. I was offering all that I was permitted to, and Phil would yell at me. There was no agent involved, and I sure wished there had been one. Cora Rizzuto, I later learned, was telling him not to take it out on me. But he did.

He was actually prepared to quit. The newspapers were all over it. I felt he would, and I felt I would be the bad guy. The New York media columnists were quoting me regularly.

Pope finally approved a decent raise, which of course made me think, *Why couldn't we do this in the first place if the money was there?* Slowly my friendship with Phil healed, and it was a great day when he was elected to the Hall of Fame. John Moore and I drove to his home in Hillside, New Jersey, to help with the throngs of visitors and media that would be descending. At my suggestion, Cora hung an American flag outside their home. It was a wonderful day, and at the end, Phil invited John and me to join them for dinner at a favorite Italian restaurant near his home.

When do you ever have dinner with a guy on the day he gets into the Hall of Fame?

In 1991, John and I produced a half-hour special on Phil's 50 years with the Yankees, which was nominated for an Emmy. We hired the fine actor Charles Durning as host. (We also did one on Billy Martin, with Phil Pepe as host, which won the Emmy…but we knew the Rizzuto show was better.) We taped much of it at Scooter's home and he was great, talking about his parents (his father was a streetcar motorman) and how he overcame the odds to be a major league player at barely 5'6". At a tryout with the Dodgers under the leadership of Casey Stengel, he was told to go home and get himself a shoeshine box. Bill Terry, managing the Giants, also sent him on his way at their tryout. But he became an MVP! For 40 years, he was the voice of our summers.

I thought that little scar in our relationship was always there in the room, but he was good to me. When there was an auction of his memorabilia and a press conference at Mickey Mantle's Restaurant, I presided. He was older; Cora and his three daughters weren't sure he could speak, but he did and he was great.

Dave Kaplan, who ran the Yogi Berra Museum, joined me in visiting him at the senior citizens home where he lived near the end. We brought cannolis and had a wonderful visit. I took a photo of him on an exercise bike, where he was looking great and showing off, and it might have been one of the last photos of him. He died not long after, on August 13 of all days—the same day that Mickey Mantle had died 12 years before. (August 16 is the date of departure for the Sultan, Babe Ruth; the King, Elvis Presley; and the Queen, Aretha Franklin.)

Phil Rizzuto at his care facility, working out on an exercise bike, and looking very good doing it!

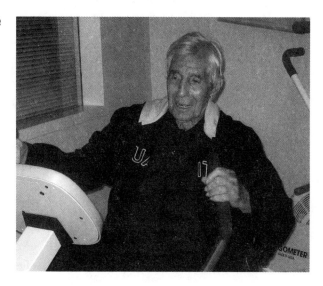

With Phil Rizzuto in our first visit to newly opened Comiskey Park.

Phil publicly said he deeply regretted that WPIX wouldn't give him the day off to fly to Dallas for Mickey Mantle's funeral in 1995. He was so upset with himself that he said he was leaving broadcasting, although he did come back in 1996 for Derek Jeter's rookie season. He went out with a world-championship season.

WPIX graciously took the heat for that, but the truth was, by this time Phil hated air travel and would do anything to get out of going to Dallas. He begged off all our West Coast trips. WPIX would not have stopped him from going; he made up the story of PIX making him stay home. To their honor, they never disputed it.

I led a memorial service for Phil at the Yogi Berra Museum with Cora in attendance. Her death, three years later, was unreported until it was included on a list of "recently deceased" at the New York Baseball Writers Dinner, bringing a collective gasp from the audience.

I was also involved in a street-naming ceremony in Phil's honor in 2022 in Queens, at his childhood home, at which time we discovered that three of his four children had passed away. From his family, only the one surviving daughter, Penny, was there.

In 1991, I was able to bring Bobby Murcer back to the broadcast booth. He'd been absent for a year, during which he was president of the Oklahoma City 89'ers Triple-A team in the American Association, and stayed active with the Baseball Assistance Team (B.A.T). He missed the Yankees, of course, and I was delighted to be able to bring him back.

A former smoker and chewing tobacco user, he had stopped both, and it had been discouraging for him when in 1987–88, he was paired with Ken "Hawk" Harrelson in the radio booth. Bobby was really low maintenance, but he did ask Harrelson if he would mind not smoking while they shared the small booth.

Harrelson refused, and Bobby suffered through some tough days. But he was happy to be there and stayed with it for many years, until he developed cancer and had to slow his work.

He was a skilled broadcaster, and his insight was never more evident than when he had the microphone for the famous George Brett "Pine Tar Game." While the events on the field, featuring a furious Brett railing at home plate umpire Tim McClelland over a home run ruled to be an out, may have seemed confusing to most, Bobby knew at once what was happening and brilliantly explained it to viewers along with Frank Messer. He was at his best.

Bobby brought a Southern charm to the broadcasts, as Mel Allen and Red Barber had once done. He "went down easy," as a scouting report might have said. It was still the days before analytics flooded broadcasts and Statcast numbers became mandatory for almost every pitch and batted ball. He remained part of the broadcast team for the rest of his life, and in his final year, he got a standing ovation from the Yankee Stadium crowd as he returned to the booth one last time after a chemo treatment.

Bobby's greatest asset, he would be the first to say, was his wonderful wife, Kay, who became an immediate friend to all she met and so enhanced the Murcer "brand." Everyone loved Kay.

I was on a train home from Brick Church, New Jersey, on July 12, 2008, returning from a memorial service for Dee Irvin, Monte's wife. My phone rang. It was Kay with a call I had feared was coming. Bobby had died just an hour before, dead of that horrible glioblastoma—brain cancer.

Only days before, he had been in New York fulfilling obligations to promote his autobiography, including appearances at Barnes & Noble and the Yogi Berra Museum, plus several radio interviews. I was doing PR for the book and was with him. Not only was he in great pain, but he was dealing with shingles as well. But he sat there and signed books and bantered with fans as though he were fine.

I could only admire his courage. And Kay was not only a great support, but also kept everyone informed, even sharing lighter notes on emails titled "tumor humor."

When I got home from that train ride, I called Whitey Ford with the sad news. Whitey broke down in tears on the phone. "You mean that little kid with the Mantle/Maris T-shirt, he died?" Whitey, like many, had somehow hoped—even expected—Bobby would beat this.

(It wasn't the only time I saw Whitey in tears. For some reason, when I told him that '60s relief star Luis Arroyo was going to be at Old Timers' Day one year, he similarly welled up with tears. I think he knew that it might be the last time he would see his old relief savior, and it touched him. He really loved Looie.)

I was among the eulogists at Bobby's memorial in Edmund, Oklahoma, on August 6. The whole Yankees team was there, having made a special side trip from Dallas, where they were playing the Texas Rangers that night.

I spoke about all that was placed on Bobby's shoulders in the '60s—succeeding Mickey Mantle, getting Mickey's locker, wearing Bobby Richardson's number, being projected to be the next superstar. If he didn't quite make it to "superstar status," he did become the team's most popular

Bobby Murcer (right) returned to the broadcast booth and our team (including Tom Seaver, Phil Rizzuto, and director John Moore) won the New York State Broadcaster's Association award for live sports coverage.

player and a wonderful role model for youngsters. He more than met his challenges.

It was a really sad time for me. My father had died at 92 on July 24, and my close friend and college roommate Barry Mandell died August 5. The always difficult anniversary of Munson's passing was August 2.

We had two other announcers in my days with the Yankees whose time in the booth was brief. In 1970, Bob Gamere, 31, who had done Harvard football in the '60s, was hired to replace Jerry Coleman, who would move on to a celebrated broadcasting career in San Diego.

Gamere (traveling secretary Bruce Henry called him "Gums Gamere") was a virtual unknown, and that is what appealed to Mike Burke, who hired him. A young guy, breaking in, learning the ropes in the same booth with Rizzuto and Messer.

Unfortunately, Gamere tried too hard off camera to impress everyone with his baseball knowledge and rubbed people the wrong way, especially Ralph Houk. At the end of the season, he was let go, essentially for the same reason he was hired—lack of experience. In his departure he revealed that his salary was only $15,000, which was hard to believe even for 1970.

He went back to Boston and hosted *Candlepins for Cash*, a bowling show, and did a nightly call-in sportstalk show. As "the Great Gamere," he ran a sports book. Then things went south.

He was stabbed four times in 1988 near Fenway Park. A year later, charges were brought by a man involving assault and sexual harassment.

Those charges were dropped, but in 2009 he pled guilty to child pornography charges and spent five years in prison, and he was banned for life from using the internet.

Then there was Dom Valentino, who had done basketball and hockey broadcasting, but not baseball. He was a friend and associate of Mike DiTomasso of Manchester Broadcasting, which acquired the rights to Yankees radio in the '70s. DiTomasso wanted Valentino in the booth, and as a rightsholder, he got his way.

Dom, a very pleasant fellow with a great laugh, worked with Rizzuto, Messer, and White, but only on radio. One day he showed up with a new microphone contraption, something that strapped onto his body like a harness, but with the mic part extending up from his belly to his mouth, always in place no matter how he turned.

I mention this because when Rizzuto entered the booth on the day Dom unveiled this, Phil's reaction reminded us of Ralph Kramden's when he saw Ed Norton wearing a Captain Video space helmet in a classic *Honeymooners* moment.

Dom suffered a heart attack while we were on a road trip in Minnesota and had to be left behind at a local hospital. There must be few things lonelier than being left behind in a strange city with no friends or family or colleagues after the team leaves town.

I loved my 11 years at WPIX, where I also headed public relations for the station. I had to learn every aspect of the broadcast industry—news gathering, sales, engineering, government regulations, ratings, license renewal, syndication, satellite transmission (we were a "superstation" because we carried Yankees baseball), community affairs, community concerns (we had to do "ascertainments" with local officials to learn of their pet interests), and much more. We even launched a nightly national newscast, Independent Network News (INN), for unaffiliated stations across the country. I kept up with about eight industry publications a week and handled all our awards submissions. There were good people in every department, and they were all helpful to me.

One thing we did on Yankees games, which was pretty advanced for its time, was the installation of two robotic cameras on the roof of the stadium, controlled with a joystick in our control room by a single engineer. One was mounted over left field and the other directly over home plate. That one was useful for viewing pitches from on high, long before the strike zone box was introduced (although I did witness a display of the strike zone box in development and knew it was the future).

As for the rooftop cameras, I told people we were using it to track Rizzuto leaving in the seventh inning, as he had a well-known tendency to leave early to beat the traffic.

WPIX once tried to buy the Yankees; Lev Pope was a huge baseball fan. But the parent company, Tribune (based in Chicago) nixed the deal—and later bought the Chicago Cubs.

As station president, Lev was faced with issues apart from Yankees baseball coverage and relations with George Steinbrenner. For instance, the station used to run Oral Roberts' Sunday morning evangelical program. It would run weekly except for during Christmas season, when the demand by toy manufacturers for commercial time on weekend mornings was great. So, the station would temporarily drop religious programing for cartoons to accommodate the toy commercial demand. And they'd make a lot of money.

One day there came a call from the security desk in the main lobby on 42nd Street, the landmark lobby with the huge rotating globe. It seemed that Oral Roberts was there, in person, asking to see Lev Pope. Lev said, "Send him up."

Roberts arrived in Pope's corner office and immediately dropped to his knees and began praying for Lev's redemption in light of his sin.

Lev, a deeply religious Catholic, was unmoved. The toy commercials continued, and Roberts' show returned in January, as planned.

Our chief engineer was Otis Freeman, a slow-talking Southerner who reminded me of Sheriff Andy Taylor (played by Andy Griffith) of

Mayberry. Otis would playfully say that he had the greatest TV show in history in his head. It would run from midnight to 6 AM and feature only an overhead camera looking down on a green felt cloth. Every 60 seconds, a hand would roll a pair of dice. That was the show. People would bet. Commercials would run. It might have been an enormous hit.

I did a lot with the station in my role as its PR director, including lunches with Cliff Robertson, Anthony Hopkins, Patrick Duffy, Pamela Sue Martin, and Jane Seymour so they could talk about their upcoming projects ("Operation Prime Time") with entertainment journalists. But my highest-profile assignment was publicizing the highest-rated syndicated special ever—the opening of Al Capone's safe, hosted by Geraldo Rivera. The safe was empty. Two hours of live television for nothing. But oh, the publicity we got for that...!

The news operation was overseen by news director John Corporon, and Pat Harper, despite her loathing of Yankees games, was our news "star." Bill Jorgensen moved over from WNYW to join her at the anchor desk. Bill had the central casting look of a TV anchorman: picture Ted Baxter (of *The Mary Tyler Moore Show*) with lots of scowls and age lines in his face. Bill spent much of his day holed up in his office with a list of his stock holdings on a white board. I don't remember his having any interest in sports, his seldom having spoken with our much-loved sports anchor Jerry Girard, or having exaggerated exhales when baseball went into extra innings. Then he'd get his act together, head for makeup and the studio. He looked right at the camera (and the teleprompter) and made everything sound important. His sign off, "Thank you for your time this time until next time," was well known in New York, as was the sign-off to Richard Hughes' editorials: "What's your opinion—we'd like to know." (He didn't actually want to know.)

One night, a few drinks into a party at a nearby saloon bidding farewell to a news employee, Pat and Bill got into an argument and she threw a drink at him. Alas, I wasn't there to do first-person public relations damage control, but it did occupy several days of Page Six journalism in the *New York Post*.

In 1987, Bill went off to his vacation home in Florida. News anchors were always taking vacations, so his absence wasn't especially noteworthy. But after a couple of weeks, he called Corporon and said, "I'm done. Life here is good. I'm retiring."

We made no announcement. And so, after 20 years on primetime television in the nation's No. 1 market, he simply disappeared. We never got a single letter or phone call inquiring about him. Not one. And that's the television news business. Today, some 35 years later, there are probably viewers who think, *Gee, I haven't seen Bill Jorgensen for a while; I wonder if he's on vacation!?*

Dave Kaplan, the founding director of the Yogi Berra Museum, visited Yogi Berra in his care facility with me during his final weeks there, as we had done with Rizzuto. Same place. Carmen Berra had already passed, and he was happy to have some familiar company. The facility had been too carefree at telling people who were visiting loved ones what room Yogi occupied. He was quite uncomfortable, of course, having strangers knock on his door.

We had a really nice visit. I brought him a book of baseball art by the great Andy Jurinko who had painted all the Hall of Famers. It must have weighed 15 pounds. We talked about how the stolen base had gone out of the game, and Yogi reflected on that knowingly, mentioning how even a big guy like Hank Bauer "could really run."

As we were departing, I heard what could have been the last Yogi-ism. A nurse came into the room and Yogi said, "What time is 3 o'clock mass?" Obviously, they hadn't always started on time, and this was a perfect Yogi-ism for the moment. He didn't want to get there too early.

He died just a week or so later. His funeral in New Jersey was officiated over by eight priests, bishops, and even Cardinal Dolan from the New York archdiocese. I went with Joe Garagiola Jr., Phil Linz, and Art Shamsky, and of course on the trip we spoke of the day 51 years earlier, when Linz played the harmonica on the team bus and Yogi, his manager, came back and smacked it out of his hands. They had long ago reconciled.

A final visit with Yogi Berra at his care facility, in the company of Dave Kaplan, director of the Berra Museum. Yogi always wore his Yankees cap, and we talked that day about what a fast runner Hank Bauer was.

Among those who couldn't make the trip was Whitey Ford, who was represented by his wife, Joan. Whitey by now had Alzheimer's and the trip would have confused him. He was really only comfortable in his own home, surrounded by the familiar setting.

When Whitey died in 2020 at 91, Yogi was proven correct again. Among the many cherished Yogisms was, "You gotta go to people's funerals or they won't go to yours." And sure enough, Yogi could not attend Whitey's, having predeceased him.

You never knew when a good new Yogi-ism would turn up. His granddaughter Lindsay, a very skilled journalist and the family spokesperson, once told Yogi that she had recently interviewed Tom Brady.

"Did he ask you out?" asked Grandpa, always anxious to see Lindsay married.

"Grandpa, please…Tom Brady dates swimsuit models!" she said.

"So?" responded Grandpa. "You got a swimsuit."

It was an understated part of Yogi's life that he had been the only baseball player who happened to be present at the Normandy invasion—D-Day. (My father, a medic, was there as well.) He was on a gunboat, protecting our troops. It was not something that we fully appreciated (his being the only one), and we certainly should have made more of it while he was an active player, coach, or manager. It took until his retirement for those facts to fully emerge, facts that further substantiated his growing reputation as perhaps the finest example of the Greatest Generation.

And on the matter of being unappreciated, we all knew that Ralph Houk—"the Major"—was in fact promoted to major during World War II, and fought at the Battle of the Bulge.

What we didn't appreciate, nor make part of his bio, was that he was the highest-ranking baseball player ever in the military. No other players reached major or higher.

I was hospitalized for two weeks in April 1975 following some complicated surgery that required a bone marrow transplant from my hip. Someone who called every day to see how I was doing and if I needed anything was none other than Jim "Catfish" Hunter, who was only in his first month with the Yankees.

People who knew Hunter personally would not be surprised. Although he was the youngest of nine Hunter children, he a had maturity and a presence that could not be missed.

He was a peanut farmer back in Hertford, North Carolina. He loved riding a tractor, working his land. He bonded with our grounds crew and would have been perfectly happy to have been part of that crew if he wasn't such a gifted pitcher.

We had famously signed him as a free agent on New Year's Eve of 1974, after he had been pursued by every team in baseball. He was the reigning Cy Young Award winner, coming off four straight 20-win seasons and three straight world championships.

Everyone who was ever a teammate or a front office employee absolutely loved Catfish. He had a great sense of humor, was a clever practical joker, and was then all business on the field. My close friend Jimmy Bank, traveling secretary of the Oakland A's, told me I was absolutely going to love having this guy on the team.

His signing, which actually preceded the free-agent system we now know, followed a breach in contract by Oakland owner Charlie Finley. An arbitrator declared him free.

His signing set in motion the rush to a free-agent system, since it was a good look at a player's true worth in an open market. It established not only true worth, but the player's right to use an agent, the idea of a multi-year contract, and the use of the word "millions" in those contracts.

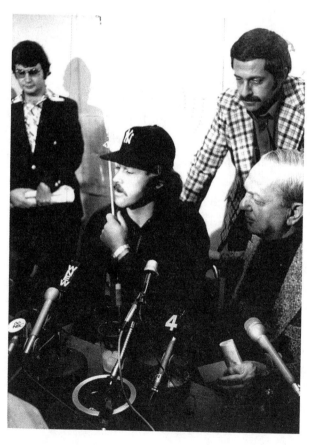

The New Year's Eve signing of Jim "Catfish" Hunter at the Parks Administration Building in Flushing Meadow. My jacket is closed so as not to reveal mimeograph ink on my shirt.

As the Yankees PR director, I had to hastily assemble the press for the New Year's Eve press conference (they were not too happy about that), which was held in our group sales office in Flushing Meadows. Hunter had flown up from North Carolina on a snowy night in a private jet, landing at LaGuardia, which was just minutes away from our offices. He flew back with his North Carolina lawyers right after the press conference, which is best remembered by me for getting mimeograph ink all over my shirt as I fumbled to get our press release printed. (It may have been the last mimeograph machine sold in America. Everyone else had migrated to Xerox copying machines by now, but Gabe Paul thought mimeograph was the wave of the future, and much cheaper.)

We brought Hunter back to New York a week later and made the rounds with a full-blown media day. There was an appearance on *AM America* (predecessor of *Good Morning America*). Reverend Jesse Jackson and Vietnam War villain Lieutenant William Calley sat with us in the green room, and Catfish told the Reverend that he looked just like Reggie Jackson, which made me cringe. Hunter then posed for a session with celebrity photographer Richard Avedon, had lunch with the New York media over Carnegie Deli pastrami sandwiches in a suite at the Americana Hotel, and went on the local NBC station with Dick Schaap. At every stop, he had me as his partner for the day.

We had dinner together at Top of the Sixes and shared Finley and Steinbrenner stories. We laughed a lot. And as media requests continued all winter, we spoke almost daily.

Spring training was another media circus, and Howard Cosell arranged for a Brink's armored car to drop Catfish off outside Fort Lauderdale Stadium for a video op.

So, we were pretty friendly by this point, and when I had my surgery, no one checked in more often than he did. I returned to work in late April, my jaw still wired shut, and he had a lot of fun passing tasty desserts in front of me.

The Yankees were determined to get their money's worth in Year 1 of his contract. He made 39 starts, hurled 30 complete games, pitched 328 innings, and won 23 games. He always gave up a lot of home runs, and he had a way of admiring them just as a fan might. In that first spring, Dave Kingman of the Mets hit one into the dark night sky in Fort Lauderdale. I was sitting with Mets PR man Matt Winick, we witnessed it together, and now, about 45 years later, we still talk about it as the home run we never saw come down. I thought I saw it when photos from the Webb Space Telescope were revealed.

Catfish retired after his five-year contract was up, having pitched in three World Series for the Yankees. He only won 20 that first year and was never the same pitcher again, but in many ways, he was a team leader who helped bring the Yankees back to their glory days.

In 1998, after he developed Lou Gehrig's disease (ALS), he declined rapidly. He lost the use of his hands. When I called to check on him, he gave me an off-color story on how he was getting along without the use of his hands. I had to laugh despite it all.

It was a blessing when his lack of balance caused him to fall backward on the pavement at his home, and he died soon after from that head injury, never having to go to the end of the run with ALS, which is so awful in its later stages.

Like Hunter, Lou Piniella was liked by everyone he met, except perhaps for some umpires he didn't agree with. He was tall and handsome with a great smile and a great sense of humor.

Those of us with Yankees connections will always think of him as a Yankee, and of course he was part of those three championship teams in the 1970s. But he also played in the Cleveland, Washington, Baltimore, and Kansas City organizations and probably had more Topps "rookie cards" than anyone. I think the rap against him as a player was his surprising lack of power, which his teammates would forever tease him about. He was a corner outfielder, a position expected to deliver big home run totals, but he never hit 20, and for 18 seasons in the majors, he only had 102. He put in seven years in the minors before winning Rookie of the Year honors in 1969. (We then had Munson, the 1970 winner, and Chris Chambliss, the 1971 winner, all in the lineup at once.)

So, he took the teasing (which included mimicking his high voice) but continued to deliver line shots into the gaps, as he rolled up a .291 career average and .305 in postseason play. The Royals traded him to the Yankees so that they could open up an outfield spot for Jim Wohlford, and his Yankees teammates were always riding him about "Jim f—— Wohlford."

He was very popular with Yankees fans, many of whom thought he was Italian, but he was a Spaniard, fluent in the language, and would serve as a translator for some Spanish players during contract talks.

As a Tampa neighbor of George Steinbrenner's, he thought he could get along with the Boss when he twice agreed to manage the team and in his year as general manager (1988). But it wasn't to be, and he admitted he should have known better. He went on to manage for 23 years in all, doing three years in Cincinnati, 10 years in Seattle, three years in Tampa Bay, and four years with the Chicago Cubs. Everywhere he went he was beloved, and with the 1990 Reds, he won a world championship on the very night that George Steinbrenner was hosting *Saturday Night Live*. With the 2001 Mariners, he had a 116–46 record, but the Yankees knocked Seattle out in the ALCS.

During Hunter's first year with the Yankees, he roomed with Piniella in the room adjoining mine at the Fort Lauderdale Inn. It was a good pairing; one could easily see the two of them becoming fast friends.

One particular night stands out. Well past midnight, the two of them returned to their room after having had, well, a couple of beers. I was awakened by their arrival, and thought, *Oh boy, what are we in for tonight!?*

To my surprise and amusement, the two of them, quite loudly, went deep into the morning hours—going over how to pitch to everyone in the American League. It was loud and profane and funny, all at once.

A fastball on 3-and-1 to Sixto Lezcano?! Are you f—— nuts? You gotta throw him a f—— breaking ball right there; game over!

I don't remember who said what, but that it was a pitcher and a hitter debating this all night long was, um, educational. They didn't agree on much, but I thought if Piniella knew all this stuff from watching games from right field, he was going to be a manager one day.

Of course, if I was truly listening to it all and taking it all in, I too could have been a manager one day. But I still wouldn't be sure what to throw Sixto Lezcano on 3-and-1.

Chris Chambliss, a gentle, soft-spoken Yankees hero, hit the pennant-winning home run for the Yankees in the last of the ninth of the final game of the 1976 ALCS. When I'm asked about my favorite memory from my years as PR director, I cite this, for it was culmination of our first year in the new stadium and the first Yankee pennant in 12 years, or since I was 16.

But Chris had another special moment that has generally been forgotten but had a long-lasting effect on the game. On July 25, 1976, en route to that elusive pennant, Chris hit a walk-off, three-run home run against Boston (the term "walk-off" wasn't actually invented yet) that gave the Yankees a win before a full house. Returning to the dugout, the roar from the crowd wouldn't cease and it came to be accompanied by shouts of, "We want Chris!" Reluctantly, and at the urging of his teammates, Chris moved up the dugout steps and waved his cap. It was the first "curtain call" that anyone could remember since Roger Maris hit his 61st home run in 1961. And it started a practice that continues to this day for big home runs.

There was another moment, less special, at Fenway Park, when Chris, standing at third base, was hit in the arm by a dart thrown from the stands. It was hard to believe a dart could travel that far—and frightening too. Chris just pulled it out of his arm and handed it to third-base coach Dick Howser, and the game continued.

Seventh Inning

I was working at MLB late in the afternoon of August 2, 1979, when my phone rang. The secretaries had gone home for the day, and when I picked it up, I realized it was a frantic George Steinbrenner.

"Mr. Steinbrenner, it's Marty Appel," I said. "How can I help you?"

"I need to speak to Bowie…right away…a terrible thing…Thurman Munson's been killed in a plane crash."

"Hold on," I said, remembering that he had little patience for holding on. I ran down the 30 feet or so to Bowie Kuhn's office—he was there but his secretary, Mary Sotos, had left. (This was for the best, because when Mary answered, she would say, very slowly, "Comm-is-sioner KUHN's off-ice" emphasizing every syllable. Mr. Steinbrenner might have hung up.) I told him I was transferring a call from George Steinbrenner, and he should pick it up when it rings. (I had no idea how it came to my line in the first place.)

Thurman and I went back to 1968, the year he was drafted and the year I started with the Yankees. So sure was everyone that he was on a fast track to being the team's starting catcher that we even arranged for his Binghamton farm team to play a game at Yankee Stadium so we could photograph him and meet him. Bob Fishel and Bill Guilfoile arranged for all the PR needs, and I more or less tagged along.

I wish Thurman could have played a few games for the Yankees that year so he could have been a teammate, however briefly, of Mantle's. Just

159

as I wish Aaron Judge had been a teammate of Derek Jeter's in Jeter's final year. With those connections in place, the dynastic quality of the Yankees would have flowed seamlessly—Ruth to Gehrig to DiMaggio to Mantle to Munson to Jackson to Winfield to Mattingly to Jeter to Judge.

We fast-forward to early in 1977 and I called Thurman and said, "How about we do a book together? Your life story. You're not talking to any of the writers, so I could be the logical one to do this with you."

At first, he was reluctant. "I'm only 29, he said. "Not much of a life story there yet."

"True, but in sports you're a veteran, and you just won the MVP award. When you win an MVP in New York, somebody is going to do a book about you! You'll have no say in it, you'll probably hate it, and you won't make a dime off it."

My sales points registered. "If I do it, I'd just want for it to be a paperback, so kids can afford it," he said.

"Well, the usual way is it starts in hardcover so libraries can stock it, and kids can read it free. Then, if it does well, it goes to paperback."

So we agreed, found a publisher, and went to work. We recorded it in the study at his home on 14th Street in Norwood, New Jersey. (He used the same building plans for his "real" home in Canton, Ohio.)

Visiting with Thurman Munson at his locker to review plans for the release of the autobiography we did together.

After our sessions, his wife, Diane, would ask if he mentioned certain people and events. It became clear he was leaving out some important stuff from his childhood. But it was his book, his story, and his right to leave out what he wanted. (After his death, "Diane" became "Diana," as though she had always been. This caught most of his teammates by surprise, as he clearly always said Diane.)

The book sold modestly. It had little controversy and made no headlines, but Munson's family and fans seemed to like it and he seemed satisfied that it didn't disrupt team chemistry, even for a day.

Why he chose to be uncontroversial, I can't say, unless he had the kids in mind. I had presided over the press conference where it was announced that he had won the MVP award, and with the team having just signed Reggie Jackson, Thurman chose that moment to announce his expectation of a new contract from Mr. Steinbrenner. That was certainly laying down the gauntlet. I was blindsided, and I said, "I'm sure Mr. Steinbrenner and Thurman will work it out." It was pure PR talk. Instinctive.

The next morning came an angry call from the Boss. "The hell we'll work it out!" he screamed. "Don't you dare say that again. He'll play under the existing contract! Period."

I think my instinct was right. The story of his winning the MVP would not have been a good time to go to war.

Thurman felt the signing of Jackson had triggered an automatic raise and that only the Catfish Hunter signing had been excluded from that understanding. He thought he was to stay equal to the highest new free-agent signing. The Boss didn't see it that way.

So the war was on. They were two hardheaded Buckeyes determined to see the Yankees win, but they dug in on the contract.

Thurman would still march up to Steinbrenner's office after batting practice, plop his clay-caked spikes on the desk, and talk about real estate, the stock market, and business opportunities. The Boss hated the rudeness of the clumps of clay on his round wooden desk, while Thurman loved it. He would tell people that it made the veins flare in Steinbrenner's neck. That battle raged on through many meetings.

When Thurman died, Mr. Steinbrenner told people, "I loved when he'd come up and put his shoes on my desk, and the mud from the field would fall off them."

Kuhn, meanwhile, was thinking about whether he should go to the funeral. He was thinking about precedent and thinking that he hadn't gone to Lyman Bostock's funeral the year before. (Bostock, then with the Angels, had been killed in a shooting.)

I advised that he should go and not worry about precedents. "Thurman was the captain of the defending world champions," I said. "You handed him the World Series trophy nine months ago." So he went, and I went separately, picking up Murcer and Piniella at the airport. They were the two teammates who were to offer eulogies and they flew in the night before, when we all gathered at the Munson home. They talked about what each one would say. (We met a third player, the former Yankee Mike Heath, at the airport and he came along, having flown in from Seattle where his Oakland A's were playing.)

"Thank god we have that book you did with Thurman," said Diana.

Now we fast-forward to 2007. The 30th anniversary of Thurman's death would be coming. His legion of fans had grown so that he was a cult figure. His leadership on those championship teams of the '70s got bigger all the time. And so too did the events around his death—both the day of and the days afterward.

My publisher reached out to see about doing a new biography, fleshing out details of his childhood and expanding on the details of the death, the aftermath, and the legacy. I took it on. A few very high-profile sports authors were thinking of doing the book as well, but they were all nice enough to call and see if it was in my plans, and they felt I was the right one to do it and stepped aside. We reached out to Diana to see if she wanted to participate, but she was reluctant. She didn't want to relive that awful day anymore. She would help with some photos, and her close friend Joanne would run an occasional question by her for me, but she didn't want to provide a foreword, and that would be the extent of it.

When the manuscript was done, my editor suggested we send it to Diana to "proofread." We wanted to be sensitive to her wishes and were prepared to edit anything that troubled her. She only asked that the details from the autopsy be removed, which they were. We did everything she asked, even if it was only that one thing.

I didn't see her often after the book came out, although we did an on-camera interview together at an Old Timers' Day for the Yankees website. (I also interviewed Kay Murcer that day about Bobby.) She was very friendly, and it was a fine interview. But she never said she liked the book, and I suspect she didn't. When you get too close to family matters, well, the family is not going to love it.

As it happened, the Munson fan base seemed to love it. I got several hundred letters and emails from them saying how much they enjoyed the book, with some even saying they were too young to remember him, but now they understand what all the love and admiration was about.

Before the book was published, I went to Yankee Stadium and photographed the backs of a lot of fans wearing No. 15 Munson T-shirts. It was a good representation of his loyal, if aging, fan base. We used the photos to line the title page.

Today I am often asked if Thurman should be in the Hall of Fame. There is a big movement for him out there. I know the fans want me, his biographer, to be supportive.

But two things keep me from wholly endorsing it. First, we had seen his best years, and by 1979, his career was starting to descend. His knees were shot. His days as a catcher were going to be limited, and how much was left in that body was hard to tell. So, it wasn't as though we were going

The Yankees had me interview both Diana Munson (above, left) and Kay Murcer for their website content at their 2003 Old Timers' Day.

to see him hit 400 homers or get 3,000 hits. We kind of knew what his career would be remembered for—the championships and the leadership. But the 11 years was just too minimal.

More to the point, though, was that I have a lot of respect for the Hall of Fame and the voting process. No proposed changes are going to result in everyone being happy. Thurman had his chances—he went 0-for-18 between writer votes and veterans committee votes. That is a big statement! I can hear Thurman now, if asked about someone else going 0-for-18, saying, "You can't say he didn't have his chances—and he didn't make it! End of story."

Would I be happy if he got in? Sure! He was my friend. But a lot of people I think should be in aren't, and that's just the way it is.

People think being a Yankee gives you an edge with the voting, but if so, where are the plaques for Roger Maris, Ron Guidry, Allie Reynolds, Graig Nettles, Tommy John, Don Mattingly, Bernie Williams, Andy Pettitte, and, for that matter, George Steinbrenner? There is no Yankees advantage, and Thurman falls into that black hole too.

I've had more than one retired player tell me they would have traded two years of their careers just to be a Yankee for a few months, if only to reap the benefits of being an ex-Yankee after their careers ended. That is probably true for appearances and accolades, but not for the Hall of Fame.

The attendance at Yankee Stadium for the first game after Thurman died was announced at 51,151. People went *ohhhh* when it was announced, thinking they were part of a miracle honoring his No. 15.

But a true confession: sometimes the numbers were tweaked a bit. When I was there, if we had a crowd of 19,000-something, we would put it over 20,000 because it looked better and make up the difference the next day, if it was against the same team. So long as that team left town whole, paid in full for their share of the gate.

I am honored to be in the New York State Baseball Hall of Fame, which has an annual induction ceremony in Troy, New York, where my guy King Kelly was born. I drove up in 2017 with John Sterling, who was being inducted with me and with Paul O'Neill. It was a great honor, and John and I had a wonderful time together on the six-hour round trip.

A year later the organizer, Rene LeRoux, called and asked if I had the phone numbers for Mickey Mantle's sons. He was planning to induct Mickey.

"Wait a minute," I laughed. "Are you telling me I got into this Hall of Fame before Mickey Mantle? What kind of a Hall of Fame inducts me before Mickey Mantle?"

I had a good run around that time. I was inducted in the various Halls of Fame, for Spring Valley High School and for Oneonta State, for my village of Larchmont, and I got a "good guy" award from the Jewish Sports Hall of Fame. They notify you months ahead of the ceremony, so I had to be on my best behavior in that stretch so as not to embarrass the award presenter.

The Larchmont Historical Society inducted me along with Lou Gehrig, who lived in an apartment on Chatsworth Avenue late in his life. I asked if the plaque they gave me could have both of our pictures—me and Lou. They obliged. I wonder what Lou would have thought of sharing the plaque with me.

I also got a "thanks, Coach" plaque when I coached my son's Larchmont-Mamaroneck Little League team to a perfect record in 1989. I believe that 0–19 mark still stands. I would have traded all my 1956 baseball cards for one win that spring, but it wasn't to be. Was it me? You start to think so after awhile, but a couple of years later I coached my daughter's softball team to a championship and felt much redeemed.

My 0–19ers did have one grand day. I took the whole team to Yankee Stadium, fit them into the WPIX luxury suite, and had Phil Rizzuto and Tom Seaver come by to greet them and take photos.

In 1985, Seaver was going to be seeking his 300th career victory. As it happened, the quest would come in New York, where he would be pitching for the White Sox against the Yankees. The opportunity to win it in New York, the day before a labor action shutdown of the game was looming, and with his family on hand, made it, to me, almost a sure victory for him.

I was at WPIX at the time, and I proposed that we roll the dice and hire Lindsey Nelson as a guest announcer for the day. Lindsey had been the Mets announcer when Seaver broke in and handled much of his Mets career. I thought it would be a great moment in New York sports, and PIX management agreed to the gamble and the expense.

Lindsey turned out to be on top of his game and added a lot to the broadcast without intruding on the work of Spencer Ross or Frank Messer, who were doing TV as the ninth inning approached. As the ninth inning arrived, Spencer turned over the mike to Lindsey for the play-by-play, something that had been discussed in advance by our director Don Carney. And Lindsey provided the perfect accompaniment to the event at hand. It was a beautiful moment; the man who had called his first victory was doing his 300th.

I wish it remained a wonderful memory for me, because it was perfect, but when I think about it, I think of Lindsey's repeated calls months afterward asking what was going on with his travel expense check from PIX. It was so embarrassing. Our bookkeeping department treated it as a routine expense, and as with other vendors, waited 90 days to pay it. I wish Lindsey's ultimate disappointment on the phone with me would go away, but it's still part of my memory.

When I worked in Bowie Kuhn's office, it was interesting—how the "government" of the game operated—but you had to leave your rooting interest at the door. You rooted for big attendance numbers, big TV ratings, long playoff rounds, but not for teams, and seldom for players. I did miss that.

At the time I worked there, the office was called Office of the Baseball Commissioner. Gloria Coleman, who ran the reception desk, would answer the phone, "Baseball Commissioner's Office!" At the same time, the other major leagues—NFL, NBA, and NHL—were rising in popularity, partly over the use of the catchy initials. It was one of many ways in which baseball was failing to keep pace with consumer marketing triggers.

The birth of the website era in the late '80s had everyone scrambling to register their company's domain name. I was working at Topps when we decided to get into the act, but some young hobbyist had already claimed

Topps.com. So, it took a lot of money to buy the domain name from him. Smart young man.

For baseball, there was an interesting sideline to the story. First, they wanted to register MLB.com, finally aware by now of the public acceptance of the term. The receptionist would now answer "Major League Baseball," and that was a start. Other divisions sprung out from the name, notably MLB Advanced Media, which became the best marketing division among all the sports leagues. Before MLB Advanced Media, one could say that the NFL pretty much did everything better than MLB, which is saying a lot.

Interestingly, MLB.com was not readily available; it was taken. It was taken by the law firm of Morgan Lewis & Bockius LLP. And by coincidence of coincidences, Morgan Lewis & Bockius LLP was Major League Baseball's law firm. Feeling that stubbornly defending their domain name could cost them a client, they agreed to become MorganLewis.com (sorry, Bockius) and for MLB.com to become baseball's domain.

As an organizer for Old Timers' Day, and as a Yankees fan, I really enjoyed keeping in touch with not only the older players but their families as well.

When Eleanor Gehrig died in 1986, that was the end of the Gehrig connection. There were no Gehrig children. When Joe DiMaggio died in 1999 (I never met his son, who died five months later at 57), that narrowed the DiMaggio connection. (Although, had she lived, I would have made a point of keeping in touch with Marilyn Monroe, for sure.)

And speaking of Ms. Monroe (and we must), one day at the Berra Museum, Yogi happened to mention that he once had dinner with Joe and Marilyn in spring training.

"What?!" I exclaimed. "Yogi, I need details! What do you remember, what did they talk about, what did she wear, did they appear like a loving couple? This is amazing!" And Yogi responded by getting right to heart of the matter.

"Well, ya know," he said, "how usually, when you order a shrimp cocktail, you only get four or five pieces? That night, they brought us eight!"

"Yogi, that's it; that's all you remember?!"

"Yeah."

After we lost Mickey Mantle in 1995, I kept in touch with his widow, Merlyn, who was always great to me, sending me a wedding gift and then gifts when my children were born. For my son's birth, we got a sterling silver piggy bank engraved with Brian's name and date of birth. I wanted to tell her that the gifts didn't mean as much without the Mantle name also engraved, but you couldn't do that, right?

I had an on-and-off friendship with the Mantle surviving sons, David and Danny. (Two others were deceased.) When their mom died, they called on me to make the announcement to the press. I worked with them when I was at Topps and saw to fruition a reissue of all of Mick's original Topps cards in 1996, for a new generation to enjoy. They liked me because they knew I was sort of the last link to their dad's playing days (aside from teammates). But when they found out I helped with PR for Jane Leavy's book about Mick, the relationship sort of cooled and I didn't hear from them much anymore. I understood.

Jane and I had flown to Mick's hometown of Commerce, Oklahoma, while she was researching her book and I was helping raise funds for a planned Mantle Museum. To see his childhood home, including the barn against which he learned to switch hit (still with dents in the metal side), was almost a holy experience.

A visit to Mickey Mantle's childhood home in Commerce, Oklahoma. The barn to the right was where he learned to switch-hit, notable for the indentations in the metal siding.

There were well-meaning people behind the museum effort, including men who had gone to high school with Mick. And the town was very rural America, right along historic Route 66. The bigger town it bordered, Miami (pronounced My-am-uh), still had the Coleman movie theater to which Mick took Merlyn on their first date. We saw the field on which scout Tom Greenwade first saw Mickey play, but it was now converted into a soccer field. A sad commentary.

Merlyn was a cheerleader at nearby Picher High School. In 2009, the year Merlyn died, and after a tornado pretty much leveled it, the city of Picher became a ghost town, effectively condemned by the federal government due to toxic poisoning in the ground and in the air. It is one of just three cities in the world that Wikipedia shows as abandoned. It simply ceased to be. There is nothing there now but the old water tower. (Old time residents return for an annual Christmas parade through the town in which they grew up.)

"She's [Merlyn] my best friend," Mick told me one spring when we were driving together in Fort. Lauderdale. I'd always make a point to pick him up at Fort Lauderdale Airport, and we had some remarkably frank and personal conversations on the 40-minute drive to the hotel. Of course, I'd always be reminding myself, *This is Mickey Mantle sitting here!*

One spring we walked across a drawbridge on Sunrise Boulevard with a few others to see *The Last Picture Show* at the nearby multiplex. It was an Academy Award–winning film about life in a small town in Texas, set in 1951–52, dealing with high school friends coming of age.

When we were leaving the theater, I noticed tears on Mickey's cheeks. "Were you crying?" I asked. (Tom Hanks' "no crying in baseball" was years away.)

"Hell," he said, "that was just like my hometown. We even had a village idiot like they did."

It was a pretty touching Mantle moment.

I once showed him a photo I had from 1957, which showed nine-year-old me in a Mickey Mantle T-shirt. He studied it and smiled. "Another one I probably never got paid for," he said. I asked him to sign it and he said, "Now you can get more for this than I did!"

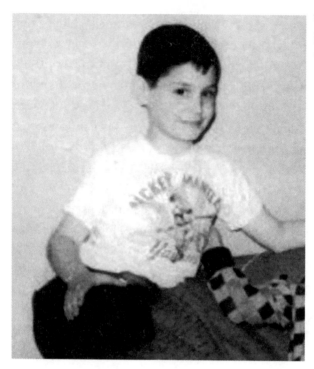

Wearing my Mickey
Mantle T-shirt, age nine,
1957.

By appearing in 12 World Series in his first 14 seasons, Mantle was undoubtedly baseball's first television star. He was on the NBC fall lineup as often as *Bonanza*, or so it seemed. He had the looks, the name, and the way he carried himself just seemed made for stardom.

He also had the respect of teammates, opponents, and fans everywhere. I was especially touched at the first Mickey Mantle Day in 1965, when he came to bat in the first inning against Detroit's Joe Sparma—and Sparma left the mound, walked to home plate, and shook Mick's hand. I've never seen anything like that before or since.

The respect can also be found in a quiet little statistic that has barely ever been noticed. Mantle was hit by a pitch only 13 times in his 18-year career. Thirteen! No one wanted to risk disabling him, knowing how fragile his legs were. It is an amazing statistic to behold. For context, Derek Jeter was hit 170 times; Reggie Jackson, 96.

I also like to remind people that when he retired in spring training of 1969, he was third on the all-time home run list, behind only Ruth and

Mays. With the passage of time his rank has of course dropped, but being third when he retired is worth repeating. And he still holds the record for World Series home runs and home runs by a switch-hitter.

So far as I know, he never lifted a single weight in all his off-seasons, other than when he ordered a double at the bar.

I have a long-running relationship with the Ruth family. Partly due to my being the Yankees official who would reach out to Claire Ruth, Babe's widow, on occasion, I found myself being a pallbearer at her 1976 funeral. I was the only one left in the front office whom she knew. It was the day after the World Series had ended; I went with Roy White, as we were both in Manhattan to cash in our unused Series tickets for the unplayed fifth game. Roy was a pallbearer as well.

Claire's daughter Julia Ruth Stevens lived to be 102, and always referred to Babe as "Daddy." She had been on their 1934 tour of Japan and maintained wonderful recall on all the details. To the end, she was a great representative of all things Ruth, and her son, Tom Stevens, a bridge engineer more my age, became a great spokesman as well as a friend. (How would you like to play Little League baseball and they find out you're Babe Ruth's grandson?) And Tom's son Brent likewise became a keeper of the flame and maintained a website, baberuthcentral.com. They all did the memory of their illustrious celebrity relative proud. Babe's other grandchild, Linda Tosetti, was the "other side" of the family (Dorothy's daughter), and the two sides had issues with each other except for when business interests forced communication. People like me did our best to not take sides.

In 2007, I arranged to bring Tom to Yankee Stadium to meet with Lonn Trost, the Yankees' chief operating officer, who was in charge of the new stadium's construction.

Tom had never met with any Yankee officials, and as I said in my introduction to Lonn, "That may no longer be the 'House that Ruth Built' across the street, but you really ought to keep the Ruth family close."

Lonn showed us the scale model and talked about the plans. The meeting went very well. The new stadium would open in two years.

Some weeks later, Lonn told me, "You know what came out of that meeting? We had forgotten to name any portion of the new stadium after Babe! And after we met, I realized it was an oversight, and we named the portion along 161st Street where Metro North passengers arrive at the stadium 'Babe Ruth Plaza.' And we'll mount the original street sign that used to be on the divider in the middle of 161st Street right there."

I felt like our visit had turned out to be a success.

On the final day of Yankee Stadium in 2008, I hosted a lunch at Mickey Mantle's Restaurant for the whole Stevens family, and later that day, Julia threw out the first pitch for the final game.

By that time, I was seated with my son, Brian, in the first row of the mezzanine deck overlooking right field. A friend from my Atlanta days, Neill Cameron, and his young nephew named Jeter were with us. Being something of a know-it-all, and showing off that evening, wearing my RUTH T-shirt, Yogi Berra button, and 1996 World Series cap, I mentioned that the right fielder when I went to my first Yankees game with my dad was Hank Bauer...and tonight, it was Bobby Abreu. And if you scramble Abreu, you get Bauer. Just sayin'.

In the ninth inning, with Mariano Rivera on the mound, I pointed out that this would be the last chance for someone to hit a fair ball out of Yankee Stadium. It had never happened in 85 years, even before the stands were expanded to include three decks. (Originally it was just bleachers, foul pole to foul pole.)

Brian Roberts, the last Orioles batter, grounded to first, and Yankee Stadium was over. We stayed in our seats for a long time while Sinatra's "New York, New York" kept playing. I had spent so many great days there. It was my second home, and a great feeling of nostalgia washed over me. And then at last, we descended to the D subway, back to the city. It was a remarkable day.

Today, I am the administrator of a private Facebook page for Yankees alumni and families, with family from Ruth, Ford, Berra, Kubek, Gomez, Ruffing, Richardson, Maris, Clarke, White, Murcer, Aker, Blomberg, Nettles, Dahlgren, Cerv, Lyle, Stottlemyre, Amaro, Martin, Siebern,

Lunch with Babe Ruth's daughter Julia and her family prior to the final game in Yankee Stadium, 2008.

DeMastri, Virdon, Sturdivant, Narron, Guidry, McDaniel, and more all regularly checking in. The eras come together, always as Yankees.

It came time for the new Yankee Stadium seven months later, and the Hall of Fame president Jeff Idelson (another former Yankees PR man) invited me to sit with him in section 214. I'm sure there was significance to that number; perhaps my lifetime Little League average. Jeff was there to collect historic items for the Museum.

CC Sabathia started against Cleveland's ace, Cliff Lee. By the fall, Lee had been traded to Philadelphia. The Phillies made it to the World Series, as did the Yankees, and in Game 1—it was again Sabathia versus Lee. Had this ever happened before? Nope. It was a true baseball oddity.

Although he was never part of a pennant-winning team, Don Mattingly, son of a mailman from Indiana, and a 19th-round draft pick, captured the hearts of Yankee fans who stuck with him even after he hurt his back and was never the same player as he was in his twenties. He brought out the little boy in those of us who simply loved the game of baseball.

It was a total joy to just appreciate his game—the work ethic, the fielding, the hitting, the lack of strikeouts, the leadership, and how he carried himself. Nobody really saw it coming. And then suddenly, he was probably the best-fielding first baseman in Yankee history, the premier player in the majors for three or four seasons, and worthy of being a captain. I wasn't there when he played; as executive producer of the telecasts, I didn't really mix with the players much. But at an event at Mickey Mantle's Restaurant years later, I went to him to introduce myself—and he knew me. He said he'd been watching me for years on the Yankeeographies shown on the YES Network. "I watched you getting gray," he laughed.

My best Mattingly memory is just watching his work ethic and his dedicated repetitions at a batting tee behind home plate during batting practice. Day after day. Grinding it out.

And then of course, there was the MVP, the batting championship, the eight-straight games with a home run and the six grand slams in a season (plus one in spring training), which were the only grand slams he ever hit.

He was my son's favorite player, and he signed a wedding invitation for Brian. In the blooper video where Donny grabs a handful of popcorn from a front row fan, the fan was a Mamaroneck High School classmate of Brian's, there with his dad who was the school's baseball coach. What a big man on campus he was!

When a successor to Joe Torre as Yankee manager was being pondered, it came down to Joe Girardi and Mattingly, two coaches under Torre. The job went to Girardi despite popular support for the Yankees hero. And Girardi was a good choice, an excellent manager. But there was always a part of me—for many fans I suppose, who would have loved to see Mattingly get the job.

Donnie Baseball.

Now there was a baseball player.

In spring training of 1995, his last, Mattingly met the Yankees' No. 1 draft choice of 1992, Derek Jeter. Mattingly tells the story of the two of them, finishing their workout in the practice field at Fort Lauderdale beyond the regular field. (I used to see snakes there.)

This was the last year of Fort Lauderdale as the team's spring training home before moving to Tampa. So, the torch was being passed, and Jeter, when he retired, would be the last Yankee to have trained there.

It was time to go to the clubhouse and Mattingly suggested they run in, not walk, because "you never know who's watching."

Jeter played 15 games in 1995 as Mattingly's teammate—three in May, 10 in June and two in September. The Yankees knew he had loads of talent, but when Tony Fernandez was injured in spring training of 1996, would the 21-year-old Jeter be ready to play such a challenging position as shortstop under a new manager in Joe Torre?

In the front office, Gene Michael, Bob Watson, and Brian Cashman debated making a trade for someone to move into the position, a bridge to Jeter, similar to their getting Isiah Kiner-Falefa in 2022 as a bridge to top prospect Anthony Volpe. They had one in mind—Seattle infielder Felix Fermin. The Mariners wanted another Yankees rookie, a pitcher named Mariano Rivera.

It has long been said that the best deals are the ones you don't make. Trading Rivera for Fermin would not have been such a good deal.

And so, Jeter went out and became one of the greatest Yankees in history. And of course, he won five world championships with the Yankees, as did Rivera, Posada, and Pettitte. (I never liked the term Core Four, because that left out Bernie Williams, who won four rings and was, like them, homegrown and a great Yankee.)

When Jeter came to bat, you seldom thought "home run." He had that inside-out swing that drove the ball to right field, but depending on the count, he could do a lot of other things with the bat. That the home run was not in our thinking was belied by his finishing in the top 10 all time of Yankee home run hitters, and third among postseason home run hitters. Of course, the numbers were accumulated because of the length of his career, but they still remain a wonder to observers.

I had lunch with his father on occasion, and his parents had me as a guest in their suite at the Stadium a few times. From that vantage point, I can attest that he did in fact seemed to have a perfect upbringing. I also loved that he spent his summers in New Jersey where he watched the Yankees on WPIX at his grandmother's home. And when his dad asked if I could send a copy of *Pinstripe Empire* to Grandma—you bet I could, and you bet I did.

Early in his sophomore season, I was working with Topps and we had the famed artist Peter Max do a Jeter portrait for inclusion as a special set of artistic cards. We did a press conference at the Peter Max studio, and Jeter brought his young wingman Jorge Posada along.

"Hello Mr. Max" said Jeter, polite as ever. He called his manager "Mr. Torre," only shortening it to "Mr. T." as the years went on.

In Mattingly and Jeter, the Yankees were blessed in having two players, back-to-back spanning 32 years, who would be worthy captains and role models for kids while also earning the admiration of everyone in the game.

The great Mariano Rivera and his near perfection for two decades gave baseball fans a chance to stand back and say, "What if someone is just too good for this league? What do we do with him?"

It even made me think that somewhere out there in the world, maybe in a country that doesn't even play baseball, might be someone who could hit .500 and have no trouble reaching 100 home runs in one season. Imagine.

Trevor Hoffman held the lifetime saves record before Rivera passed him, but many onlookers were tempted to ask, "How many were before a

Early in his sophomore season, 1997, Derek Jeter attends the unveiling of a baseball card painting by Peter Max (center).

national audience?" The answer would be nearly zero, and that's not a knock on Hoffman, just a statement about the good fortune of being on a winning team with lots of "Game of the Week" and postseason network exposure.

The thing about Rivera was that in any given year, he wasn't necessarily the best reliever in the game. He only led the league in saves three times. As baseball wound toward the 2020s, it seemed like throwing 100 mph was no longer a big deal (Rivera didn't do that), but that most teams seemed to find that special someone who could shut down opponents in the ninth inning.

What made Mariano great was the length and durability of his career and how he was always on the mark. Yes, he would have a bad outing every now and then, but he seemed to easily shake it off and was fine the next time out. The psychology behind Rivera's performances should be studied by anyone in a high stress job.

I attended an old-fashioned "hometown parade" for Mariano the year of his Hall of Fame election. It was held in New Rochelle, where he had lived and where he had rehabilitated a church on North Avenue. It was a wonderful day and it felt so "old timey," the kind of thing they had for Mickey Mantle in Commerce, Oklahoma, after his rookie season.

At the reception afterward I just wanted to tell him what he had meant to the franchise and to its fan base. It was easy to feel emotional with this great man. We had met before, but we weren't exactly "old friends." And here I found myself telling him about the meaning of Mariano, even placing my hand on his shoulder as we spoke. He was fine with that.

I walked away thinking, *I shouldn't have done that! What was I thinking? You don't touch the Great Mariano!*

In some gymnastics and swimming competitions, we see that there are some events in which judges discard the high and low scores in compiling total points. It got me to thinking—what if we did that with relief pitchers?

Almost every reliever, including Rivera, has that one awful game where they give up something like four runs in a third of an inning. Since they barely pitch 60 innings in a full season, that one awful outing plays havoc with their ERAs.

With Mariano Rivera
in New Rochelle, New
York, following a parade
to honor him for his
Hall of Fame election.

I'm not suggesting that the system of crossing off the one bad outing
should be applied to the pitcher's record—that would negate comparisons
to history. But if I was a general manager looking at relief pitchers across
baseball, I might tell my analytics people to "give me everyone's ERA
while crossing off that one bad outing." That might be interesting to see.

So, I took on this exercise. And in 2007, Rivera had an ERA of 3.15
after four straight years under 2.00. But on April 27 in a game against
Boston, he allowed four earned runs in just ⅓ of an inning. He spent the
rest of his season making up for it. If we wiped that one bad outing off
the books, his ERA for the season would be 2.66. While that was still not
Mariano-like (if you wipe out 2007 altogether, had had eight straight years
of under 2.00), it becomes a good example of the point of this exercise. In
fact, it would even have turned his career 2.21 into 2.18—although either
number still ranks first among pitchers since 1927.

He entered that April 27 game in the ninth inning with the Yankees
trailing 7–4. Seasoned Mariano watchers would tell you that he was never
quite the same without the pressure of a save on his shoulders. And sure

enough, that day, after retiring the first batter, he gave up three straight singles, and you know the fans were murmuring, "You don't bring him in with the Yankees down by three!"

Rivera became the first player ever elected unanimously to the Hall of Fame (a year later, Jeter missed by one vote). People asked, "How could Ruth, Cobb, Mays—all those guys—have missed being unanimous?"

The answer was that for many, many years, the Hall of Fame was catching up with there having been no voting until 1936. Those earlier ballots were filled with deserving candidates who hadn't been voted on, so getting named on all ballots was tough.

The Joe DiMaggio situation was frequently brought up. He wasn't elected until his third year of eligibility. Why? Well by the early '50s, there was already sentiment among the baseball writers that there should be a waiting period. Some were influenced by that. The five-year waiting rule was enacted in 1954, the year Joe was finally elected. He was the last player elected in less than five years (aside from Roberto Clemente, by special election after his death). It looks odd now to see that Joe waited so long but digesting all the facts (some may have noted his only playing in 13 seasons) helps bring about an understanding.

One last note on Rivera. The 1996 Yankees had two Marianos—Rivera and Duncan. As this is written, they are the only two Marianos who ever played in the major leagues, out of almost 23,000. I thought that was, well, interesting. Nothing more.

As I mentioned earlier, I am a member of a group of sportswriters who meet monthly for lunch. Lots of baseball talk, with a little politics thrown in depending on the news of the day. Only a few of us are Yankees fans. Most are Mets fans, but we have an Orioles fan, a Tigers fan, and some general unaffiliated baseball fans.

Since I have a lot of friends from the literary community, they tend to be Mets fans more than Yankees fans, because the Mets, along with the Red Sox and Cubs, have represented long spells of heartbreak and failure, which are traits that seem to appeal to the literati.

The group began in 1990, so we're talking about more than 30 years of monthly gatherings.

The founding father was Larry Ritter, author of the baseball classic *The Glory of Their Times*. (That book heads most "greatest baseball book ever" lists.) Some of our members besides Larry have passed away, including Ray Robinson, Al Silverman, Stan Isaacs, Michael Gershman, and Bob Creamer. Others have joined, but only one, Darrell Berger, seems to have embraced analytics as a way of measuring baseball.

A quick word on analytics here: I once asked several analytics-heavy historians whether we have learned of any players whose greatness was overlooked because of a lack of analytical research in their day. The best they could come up with was the old Yankee outfielder Charlie Keller, DiMaggio's teammate, who tied for 32nd place in OPS+ (DiMaggio himself is tied for 24th with Willie Mays, Hank Aaron, and Mel Ott). If only we could revisit Old Timers' Day and have Mel Allen say, "Our next guest is tied for 32nd in OPS+, let's welcome the great Charlie Keller!"

I more prefer my analytic comments to be closer to the observation that when Andy Pettitte faced Mickey Tettleton, it was the first time in baseball history that two guys with four "t's" in their names ever faced each other.

Rittter, who was also a noted economist, died in 2004, but we continue to honor his most important wish, which is that we meet around a round table, so that most discussions have everyone participating. With a rectangle, there are always two or three conversations going at once. (He was truly a respected economist, and at his memorial service at Mickey Mantle's Restaurant, no less than Paul Volker, head of the Federal Reserve, was among the speakers. I never expected to be introducing Paul Volker as a speaker, anywhere!)

I once asked Larry why, after I had listened to the original tapes of his interviews with old ballplayers, there was no swearing. In normal conversation, that would be expected among these old-time players.

"I suspect it was because I had my young son along," he said. "The players watched their language in front of him."

Our lunches have contributed nothing to society, other than our tips to the restaurant workers. It's just a monthly event to celebrate baseball and friendship, and then off we go back into real life. It's generally the only lunch table in New York where Sibby Sisti's name might come up.

I spoke recently with Al Clark, a retired American League umpire (when the leagues had separate crews) and the only umpire to ever have his name on his cap (AL). I always get good tidbits from Al about his profession. His father, Herb, was a sportswriter and an unabashed Yankees fan who used to sit by me in the press box, and who, despite his son's profession, was always complaining about the umpires "cheating" the Yankees.

Al would tell me little things about his colleagues that were sometimes quite amusing, like Steve Palermo announcing the count after every pitch as though he were a broadcaster. It was to make sure everyone—batter, catcher, and himself—were on the same page. He didn't use a ball-strike counter, which most umpires clung to in their palms.

"You can't ever trust the scoreboard to be right 100 percent of the time," he'd say.

One day I asked Al about the movement to praise catchers for their ability to "frame" pitches. I always thought that was an exaggeration. Could umpires be fooled so easily? And of course, it bordered on cheating, moving the pitch into the strike zone when it didn't land there.

He told me I was right. "Framing the pitch means nothing, absolutely nothing," he said. "We call the pitches at the same moment the hitters do—as it is just crossing over the plate. That's when they decide if they're swinging, and we decide with them if it's in the strike zone."

Umpire Phil Cuzzi takes it a step further, explaining to me that the process of framing can backfire and result in a borderline strike being called a ball. "[I'm talking about] that borderline pitch that is on the edge and in the strike zone. By pulling that pitch into the middle of the strike zone rather just "sticking" it where it's pitched, it looks more like a ball than a strike. The catcher's job is to make the pitch look like a strike, but when he pulls the pitch in such an aggressive manner there is no way that pitch looks like a strike and more often than not called a ball," he says.

I've taken to giving the umpires more slack. If we see a home plate umpire miss one, especially with that strike zone box shown on every telecast, think of how many the batters miss, taking a swing at a bad pitch. The batters and the umpires are paid to know the strike zone. But they're human, and they are going to miss some. And umpires miss a lot fewer than the batters.

"One more thing," Clark added. "The centerfield camera is not directly behind the mound and the plate—or the plate would be blocked. It's off a little bit, and so too is that box. It may not seem to be far off, but it's not perfect."

Have you ever seen a first- or third-base umpire shrug his shoulders as though to admit he "wasn't watching" on a check swing? Me neither. (Phil Rizzuto used to have ww all over his scorebook in the broadcast booth.) But surely, on rare occasions, they are not concentrating, not focused on the batter on every pitch. It must happen. Yet they always rule on the check swing.

I once asked another umpire friend about this, and the response was, "Oh yes, they aren't paying attention a lot of times. But it's mostly in the minors, and those guys don't usually make it to the majors. In the major leagues it's rare. But when it happens, you call a check swing. You don't want to penalize a hitter if you aren't watching."

In the '60s and before, umpires seemed to possess names that commanded attention. There were few "Bill Millers" or "Al Clarks" out there. (Although we do have a John Randazzo now.) They all seemed to have names like Dusty Boggess, Chris Pelekoudas, Harry Wendlestadt, Frank Secory, Jocko Conlan, Babe Pinelli, Joe Paparella, Shag Crawford, Tom Gorman, Jim Honochick, Bill Jackowski, Frank Dascoli, Frank Umont, Ed Runge, or Augie Donatelli. Names to be reckoned with. Unforgettable, fearsome, formidable names. Lots of syllables. Those were names!

Nester Chylak, now in the Hall of Fame, was another great name. He lived in Pennsylvania, and each winter in the '60s and early '70s, the Yankees PR department would charter a bus and visit media in outlying regions, interested in generating publicity to stimulate early ticket sales.

When we went to Scranton–Wilkes Barre, we would invite Nester to say a few words. It was perfectly appropriate.

But one year, when he got up to speak, he said, "I don't mind saying this, and of course I'm always impartial, but I'm a Yankee fan. Always have been. When the Yankees are good, it's good for baseball, and so I root for them to do well."

A lot of us in the room were shocked by this confession, and of course, it didn't mean that he ever gave the Yankees a favorable call. Still, baseball is very much about remaining above suspicion, so we looked at each other with eyebrows raised. But that was the umpire profession of that generation. They were all extremely self-confident people, and if Nester wanted to say that, he was going to say it.

It was on one such caravan that we learned of the passage of the Designated Hitter Rule, announced while we were actually engaging in a Ralph Houk–led press conference in 1973 in southern New Jersey. We did not know that announcement was coming that very day, so we were all caught by surprise.

Capturing the early reaction was a question from a local journalist, who asked Ralph, "How often do you expect to use a designated hitter?"

My recall may be imperfect on this one, but I'm pretty sure Ralph immediately said, "Every day!" (He was right.)

The DH was used throughout spring training by American League teams (in AL parks), so it wasn't a shock to the system when opening day rolled around. We were all quite used to it. On that day, the Yankees played in Boston, and thanks to an early start, the first DH would emerge from that game. That turned out to be Ron Blomberg, who hadn't been a DH all spring, but an injury now forced him to not play in the field.

In the first inning, batting sixth with the bases loaded, Bloomie walked and got the first DH run batted in. After the game I asked him for his bat, and thus it became the only bat ever used for a walk that is in the Hall of Fame.

Blomberg was a character, a product of the Atlanta public school system where he starred in baseball and basketball in high school. He was outgoing and sometimes outrageous, and he kept in the eye of baseball fans long after his short career by "owning" the "first DH" niche.

He was the first draft pick in the nation in 1967, by virtue of the Yankees' last-place finish in '66. The Yankees admitted that his being Jewish had some part in the selection, as the Yankees had never had a Jewish star. Fingers were crossed because he had great natural ability, but alas, some horrific injuries cut short that journey.

I suspect that even in his seventies, he could still wake up in the middle of the night and demolish a fastball from a righthanded pitcher.

The most fun I ever had with a book project was when I worked with the umpire Eric Gregg on his autobiography in 1990.

Eric was a National League umpire who was easy to spot on a baseball field. He was only the third Black umpire in the major leagues, and he weighed, on occasion, almost 400 pounds. But he met the physical demands of the job, even as people worried about all the weight he was carrying.

We agreed to do his autobiography together, capturing his childhood experiences growing up in a row house in West Philadelphia, and his rise to the major leagues as an umpire, which was the only way he could get to the majors.

The naivety of his youth was so colorful. He was never on a plane until he went to the Barney Deary Umpire School in Florida (where he was told he was too young), and as the passengers boarded, he thought "first class" meant first come, first served. So, he went to the head of the line. That was just a sample of his lack of sophistication as he worked his way up.

His stories were really funny, and many were very touching. He was pretty much on his own outside the ballparks, as his three partners would go to dinner without him. He was left to develop his own network of friends in each city, which he did.

He was working the San Francisco–Oakland "Earthquake World Series" in 1989 and his colleagues laughingly blamed him for causing the quake by falling off the trainer's table.

He married a beautiful Dominican girl and they had four children, one of whom, Kevin, became the PR director of the Red Sox and then his hometown Phillies. Eric took great pride in saying that they were going to the "same school as Mike Schmidt's kids."

We collaborated on the book seven years before he umpired an Atlanta Braves playoff game in 1997, in which he didn't appear to call too many pitches correctly. Atlanta fans still talk about that game, the "Eric Gregg Game," visible to all on national television. Livan Hernandez of the Marlins struck out 15, and *Baseball America* called it the third-worst umpire performance in the 1975–2000 era. It was his last postseason assignment.

We taped many hours together at Drexel University, which was near 30th Street Station in Philly, so it was easy for me to get to after an Amtrak trip down there. He not only had great stories, but he was a great storyteller. We laughed and laughed at his tales, and the manner of his delivery made him a popular public speaker. He drove me around his old neighborhood—"The Bottom," he called it. He had a brother doing a long stretch in prison, a sister who died from drugs, and another sister who "gets by." Their father, a big drinker, worked sanitation in Philadelphia but got into a lot of fights. He and Eric didn't speak much. We even drove past his old residence and didn't stop, even though his father was sitting on his front porch.

The book was called *Working the Plate*, which had a double meaning of course, because oh my, could he eat. Eventually the league sent him to a weight reduction program at Duke University, which worked for a time. But he admitted to being on a see-food diet—"see food, eat it"—and inevitably, the weight returned.

Making fun of people's weight is not "well intentioned," and people like Eric, who had a naturally good nature, took it and laughed along. (Once a player left a hamburger on third base when he was working there.) But obviously it was a serious health issue and surely must have contributed to his early death.

He lost his beloved job when the major league umpires staged a mass resignation, a misdirected negotiating ploy by their agent, Richie Phillips. Most of the umpires were rehired, but Eric was among the ones who weren't. Twenty-six members of the House of Representatives wrote a letter to Commissioner Bud Selig urging him to rehire Eric. But he didn't.

He wound up working at a concession stand at Veteran's Stadium.

Eric died of a stroke at age 55 in 2006. Bill White and I were two of the eulogists at his funeral in Philly. Bill had been his boss as National League president. I was pleased to see a number of his former umpire colleagues present at the funeral.

A book of which I am really proud is *Pinstripe Empire*, which was published in 2012. It is a narrative history of the Yankees, and I use the term *narrative* because, although it has two photo sections, there have been other nice team histories which were photo driven.

Originally this was going to be a biography of Colonel Jacob Ruppert, the beer baron who owned the Yankees from 1915 to '39, in partnership for a time with Tillinghast "Til" Huston. I thought he was due one, but in conversation with my agent Rob Wilson, and with editor George Gibson of Bloomsbury Publishing, we expanded the idea to being a full history beginning with the team's birth in 1903 and the events leading to that.

As I outlined the book, I realized that it would be the first team history since Frank Graham wrote *The New York Yankees* for Putnam in 1943. (That book was updated a few times into the early 1950s.)

Putnam would go on to publish team histories for all 16 clubs (plus an umpire book), with all bearing the team names except for the Philadelphia Athletics, whose book was called Connie Mack.

I had read some of those books in my teen years, and although they lacked an index, they were valuable reference tools, because the authors had witnessed much of their histories in person.

Graham started covering the Yankees for the New York Sun in 1915, so he knew the earlier sportswriters like Fred Lieb, Mark Roth, and Joe Vila, who played a role in bringing an American League team to New York. Graham also wrote *Lou Gehrig: A Quiet Hero*, something I did book reports on in elementary school several times. (I was big on repeating book reports; after all, who could check? I think I did Gene Schoor's Mickey Mantle biography four times.)

So, I began writing *Pinstripe Empire* (the name suggested by Tom Villante), and as it unfolded I realized that my original instinct was indeed worthwhile—Ruppert was going to be a major figure in the story. When asked, "What did I learn while doing the book?" my answer was that Ruppert's significance was much greater than I had believed.

Here was a fellow who inherited a major New York brewery from his father after serving four terms in Congress. Although American-born, he spoke with a German accent, which could grow more pronounced depending on the situation.

Ruppert not only bought Babe Ruth and built Yankee Stadium; he elevated the Yankees, and with them the whole baseball industry, to greater prominence. He did small things to move the Yankees "brand" into top-tier status, even things like making them the first team with an extra set of uniforms to wear in second games of doubleheaders. All the other teams took the field with sweaty, dirty, first-game uniforms.

He was a very wealthy bachelor, so in Ruppert we learn what opulence meant in America in his time, complete with a Fifth Avenue mansion and a country estate. And he accomplished all that he did with the Yankees, first during Prohibition, when his brewery was effectively closed, and then during the Great Depression when fans could barely afford a ticket. Not to be stymied, he built an empire—the Pinstripe Empire.

I got Yogi Berra to write a foreword and Bernie Williams to write a preface (I never really understood the difference), and these weren't written by me subject to their approval (that happens a lot), but based on conversations with them. I was especially glad to have Bernie aboard, because unlike Jeter or Rivera, he had come up when times were bad, and could fully appreciate the rebuild of the Yankees of the '90s.

It was of special meaning to me that I reached out to Frank Graham Jr. for a "special introduction" in which he talked about his father's original book and his growing up surrounded by Yankee history. Frank Jr. had worked for the Brooklyn Dodgers but eventually left baseball and wrote a fine book called *A Farewell to Heroes*. When I found him, he was a longtime "field editor" for *Audubon* magazine, living in Maine. I loved how his introduction connected his father's earlier work with mine, and we included a photograph of his father's book jacket. We last emailed in July 2022 as he turned 97.

To do the book, I first made a list of all significant Yankees moments in history and then a separate list of significant Yankees. I knew that the book was not complete without their inclusion, and I crossed them off as I wrote about them. Then I filled in lesser events and lesser (but interesting) players. There was something empowering about being the one to decide, "Is this in or out?"

I spoke to a lot of old players, or their wives or descendants. I spoke to a lot of retired sportswriters. K. Jacob Ruppert, the great-great-grandnephew of the Colonel and keeper of their family history, was one of many descendants of Yankees figures who helped. Whitey Ford was especially forthcoming because he really paid attention to all that was going on around him. I discovered Mary Lou Doyle, whose great-grandfather Slow Joe Doyle pitched for the Highlanders. (Did he work slow, or throw slow pitches? We never could get to the bottom of his nickname.)

(I helped arrange a "reunion" at a Yonkers, New York, bookstore between K. Jacob and the great-grandson of Red Sox owner Harry Frazee, Max. It was an author event with Max as a guest, and I arrived with Jake and made the surprise introduction, which had all the guests dazed in amazement. That was a fun evening, but the sale of the Babe was not rescinded.)

As I was writing *Pinstripe*, I came to the 1955 World Series, which is where I came in as a fan. From there forward, the writing became a bit

A meeting between descendants of Harry Frazee, Max (in Yankees cap) and Jacob Ruppert (K. Jacob), that I helped arrange at a suburban bookstore. The Babe Ruth sale was not reversible, and the Yankees maintained their 27 world championships.

easier, for I had witnessed it all and less research was needed. In the end, the 1955 World Series appears on page 310 of what would be almost a 600-page book. So, I'd lived half of it.

The first two words in the book were "Phil Shenck," the name of the Yankees original head groundskeeper, who had to whip Hilltop Park into shape for the team's first opening day.

Bloomsbury hired a professional voice actor to record the audio version of the book. When it was sent to me, it spoke, "Bill Shenck." He got the first word wrong! It was corrected.

I end the book with the current head groundskeeper Danny Cunningham, who oversees the current stadium, which made for a good bookend.

Pinstripe Empire grew into a brand. A paperback update was done in 2015, and an update on the eBook edition was published in 2021, bringing the book up to date through 2020, the strange "Covid-19 season." Billy Crystal lent a "celebrity endorsement" on the cover.

We created a Facebook page called Pinstripe Empire, populated by thousands of Yankee followers, and then did a children's version called *Pinstripe Pride*, for which Michael Kay wrote a foreword. We created a course called Pinstripe Empire at New York University, and did lectures with that title at Syracuse, Fordham, Clemson, Washington University, and other colleges. I was even invited to speak at the Smithsonian in Washington, D.C. And this book you're reading now can be called part of the brand extension.

Yankees officials did not formally endorse the book as the definitive team history but told me they viewed it as such individually. COO Lonn Trost told me he found himself reading every page twice and learning so much new. It was better not to have the team's endorsement, because that might have meant it would be perceived as a sanitized telling.

As it was, it dealt with the team being slow to integrate, being perceived as arrogant, "like rooting for U.S. Steel," and its unpleasant cutting of ties with popular players, managers, and broadcasters. An example: Vic Raschi won 21 games in 1949, 1950, and 1951. He was 16–6 in 1952 and then 13–6 in 1953. So, they sent him a contract calling for a pay cut. When he sent the unsigned contract back, he was sold to the Cardinals.

I was cautioned by friends who root for other teams, "When you're writing, remember—Yankees failure was a time of rejoicing by other clubs and their fans." And I did not forget that, so I think it came across as a balanced history.

I hope there will be a market for continuing updates. After all, if one cares about baseball history, it is hard to study that without Yankees history.

There is a mystery woman in Yankees history, someone who has long intrigued me.

Her name was Helen Winthrop Weyant, originally from Winthrop, Massachusetts, and known to close friends as "Winnie." A paid death notice in the *New York Times* on July 28, 1985, said she died in Scarborough, New York, on July 26. "Sister of Pamela Donald and the late Lillian Foster and Rex Weyant. Funeral private. For further information contact Beecher Funeral Home, Pleasantville, N.Y."

When I discovered that small death notice, it was the only public record I could find for a woman who once owned a third of the New York Yankees. The funeral home later filled in a few blanks; she actually died July 25 at the Brandywine Nursing Home in Briarcliff Manor, after residing in Scarsdale, and her funeral was handled by a Manhattan law firm, Gilbride, Tuse and Monrow. Her cremains were buried at Sleepy Hollow Cemetery in Sleepy Hollow, New York.

Winnie had been a friend and companion for Colonel Jacob Ruppert, the bachelor owner of the team. She accompanied him to many social events and resided at his country 400-acre country estate in Garrison, New York, when he was there. She never attended games. When the *World-Telegram's* Dan Daniel visited the Colonel there, he found Miss Weyant to be very much engaged in the team's operation, and very much a student of baseball. Her most notable public appearance had been at Ruppert's side when he announced that he would be helping to fund Admiral Richard Byrd's Antarctic expedition in 1934. She told Daniel that her father George had a longtime friendship with Ruppert. She and the Colonel were introduced by George Weyant, in 1925, and spent 14 years together.

Otherwise, she remained a mystery woman, although her brother, Rex, was assistant to the traveling secretary (George Costanza's fictional job) and then traveling secretary in 1944 and 1945, after Mark Roth died. He is in the team photos, and he lived until 1981.

Winnie was 37 when the Colonel died in 1939, which would have made her 81 at her death. She had been an off-Broadway actress under the name Winthrop Wayne, but she retired in 1929, presumably to devote more time to Ruppert.

Imagine her surprise when someone knocked on the door of her West 45th Street apartment to inform her that the Colonel had named her a one-third recipient of his estate.

The other two-thirds went to two nieces, Helen Ruppert Silleck-Holleran and Ruth Rita Silleck-McGuire, both of Greenwich, Connecticut.

Upon receiving news of her inheritance, Winnie was "semi-hysterical... and had no idea why so much money had been left to her," according to the *New York Times*. She was suddenly a one-third owner of the New York Yankees.

"I feel very honored by it all," she told the *Times*. "I'm surprised and frightened."

She needn't have been frightened. The business affairs of the team would be handled by a group of four, including the Colonel's brother George Ruppert and Ed Barrow, the team's business manager (today, called general manager).

"There was nothing as frightening as being summoned to see Mr. Barrow," said Phil Rizzuto. "His eyebrows were the scariest things you ever saw."

And so, Winnie disappears from view. K. Jacob Ruppert, now a magistrate in Louisiana, believed that she remained single for her whole life, devoted, he thinks to Catholic Charities, and probably died in a Catholic-run nursing home in Westchester County.

Barrow headed up the sale of the team to Larry MacPhail, Dan Topping, and Del Webb in 1945, but ultimately, the Ruppert fortune wasn't such a fortune after all, and Winnie was probably not a rich woman. She would have been an interesting interview.

Eighth Inning

I can't say I had much of a relationship with Jackie Robinson, but it was always an honor to be in his presence. The first time was when I was in college. He was a guest speaker at nearby Hartwick College in Oneonta, and I drove over to hear him.

Jackie was a terrific public speaker as he recalled his career and its aftermath.

I was sports editor of my campus weekly newspaper, so I got to ask him a question, and I remember saying, "It's hard to believe it has only been 20 years since you broke the color line; do you think the game has progressed as much as you expected?"

This was 1967, and baseball was happy to feature Black stars, but the relief pitchers and bench players were generally all white. Forget about coaches and managers and front office people. The Yankees had just hired their first Black secretary, Pearl Davis, which was progress, and that was led by the enlightened people leading the organization at that point, Michael Burke, Howard Berk, and Bob Fishel.

(Through 1966, there had only been 12 Black Yankees players, beginning just 12 years earlier with Ellie Howard. Then came Harry Simpson, Hector Lopez, Jesse Gonder, Marshall Bridges, Al Downing, Pedro Gonzales, Elvio Jimenez [one game], Arturo Lopez, Roy White, Horace Clarke, and Ruben Amaro.)

He did not like the lack of progress, and he talked about how slowly things had moved since he broke in.

Jackie would always be invited to Old Timers' Day, and the Yankees in those days always made a point of inviting ex-Dodgers and Giants, especially if they lived near New York. Jackie lived in Stamford, Connecticut.

As was our practice, we would call the "no-response" invitees to see if we could persuade them. On a few occasions, it would fall on me to call Jackie. It was a bit frightening because I had a feeling the call wouldn't be well received.

It would go something like this.

Me: "Jackie [baseball is a very first-name industry], I'm following up on our invitation to you for Old Timers' Day in a few weeks...we would love to have you with us. Is there a chance we can persuade you to attend?"

Jackie: "Thank you, but I have to tell you, until such time as baseball demonstrates progress in hiring Black coaches, managers, and front-office people, I will not be attending any of these functions."

Me: "Well, thank you for taking the call, Jackie, and I hope we can see you sometime in the future. You mean a lot to all New York baseball fans."

He died at 53, and didn't get to see baseball move forward, however slowly. He didn't live to see Frank Robinson hired to manage Cleveland in 1975.

Ellie Howard had been a coach with us since 1969, something I could have brought up on my phone calls with Jackie, but I assumed he knew that and I was reluctant to debate the issue with him, or to make it seem like that made everything right.

By the way, I was at Frank Robinson's managerial debut in Cleveland. It was opening day at Municipal Stadium and the Yankees were the opponents. As a designated hitter (yes, he was a player/manager) before more than 56,000 fans, he hit a first-inning home run off George Medich. A memory I have of that at bat is that the Cleveland PR people allowed still photographers on the field—just feet from the batter. It looked like baseball did in the 1930s, except of course, for the red uniforms worn by Cleveland.

A year later, Cleveland fans voted that the most memorable moment in franchise history, surpassing all their old championships and legendary players.

I had a really strange conversation with Al Downing during a fantasy camp in 2012. Al had broken in with the 1961 Yankees and was a mainstay of the Yankees dynasty of the early '60s.

I happened to mention to him something about being the first African American pitcher in Yankee history.

And he said, "No, I wasn't. It was...." I don't remember who he said, but he was wrong; it was him. How could have been unaware of such a thing for more than 50 years?

We talked about his giving up Hank Aaron's 715th home run to break Babe Ruth's record, and about other things, but I couldn't believe he was not aware of his "first," which is always a big conversation starter.

It was such a pleasure to know Elston Howard, who was a coach for most of my time with the Yankees. He was universally loved, and a lot of us were hoping he would succeed Ralph Houk after Houk resigned as manager following the 1973 season. The job first went to Dick Williams, who had taken the Oakland A's to the world championship, so few could quibble with such a high-profile signing. But when the American League president Joe Cronin voided that signing (Williams still being under contract to Oakland), the Yankees turned to a former farmhand but by then a longtime National Leaguer, Bill Virdon.

Here was where disappointment settled. Virdon was a good man—I personally liked him a lot. But we thought this was Ellie's turn. He had expressed interest in managing and certainly had the baseball smarts.

Some were not as high on him.

"Ellie has a lot of attributes, but when he walks into a room, is he a commanding presence?" was said. "Do heads turn, knowing this is our leader?" It is not a knock on Ellie to say that his gentlemanly demeanor and soft spoken presence would be held against him on this judgment. But it was sad that he never had his shot.

Bill Kane, our traveling secretary, often had a down-to-earth view on the promotion of some people. For instance, he thought that our third-base coach Dick Howser would never manage, let alone take a team a world championship as he did with the 1985 Royals.

Bill thought that Howser being 5'8" would make him ineffective. "This is a physical game; athletes respect size," he would say. "There needs to be unspoken authority, like, I hate to say it, like the manager could beat you up if you were out of line. Like Houk. Like Walter Alston. Fred Hutchinson. Hank Bauer. Players respect size and strength."

This sounded awfully schoolyard to me.

Howser disproved this by getting named to manage the Yankees in 1980 and winning 103 games to finish first in the division. So much for Kane's theory. But Bill was a smart guy and I tended to listen to him. And I didn't want to see Howser leave. He wore a 7½ shoe, and when I had to borrow baseball shoes to play in writers' games, his was the only pair that fit me. He eventually gave me a pair of my own.

Like my calls to Jackie Robinson, I had a similar experience with Roger Maris.

I had rooted for Mantle during their epic 1961 home run race, but I never rooted against Maris and certainly never booed him as many fans did when the press turned against him with the passing years.

He didn't help himself in that time frame, not really caring what the press thought of him and perhaps not appreciating how they could turn the fans against him. Still, he was Roger Maris, and his legend grew with time.

So, I would call Roger and encourage him to attend, and one year I met him at a Cracker Jack Old Timers' Game gathering in Washington, re-introduced myself, and told him how much it would mean to have him back in Yankee Stadium.

He was quite soft-spoken, even mellow. But he said, very politely, "Ah, what do I need to come back for and hear all those boos."

I told him that in my own opinion, I didn't think there would be boos. I think his feat had risen to legendary proportions and that the fans would embrace him, especially after such a long exile.

But he wasn't interested. He thought he would be booed, and that mattered.

After the Yankees won the 1977 world championship though, George Steinbrenner called him himself. Mr. Steinbrenner was now an Ocala resident, and Roger lived in Gainesville, Florida, about 40 miles north. So, he called him as a neighbor, and oh yes, someone who owned the New York Yankees.

And he talked him into coming for opening day in 1978 to raise the world championship banner with Mantle.

The Boss often took advice on ceremonies and staging from his Broadway partner James Nederlander, who knew how to produce dramatic moments.

And Roger accepted.

Making sure to avoid any chance of booing, Mr. Steinbrenner made sure that Bob Sheppard's announcement would be, "…We direct your attention to the flagpole in Monument Park, where the 1977 world championship pennant will be raised by…Roger Maris and Mickey Mantle."

By saying Mantle's name second, in the same breath as Maris', with no time for booing, the mission was accomplished, and all Roger could hear was loving cheers. It led to his returning several more times before he died of lymphoma in 1985, and I'd like to think he felt he was at last appreciated by Yankee fans.

General William "Spike" Eckert was selected to be the fourth commissioner of baseball following the retirement of Ford Frick in 1965.

General Eckert was a compromise candidate, and it is safe to say that no one in baseball knew him, and no one wanted to take credit for suggesting him.

Upon Eckert's selection, Larry Fox of the *New York World-Telegram* and *Sun* said, "My god, they've chosen the unknown soldier!"

Even while he served, Lee MacPhail ran the Commissioner's Office and even received the *Sporting News'* Executive of the Year award in 1967.

Baseball people seemed to go out of their way to stay away from Eckert, who was turning into a joke. It wasn't his fault. It was just a bad selection.

All you need to know about General Eckert is that he was invited to Old Timers' Day at Yankee Stadium in 1968, as commissioners always were, and during the pregame batting practice and the mingling of writers and players on the field, he found himself standing next to me, and engaging in conversation with me. I was the summer fan mail clerk. There was no one he knew to talk to!

Poor General Eckert. They put him out of his misery the following year, and he died in 1971 at 62.

Marvin Miller, as head of the Players Association, did amazing things for players, with the most noted being the structure of free agency, the creation of an arbitration process, and the financial benefits they reaped.

He did something else which is seldom cited. He was a strong advocate for player safety, and one of the things that came about in his time was padded outfield walls. It was an issue that seldom came up in conversation.

It wasn't a negotiated item; it was just a safety measure that both sides faced responsibly. "I think as time went on, there was just general recognition by all parties to ensure player safety," says Tal Smith, with whom I worked at the Yankees. "Safety concerns were brought to the attention of the clubs and addressed along with the need for filing grievances."

The result of that has been remarkable, as outfielders play the position unlike their predecessors, with almost reckless abandon, making spectacular catches with little concern for injury. If we watched games from decades ago, it would amaze us how many balls hit the walls for extra base hits as outfielders slowed down once they hit the warning track. Next time you see such a "circus catch" at full speed into the wall—think first of Brooklyn's Pete Reiser, whose career was cut short in 1952 running into those walls.

Other things have come about more slowly. In 2017, shortly after Todd Frazier joined the Yankees, he hit a line drive foul ball down the third base side that seriously injured a little girl who was at the game with her grandfather.

This sort of thing had been going on forever, of course. We all cringed one day in the '70s when Phil Rizzuto said, on air, "Holy cow, it's a wonder why more people aren't injured coming to the ballgames."

The small print on ticket always claimed that the clubs were not responsible, but that was seldom tested in court.

For some reason, the Todd Frazier moment set in motion a rapid plan to expand netting almost from end to end of foul territory at all ballparks. To see MLB move with such speed was amazing, because the game simply doesn't adapt that quickly. The game did move quickly after Yankees coach Don Zimmer was struck by a foul ball in the Yankees dugout during the 1999 postseason. By Opening Day of 2000, all dugouts had protective screening.

After Cleveland's Ray Chapman was killed by a pitch in 1920 in a game against the Yankees, it took some 35 years for helmets to be introduced. And it wasn't as though they couldn't manufacture them—after all, soldiers wore helmets in World War I.

Eventually helmets were mandated, but among the holdouts who were grandfathered in and wore inner cap liners instead were Detroit's Norm Cash and Boston's Bob Montgomery. I think the last players to resist ear flaps were Dave Winfield and Candy Maldonado.

The first Yankee that I recall wearing protection other than a helmet was Tom Tresh, who took to donning a shin guard after fouling too many pitches off his lower leg. Today, of course, the batters wear acres of body armor.

I remember Tresh as well for a courageous act during a game at RFK Stadium in Washington. Suddenly, a bat—not a piece of baseball equipment, but the flying mammal—flew out of the stands and landed in short left field. Thinking it was necessary to remove it for the game to continue, Tresh ran in, scooped up the intruder with his glove, and ran it into the dugout where, presumably, Washington groundskeepers figured out what to do with it.

Tresh looked like a classic powerful switch-hitting Yankee, and the fans hoped he would be the next hero in waiting. After Mantle, his was the Little League bat kids most wanted to receive at Bat Day. He won Rookie of the Year and was a two-time All Star. He made a great catch in left field in the 1962 World Series, after adjusting from shortstop only weeks before. (Tony Kubek having returned from the Army.)

But injuries started to arrive in 1966, and he plummeted to .219, .195, and .211. He was at .182 in 1969 when the Yankees dealt him to Detroit for Ron Woods to wrap up his abbreviated career. He had been in a four-year slump.

I have wondered over the years about players who had the misfortune of starting out in a slump. Slumps happen.

Surely there have been some players who go 4-for-37 starting out and get sent down, perhaps never to be heard from again. If a veteran player has a 4-for-37 slump in the middle of June, it's barely noticed and he continues his career. But I'm pretty sure some guys picked the wrong time for failure—like the start of a career. Like Munson's 1-for-30 with an 0-for-24 in there. Sometimes, a patient manager (as Ralph Houk was) is an important part of the story.

Another thing that I felt was noteworthy about Tresh was his ancestry. When he arrived in the majors, we learned he was the son of a former major leaguer, Mike Tresh, a catcher, mostly for the White Sox, who played from 1938–49. I had never heard of Mike Tresh, and by this time, I had pretty much heard of most major leaguers who had played for a substantial amount of time.

As Tom's career took off, I began to see that he was exceeding his father's accomplishments. (Mike, for instance, hit two home runs in more than 1,000 games.) And as the years moved forward, I began to see Tom as one of the first sons to exceed his father's career. The *Encyclopedia of Baseball* (the "Turkin-Thomson" version) listed fathers/sons who had played in the majors. A number of Hall of Famers produced sons who made it—Earl Averill, Eddie Collins, Freddie Lindstrom, George Sisler, and Ed Walsh, to name a few, but none could match their dad's career. With Tresh, that started to change. And now you have a lot who exceeded Dad, possibly because their fathers were earning good money and could afford to send their sons to strong college baseball programs. They may have even had workout equipment or a batting cage at home. Even without the money, athletes get better by generation just with better health and medicine available. In my mind, Tom being better than his dad was a milestone moment.

Tresh moved to left field to allow Kubek back in the lineup, but months before, one of the best spring training competitions had taken place with Fort Lauderdale's debut season as a spring training site, pitting Tresh against Phil Linz to see who would win the shortstop job in Tony's absence.

The two of them were two of four rookies to make the team in 1962, along with Joe Pepitone and Jim Bouton. There were four open roster spots because the expansion draft to stock the Los Angeles Angels and the new Washington Senators had all teams losing players.

Pepitone, a genuine Brooklyn character, had power and was a terrific fielder, but his autobiography, *Joe You Could Have Made Us Proud*, really captured his career in seven words.

On more than one occasion, he was late showing up for games and the Yankees front office quietly called their contacts at the local police precinct to express concern for his well-being. Fortunately, he always arrived intact. And frankly, no one on the Yankees would have predicted that among Pepitone, Tresh, Linz, and Bouton, Joe would live the longest.

Linz became a good friend, and, ultimately, we would hang out with Art Shamsky in Manhattan. I once said to him, "Phil, in that famous spring training competition, Pete Sheehy gave Tresh No. 15 and you got 34. Did you ever really think you had a chance?"

And he said, "Oh no, not once those numbers were handed out!"

Linz, Shamsky, and I went to Yogi Berra's funeral together, and Linz, of course, had famously played "Mary Had A Little Lamb" on his harmonica on the team bus in Chicago after a September 1964 loss. Yogi had hollered to the back of the bus, "Knock that shit off!" and when Linz asked, "What did he say?" Mantle said, "He wants you to play it louder."

With the encore, Yogi walked back and smacked it out of his hand. It flew into the air and landed on Pepitone's knee.

The incident, witnessed by the press who traveled with the team, made headlines for days and got Linz an advertisement for Hoerner harmonicas on the back cover of the 1965 Yankee Yearbook.

I sat with my pal Joe Garagiola Jr, who was representing his dad. Joe Sr. and Yogi grew up on the same block in St. Louis. But he was up there in years and the flight from Phoenix was a lot. Joe Jr. was prepared to speak about the remarkable friendship between these two guys, but he was never called on. It would have been a heart-warming moment.

Tony Kubek, quite shy as a player and frankly, a lousy interview subject, shocked many when he became an NBC broadcaster, doing not only Game of the Week but the jewel events—the All-Star Game, the playoffs, and World Series. "Was this the same guy?" wondered his old teammates. He went on to win the Ford Frick Award for broadcasting, earning him a place in the broadcaster's wing at the Hall of Fame.

Tony's earlier claim to fame was in Game 7 of the 1960 World Series, when a grounder hit by Bill Virdon took at bad bounce off a pebble and struck him in the throat, sending him to the ground clutching his neck and seeking to find his breath. It was a scary moment, and a momentous one, in that it led to the Pirates tying the game, and eventually winning it on the Bill Mazeroski home run. (I still wonder how after 51 years of sweeping the infield, there could still be a pebble at shortstop.)

Tony was kept overnight in a Pittsburgh hospital for observation, and the next day, with the Yankees having flown home, he had a visitor. It was his rival shortstop, Dick Groat of the Pirates. A very nice gesture indeed.

The problem was, when Groat entered Tony's room, Kubek had absolutely no idea who it was. Only after several minutes of conversation did he realize it was Groat.

Dick, you see, was bald, not something one recognizes on the field unless it is during the playing of the national anthem. Tony apparently wasn't looking and had no idea it was Groat.

The Mazeroski game remains one of the most talked about baseball games ever played. The score was 10–9, there were 24 hits, nine pitchers, five walks—and not a single strikeout.

I once mentioned this to Ralph Houk, who coached first base that day, and he acted like, surely, I was making this up, this couldn't be true.

"You don't say, you don't say," he kept repeating. But as Casey Stengel, managing his last Yankee game, might have said, "You could look it up."

After winning three pennants in three years as Stengel's successor, there came the awkwardness of Houk moving to the front office where he wound up firing Yogi as manager after one season (and an American League championship), and those close to Yogi couldn't help but ponder that this onetime backup catcher to Yogi had moved into a position where he could fire him. It put an awkward strain in the relationship, for sure.

I worked for a time as a spokesperson for the public relations firm Ogilvy, Adams, and Rinehart, handling the MLB's Player Relations Committee account during tense negotiations in seeking a new Basic Agreement in 1993. When the head of the PRC, Richard Ravitch, told me that he found the players to be a "most collegial bunch," I had a feeling he might be just a bit out of touch with on field language, and that "collegial" wasn't going to get him very far. (It didn't.)

When those negotiations ended, I stayed at Ogilvy to work on the account of the reclusive billionaire heiress Doris Duke, whose father founded American Tobacco and Duke University, and whose life was being scrutinized over her adoption of a 35-year-old woman who she felt was the reincarnation of a child she lost in 1940, and the management of her estate by her suspicious butler. You can't make this up, and believe me, I'm barely touching the surface. I was part of a team that visited the University on her behalf to help coordinate a large donation, mostly to earn her good press. I was very well received, as you would imagine. (I took advantage of a trip to Duke University to take in a Durham Bulls game.)

The assignment didn't last long; Doris died just two months later.

I was then recruited by Sy Berger to become the first ever in-house PR person for the Topps Company. (I was formally hired by Arthur Shorin, a son of the founding family, and J Langdon, the president.) The baseball card business was booming and had become a billion-dollar industry, fueled by the sale of vintage cards on what was called the "secondary market." The manufacturers didn't make any money on those resales, but people were buying new cards too—thinking if they saved them, they might pay for their kids' college one day.

So I was back in baseball, working at one of the businesses that influenced my childhood. I knew Sy Berger well from his frequent visits to Yankee Stadium, where he would sign up players to contract extensions and help them receive items out of a gift catalog. Perhaps even a new toaster oven.

But it was a much bigger business now, and while I was there, the company moved from its somewhat worn-down building in the Industry City section of Brooklyn to sleek new headquarters near Wall Street. (The factory that printed, packed, and shipped the cards was in Dureya, Pennsylvania.) The Brooklyn location was famous for Sy having hiring a scow with a collapsible portal, from which he dumped many uncut sheets of 1952 cards, which included Mickey Mantle rookie cards. Cards which in mint condition would come to be worth…millions!

Of course, when he did this in 1960, the cards weren't worth much at all, and he had no idea who was on the uncut sheets. It was just a spring cleanup and the water into which it was dumped was at the end of our street into the Bay Ridge Channel, off Bush Terminal Piers Park.

Sy himself, a wonderfully personable, bright, and generous guy, was happy to tell the story himself years later, because the dumping of the 1952 cards helped elevate the value of the Mantles by emphasizing scarcity. He befriended many ballplayers through his personal connection to them, none more than Willie Mays, who was genuinely a BFF to Sy.

The other good Sy Berger story was his 1964 visit to London to meet Brian Epstein, the Beatles manager. The Beatles had hit it big (with no greater fan than me), and people were flocking to Epstein to try and get a license to produce product.

Sy got him to agree to do trading cards (Topps had earlier done Elvis Presley), by speaking Yiddish to him when they met. How he knew Brian would respond to that escapes me, but he knew Epstein was Jewish, so he took a chance. And a deal was made.

Sadly, although we always remained close friends, Sy and I parted ways when it came to the Beatles. He regretted Topps having done the cards when it was reported that they smoked marijuana. He didn't even like to talk about it.

My time with Topps drew to a close when the company's revenue fell dramatically in the years following the 1994–95 shutdown of the baseball industry. Kids were no longer buying cards without the games being played. The industry never really recovered but I stayed with them as a consultant for a number of years. It was a new business experience for me—the idea of putting goods on shelves and the whole distribution system of moving packaged merchandise was something I had never done before. It was very educational, and I never walk through stores without taking note of product placement, end-aisle displays, and how milk is always at the far end of the store so a consumer has to walk through everything else to pick up a quart.

In August 2021, after 70 years of doing baseball cards, Topps lost its license with MLB and the Players Association. Even high-placed Topps executives learned of the event on social media or on calls from friends who had seen it online. I hadn't worked there in more than 20 years, but the news hit hard. I have a loyalty to all my former employers and keep in touch with colleagues from each stop. For generations, Topps was Americana. But I suppose nothing is forever, and personally, I hope the successor brand owner, Fanatics (which purchased Topps and retained its employees), decides to market the cards to children again, something Topps abandoned along the way in favor of adult collectors.

So nothing is forever. There's no more McRib sandwich, except for an occasional rollout. My Rice Krispies no longer go snap, crackle, pop, and no Quaker Puffed Wheat in the store. I can't buy Yankee Doodles anymore, something I would occasionally set up at press conferences. And there are no more Cott or Hammer sodas, or Welchade grape drink, or Hydrox cookies, which played to my sweet tooth throughout my childhood.

Pat Tabler, who some may recall, had a lifetime .489 batting average with the bases loaded; 43-for-88. You would find that most batters hit higher than their usual average in such situations. People are quick to say "great clutch hitters."

And while they may indeed be great clutch hitters, there is much more going on. First of all, why are the bases loaded? Things are obviously not going well for the team on the field, and unless it's a new pitcher, the guy on the mound is not at his best. He's either lost the strike zone, or command of his pitches, or has been getting hit.

Naturally, the batter is going to take advantage of an unsettled pitcher forced to throw strikes, and naturally that will be reflected in batting average with bases loaded. It's not just that he's a great clutch hitter. In fact, even if it's a new relief pitcher, the distraction of three men dancing off their bases, and the pressure of getting a strikeout or a ground ball in his brain, is going to make him somewhat less effective.

And yes, the concentration level for the hitter rises with the chance of picking up a couple of ribbies. So, you will almost always find that batting average with bases loaded is a lot better.

Bobby Murcer was the most popular Yankee after the Mickey Mantle era ended, and although the Yankees were generally not pennant contenders during his best years, he had star quality and the fans readily embraced him. He was never going to be Mantle, but he had a great Yankee Stadium swing and was the poster boy in a time of posters in kids' bedrooms.

As a teen making his major league debut, he posed for a picture with Mantle and Maris, wearing a Mantle/Maris T-shirt. He looked like such a kid.

Bobby could be very fastidious. He liked everything just so. The sight of a dugout floor as a game wore on rather disgusted him—but he never let on. And believe me, you would not want to see a dugout floor at the end of a game.

He had style. In 1972 we needed someone to model the Yankees' new 1973 double knit uniforms. (All but one other team, the Giants, had already switched from flannel to knit in '72, but the Yankees were, well, they were the Yankees. They were never going to be like everyone else.)

So, we asked Bobby to be our model, and he was perfect. He knew how to pose, he knew what we needed, and it was apparent that we picked the right guy and that we were smart not to use a professional model.

Shea Stadium seemed to do Bobby in, as he couldn't find the stroke that would put the ball over the right field wall. In 1974, our first year there, he didn't homer there until September 21, and then again the next day.

Mr. Steinbrenner had been down on him since Lee MacPhail signed him to a $100,000 contract in 1973, making him only the third Yankee to reach that mark, after DiMaggio and Mantle. It wasn't outrageous by 1973 standards though; it was becoming quite acceptable for really good players who were "the franchise." Bobby said that Mr. Steinbrenner told him he would always be a Yankee, but even if he said that, he was yelling at Gabe Paul to see what he could get in return.

On the morning of October 22, 1974, Gabe summoned me to his office. He wanted me to listen to a phone call he was about to make.

"Pearl!" he shouted to Pearl Davis, his secretary, "get me Bobby Murcer."

Of course, I could only hear Gabe's side of the call.

"Bobby? It's Gabe Paul. Sorry to wake you, but you know the saying, only whores make money in bed.

"Anyway, I have some news for you, and I think you'll like it…we've traded you to the San Francisco Giants."

Gabe turned to me, covered the phone, and said, "What's his wife's name?"

"Kay," I responded, as I sat there stunned, but surely less stunned than Bobby was down in Oklahoma City.

"I know you and Kay will love San Francisco. It's a wonderful city; great restaurants. The Giants are a first-class organization."

There was silence for a minute or so while Bobby spoke, I think expressing his own shock and perhaps recalling Mr. Steinbrenner's words about being a Yankee forever.

Then Gabe said, "What's that? Oh, Bobby Bonds.

"Have a great day; best to, uh, Kay."

I had never been present for such a call before. I don't know why Gabe wanted me there, unless he recognized the historic significance. Bobby was the face of the team. But Gabe and the Boss had only had him for two seasons (Mr. Steinbrenner was suspended for much of that time), and I think the "franchise player" thing didn't really mean much to them.

And as Tal Smith, our general manager, said to me later, "Listen, anytime you can get one of the top five players in baseball…you pull the trigger."

Bonds was that. A magnificent athlete, who gave the Yankees their first ever 30-homer, 30-steal season, even if he did it while playing through a knee injury sustained while chasing a long drive heading for an unpadded wall in Comiskey Park.

Bonds and I became friends in that one season with the Yankees, before he was traded to the Angels for Mickey Rivers and Ed Figueroa. (A very good trade.) I picked him up at LaGuardia for a winter press conference, helped him find a nice apartment in the Riverdale section of the Bronx (near where I lived), and in spring training, when he seemed near tears after breaking his sunglasses, I drove to a nearby drugstore and bought a replacement pair for five dollars that looked like the broken one to me. He was so happy! (An overreaction, for sure.)

People made a lot out of whether Bonds had a drinking problem. I never saw it. What I did see was a classy guy. That season that we had him, the Red Sox asked me if I could bring Bobby to the Massachusetts State House where a hearing was being conducted on legalizing sports betting. The Sox were hoping Bonds could speak out against the measure. Bobby agreed to go, and was eloquent in opposing the bill, talking about the undue pressure it would put on players, and the suspicions that would go with a bad game or a bad at bat. He was great. The bill did not pass.

Bobby Bonds was probably the greatest Yankee to never play in Yankee Stadium, along with a few New York Highlanders who made the Hall of Fame like Jack Chesbro and Willie Keeler, and one who didn't, Hal Chase. He was just a one-year player, while we played at Shea, but it was a privilege to see him play.

Pretty much everyone who ever met Bobby Murcer came away feeling he was a great guy. And he was.

But I have met so many people over the years who translate a quick encounter with a celebrity into a decision about what sort of person they are.

Yes, it's possible they were rude, or ignored an autograph request, or didn't stop to chat or make eye contact. But really, people, is it fair to someone to judge them on that brief moment in time? A moment in a lifespan of many decades?

Would I want to be judged based on my phone conversations with customer service people?

When someone tells me that so-and-so "was an a-hole" in their brief encounter, I want to say, "Would you like to be judged on that small moment in time—and then have that person tell everyone he meets for the rest of his life what an a-hole you are?" On Facebook I see a lot of those "lifetime" judgments passed along. "Great guy" or "a-hole" seem to be the prevailing sentiments when a celebrity encounter is mentioned. How shallow it is to then tell hundreds of people about that moment in the shorthand of quick judgment.

Of course, given the benefit of a longer association, we can indeed accept such findings. The favored story from the "Murderer's Row" days of the Yankees came in assessing the outfielder Bob Meusel, who apparently never had a kind word for the writers.

By 1929, when his Yankee career was apparently winding down, he showed up in spring training as a new man, full of charm and wearing a smile.

Wrote Frank Graham: "Bob Meusel learned to say hello…just when it was time to say goodbye."

Gabe Paul's secretary, Pearl Davis, who had an outsized personality and was extremely lovable, eventually left the Yankees and went to work for the spike-haired boxing promoter Don King. She showed me once how to always leave her electric typewriter running with a half-typed paper in it, along with a sweater draped over her chair. That way in the morning, her boss would think she was already there, just away from her desk.

At Don King's Manhattan brownstone office, she occupied a street-level workstation, with King on the third floor. One day three tough-looking guys arrived and said to Pearl, "Is he upstairs?"

Pearl said, "Who shall I say is calling?"

That was good enough for the three guys; they figured out he must be upstairs. They hustled up the stairs and the sound of King getting beaten up could be heard on street level.

Pearl quit the next day. I'm not sure if she left her typewriter on.

After Tony Kubek retired in 1965, the Yankees were left without a shortstop. Over the next few years, Horace Clarke, Ruben Amaro, Dick Schofield, Dick Howser, Jerry Kenney, and Tom Tresh took turns out there, but finally in 1968, Gene Michael claimed it, and would remain the team's regular until 1974. While he was a slick fielder, he didn't hit much (.233 in his Yankee career with 15 home runs), and Yankees fans were impatient for more. Two attempts to unseat him—by Frank Baker and Jim Mason—did not succeed. (This was the franchise's second Frank Baker. The first, Frank "Home Run" Baker, is the Hall of Fame. This one was more like Frank "No Run" Baker, whose .191 average put him below the Mendoza Line.)

But "Stick" was a smart player, liked by everyone. He was a "master of the hidden ball trick," in which he'd disguise the ball still in his glove and tag the unknowing baserunner out. He got away with it three times, until the PR department (me) foolishly decided to publicize it. We put it in the press guide under his mini bio.

"What are you doing?" he asked. "This will end it!"

And it did. He never was able to do it again. Error on PR. He was still reminding me of it in the 21st century.

Michael was very close—a mentor, really, to Thurman Munson, who like him had gone to Kent State. He was nine years older than Thurman but came from Akron, near Thurman's hometown of Canton, and the two got along like brothers.

Lee MacPhail once said he'd like to hire Gene to negotiate *his* contract, so good was he at that skill, when players still had little leverage. He wound up making twice what Horace Clarke made, although one could make a case for them being equally valuable to the team.

In his time as a Yankee, he proved to be a very popular speaker, doing tons of Little League and Boy Scout banquets, telling his stories and showing great charm with the fans.

In 1976, having moved on from his Yankee years, he went to spring training with the Red Sox in Winter Haven, Florida. I saw him there and he was the same smiling Stick, but he was now 38 and he knew his career was winding down. He was thinking of managing in winter ball and we talked about that a little.

He made the Red Sox opening day roster, but never got into a game, and was released on May 4. I read it in the small print in the *Daily News* under "transactions." He would be one of those players who wore the uniform, got the paycheck, but you can't find him on the all-time Boston roster. Sort of a ghost player. The Yankees had a few of these during my time there, usually emergency catchers called up for a weekend, if Munson or John Ellis were off on Army reserve duty. Some never got into a game. Rick Stelmaszek was one such catcher.

Without even talking to him, I went unannounced to Mr. Steinbrenner's office, just walked in, and said, "The Red Sox just released Gene Michael. I know you don't know him well, but let me say, he is a great organization man, someone you'd love to have back here. I went on many speaking engagements with him, and he won so many fans over to the Yankees. And he really knows his baseball."

I had in mind some sort of speaker's bureau function, and to my delight, the Boss said, "Have him call me."

So, I set up the call and Stick got hired to be a major league scout, traveling to see other players and sending in reports on them. No speaker's bureau.

In midseason he was with us in Chicago, sitting in the press box and using a walkie-talkie to communicate with the dugout on positioning of players. It was never considered illegal, but it was a new concept, and we were pushing the envelope with it.

White Sox owner Bill Veeck was not amused. (He usually watched games from the press box.) He ordered Michael to knock it off, and I believe this was the same day he hung up my payphone while I was doing play-by-play for Mr. Steinbrenner.

Veeck said that the next day, he would provide a seat for Michael outside but next to the press box. And he did.

He also hired a guy in a clown suit to sit in the seat next to Michael. So, for the whole game, Gene did his walkie-talkie thing, and the clown did nothing, he just sat there, looking like a clown.

It was very funny and, of course, embarrassing for Michael, but Veeck was a master showman.

At the World Series in Cincinnati that year, Michael and two other Yankees scouts were back in the press box with walkie-talkies. Commissioner Kuhn ordered the game stopped and had them removed from the press box.

After the game, all Yankees personnel, including me, were ordered confined to our rooms by Mr. Steinbrenner for the embarrassment we had caused the franchise. Even Gabe Paul was told he couldn't leave his room. (We were staying in a motel about 40 miles outside of Cincinnati.)

"There will be no hospitality, no parties, for losers," said the Boss. And we had lost that game 5–1.

Gabe Paul, of course, disregarded the lockdown and stayed downtown for the hospitality. If someone else was throwing the party, Gabe was going to be there. Me, I obediently stayed in my room, preparing the next day's press notes.

Things moved along nicely in the Gene Michael career. After a couple years of scouting, he became manager of the Yankees Triple-A farm team at Columbus, Ohio, in 1979. He would return to Yankee Stadium as general manager in 1980, when Dick Howser was named manager. Howser was fired after losing the ALCS despite winning 103 games in the regular season, and Michael became manager. He dared the Boss to fire him during that 1981 strike-interrupted season, so frustrated was he with phone calls from above. And sure enough, he was fired in September, rehired in 1982 and fired again in September, returning to the coaching lines again in '83. I asked him if he was angry with me for recommending that he be hired, and he said, "Sometimes."

He managed the Cubs in 1986–87, and then returned to scouting for the Yankees before being named general manager in August 1990.

That was the beginning of an era of good will in Yankee land. Suddenly, players like Williams, Rivera, Jeter, Posada, and Pettitte were being signed and developed, without the tendency to trade off good prospects for aging veterans. Further, the Yankees were becoming likable, maybe for the first time. It had long been fashionable to hate the Yankees for their winning ways and the perception of Yankees arrogance, which extended to their fans. But now, who could root against Joe Torre? Derek Jeter? Mariano Rivera? Bernie Williams? It was a beautiful time.

Stick was credited with bringing stability to a crash-and-burn franchise that had really fallen on bad times.

Although fired again in 1995, he came to be widely admired in baseball for adding good sense and stability to the Yankees.

He became a superscout, taking on assignments as needed, but living a much more relaxed life as he aged into his late seventies.

I called him when I was doing *Pinstripe Empire* to get the backstory on the development of Mariano Rivera. He loved telling that story, of how he and Rivera, salsa music on the radio (Rivera spoke no English), made a long drive in 1992, from Fort Lauderdale to Vero Beach, to see Dr. Frank Jobe, the Dodgers' trusted physician. (Jobe is credited with inventing Tommy John surgery.) Jobe thought that was not necessary from Mariano, but he did clean out some bone fragments.

After mixed success as a starting pitcher, a radar gun was suddenly clocking him in the mid-90s. He'd never been near that.

"I asked around to see if the gun might be wrong," said Michael. "I quietly asked Jerry Walker, a scout for the Tigers (and formerly a pitching coach for the Yankees), and he confirmed that it was what he had on his gun too."

The rest of course, is history, all the way to Rivera becoming the first unanimous selection for the Hall of Fame.

I asked Michael on a few occasions if he'd like to write a book. I'm sure others had asked as well.

"It would be some book, wouldn't it?" he'd say. "But honestly, so long as they send me a new contract every year to keep scouting, I can't do it."

We never did that book. He died in 2017 at age 79, still drawing a baseball salary for the 59th year in a row.

It would have been a good one.

People in baseball were spooked by Jim Bouton's *Ball Four*, which came out in 1970. That tell-all book was revolutionary for the conservative sport, and baseball writing has never been quite the same. Jim Brosnan had almost gotten there with his two fine books, *The Long Season* and *Pennant Race*, but Bouton broke new ground, and in a sense, even some of the material in this book would not have been possible without *Ball Four*. Material that reads quite innocent today.

After everyone finished criticizing Bouton for breaking down established clubhouse confidences, the door was still open to go forward. Mantle and Ford did a "tell-all" with Joe Durso a few years later that repeated many of the same stories.

I first met Bouton in my first year, 1968, when filmmakers hired a bunch of real Yankees to be extras in some ball playing scenes while making *Paper Lion*, a book about George Plimpton's adventures in trying to be a real player. The extras probably got $100. And they came in on an off day for the $100. Alan Alda played Plimpton.

Bouton was sitting in the dugout when I walked over and introduced myself. He invited me to sit with him, and we found ourselves talking about world events. It was the year when Martin Luther King Jr. and Robert Kennedy were assassinated; there was no shortage of material to discuss.

When the book came out two years later, I as a Yankee spokesman naturally had to express the team's outrage, and I did, quite professionally.

I think Bouton knew I was only doing my job, because he soon became a television sports reporter and we were fine together. He came to spring training the following year and was pretty much boycotted and refused entry. I think Fritz Peterson wanted to give him an interview but knew that would be bad in front of his teammates. And I think Munson wanted to punch him out.

Pete Sheehy, whose clubhouse was the scene of the crime, would never give another player No. 56 so long as he was in charge of the clubhouse. (As time went on, he broke his own rule.)

I liked Pete, who would from time to time share some confidences of his own. He was a character, with very long fingernails he seemed to never trim and the ability to keep a two-inch ash on his cigarette before flicking it off. He'd been working the Yankee clubhouse since 1927 when he was hired to assist Pop Logan, who went back to the 1903 Highlanders running the clubhouse.

Pete had a thing about left-handers. He thought they were all a little crazy. If someone told him about someone doing something zany, he would flick his left wrist as though releasing a curveball but using it as a signal that the culprit must surely be a left-hander. (Bouton was right-handed!)

I was a guest on a radio show not long ago when the host mentioned the "wife-swapping episode" of Fritz Peterson and Stan Bahnsen.

"No, no, no," I said. "It wasn't Bahnsen, it was Mike Kekich." And with Pete's hand gesture in my mind, I said, "A right-hander would never do such a thing."

I loved when Pete took me into his confidence. I spent a lot of time in the clubhouse with the two Petes who ran it: Big Pete Sheehy, and Little Pete Previte. Big Pete was famous for keeping secrets, and the players all respected him for it. After a few months, I thought I'd earned his trust, and sitting at the black picnic table in the middle of the clubhouse, where all the balls sat awaiting autographs, I said, "Pete, today's the day…tell me all about the Babe!"

He was quiet for a brief moment.

"Never flushed the toilet," he said.

And that was going to be enough for the day for both of us.

When we opened the refurbished Yankee Stadium in 1976, I suggested we name the home clubhouse for him, and it happened. I also suggested a plaque for Casey Stengel in monument park, and Gabe Paul said, "Let's do Joe McCarthy too." I wrote the copy for both. McCarthy was still living, and I got him to record a message of appreciation, which we played on the PA system in the new stadium. I was glad Gabe thought of that.

Years later I was working with Bowie Kuhn on his book *Hardball: The Education of a Baseball Commissioner*. My job, besides writing the first draft, would be to guide him through topics and keep him on a timeline.

The only real disagreement we had with the editorial contents was that he wanted to leave out the whole Ball Four controversy, during which he had summoned Bouton in to tell him to denounce his own book. Bouton alerted the media and the book became a bestseller. Kuhn felt duped. And he was.

I tried to impress upon Kuhn how important this book was, not only at the time, but going forward. It changed baseball writing.

In the end, he gave it three paragraphs. I was pleased.

After the Kuhn book was published, my wife and I decided to throw a dinner party in our Larchmont home to celebrate the culmination of the effort. This was a social event a bit out of our comfort zone, but we decided to go for it as though we belonged in that social strata.

So, we invited my WPIX boss, station president Lev Pope, and his wife, Martha (Lev lived in the next town to us and they were really nice people). Then we invited Robert and Marion Merrill, who also lived nearby in New Rochelle, and although he was an internationally celebrated opera star, he was also a Yankees national anthem singer who had a uniform jersey with a 1½ on the back and I thought he would be a lively addition.

Then I decided to really reach out. I sent an invitation to Richard and Pat Nixon, who lived in New Jersey. It was a long shot, but the three guests would love it, and I suppose I could handle it for one night, for, after all, he was a former President of the United States, a big baseball fan, and he knew Kuhn. He didn't exactly know me, although I sat behind him at Billy Martin's funeral at St. Patrick's Cathedral.

I got a polite turndown from his aide, and I was kind of relieved but pleased that I had made the effort.

We prepared the dinner ourselves, thinking that "catered" was above our station and might look pretentious. And it was a great evening! After dinner, we retired to the living room where Merrill regaled us all with stories of his world concerts and included a few bars of opera here and there to accentuate his stories. What a night!

I had four other presidential encounters over the years. When Jimmy Carter came to WPIX to talk up his latest book on our newscast, I was the station official who greeted him at reception and walked him to the studio. It was not a big deal.

I saw Bill Clinton speak at the New York Public Library after his presidency, shook his hand on a receiving line, and snapped a photo of him. At the event, he spoke about the roots of racism, and I followed up

We did it up for a home-cooked dinner for the Bowie Kuhns, the Robert Merrills, and the Lev Popes to celebrate the publication of Kuhn's book.

with a letter to him expressing some disagreement, which he acknowledged and agreed with in a letter back to me.

After they left office, WPIX hired former presidents Ford and Reagan to be speakers at a convention at the Century Plaza Hotel in Los Angeles.

We paid Jerry Ford $20,000, and while awaiting his introduction to the main ballroom, I found myself alone with him in a staging room nearby. To make conversation, I mentioned that I was from New York and had met Nelson Rockefeller on occasion. Rockefeller had been Ford's vice president after serving as New York governor.

"I never really got to know him," said Ford to my surprise. "Oh, he'd be at cabinet meetings and all, but we never socialized. And he wasn't the sort of governor who went out campaigning for other Republicans. So, our times together were few."

Well, there was a bit of history for me. That was really interesting.

Together with a WPIX colleague, I then co-produced a "Conversation with President Ford," conducted by our fine news anchor Morton Dean, who had recently joined us after a long career with CBS News.

Reagan came the following year, just one year after leaving office. (He waived a speaker's fee because it was a journalist gathering.) Same hotel, same drill. And same "alone time" in the same room where I was left to make small talk.

I was going to tell him that when he hosted a White House event for Baseball Hall of Fame members during his first year in office, a press aide in the White House informed me that my book on the Hall of Famers, *Baseball's Best*, was on his nightstand as "overnight briefing material." Surely that would be a good thing to mention. (It was just three days before he was shot outside the Washington Hilton.)

We sat about three feet apart, maybe as far apart as his Secretary of State would sit at cabinet meetings. And I soon realized, he wasn't hearing anything I said. He was, it seemed, nearly deaf in his left ear. I read that it related back to his Hollywood days when a pistol was fired close to him while shooting a Western and his ear drum was damaged.

So that was interesting too! Left to have a one-on-one conversation, he was no longer capable at age 79 of properly conducting one. Was this what it was like at 78—when he was still in office? Biographies suggest that might well have been the case.

Do you think security at the White House has changed over the years?

My longtime book agent Bill Adler decided to do a book called *Kids' Letters to President Kennedy* in 1962. He wanted real letters. So, he wrote to Kennedy's press secretary Pierre Salinger to outline his idea, and Salinger realized it was good PR for the president. He invited Bill to the White House mail room to select actual letters.

Bill arrived at the appointed time and was shown to the mail room. By 5 PM, when it was time for civil-service employees to go home, he hadn't finished.

"That's okay," said the senior mail clerk. "You can stay. Just close the door behind you when you leave."

With Jim Bouton, promoting a vintage baseball league. Fittingly, the press event was held at Delmonico's in lower Manhattan.

Bill stayed until almost 10 PM, found his own way out of the White House unescorted, and went home.

Things might be a little tighter today.

I kept in touch with Jim Bouton for nearly 50 years. We did some events surrounding his involvement in a vintage baseball league, with games played under 19th century rules. We did a press conference for that wearing derby hats at an old landmark Manhattan restaurant, Delmonico's, near Wall Street.

We shared a SABR panel together as his health was declining and his wife had to finish sentences for him. But he still had that twinkle in his narrow eyes that indicated he knew more than he let on.

He called me in 2018 and described a photo he remembered of him with Mantle in the Yankees dugout. He had taken up oil painting and wanted to do a painting from the photo: Could I help him find it?

I loved challenges like that, where I knew if I entered Bouton-Mantle and searched in Google images, it would come right up. I emailed it to him in less than two minutes, and he was so pleased.

I asked his widow about it at his memorial service in Great Barrington, Massachusetts, after he died the following July. Sadly, he never got to the painting.

Ninth Inning

Working with the former Baseball Commissioner Bowie Kuhn was an honor, because after all, he held that position for 17 momentous years. He may not be well thought of today as a commissioner because he lost seemingly all his battles with Marvin Miller, but he took baseball from a small business and taught it to better market itself and to grow exponentially. He was a Wall Street lawyer; he didn't look like a guy who could grow the industry with marketing and television, but he did.

When he asked me to assist on the book, I couldn't resist. I'd be up close with the man who presided over the game for all those years, and the characters we would write about would be fascinating. Steinbrenner, Veeck, Finley, Autry, Busch, Selig, Yawkey, Fetzer, Griffith, Kauffman, O'Malley, Stoneham, Turner—what a list! And I'd be there to hear it all, including the stories that didn't make the book.

He was quite open about the charges that he just followed what Walter O'Malley wanted. While listing the times he didn't, he unapologetically said, "I would have been a fool not to. The man was brilliant."

We talked about *Time* magazine suing him over the issue of women reporters in the clubhouse.

"O'Malley called and said, 'You'll lose this one, but it's one you need to defend. That's what you're paid to do.'"

And he did fight it, but the tide was turning, and the right way. He knew it. He just followed his obligations.

(One turning of the tide was the elimination of "Ladies' Days" at ballparks. The Yankees were sued for the discrimination against men—and lost. That was it for Ladies' Days.)

One thing that he said—not for inclusion—was, "All the great things we accomplished came without ever finding another Mickey Mantle."

He meant the story of Mantle—how he was discovered, overcoming injuries, how he succeeded DiMaggio, how he rose to fame, his Hollywood glamour, even his alliterative name—would probably never happen again because of the sophistication of the game today. The days of finding a diamond in the rough, undrafted, were over.

He didn't include it because after thinking it over, he felt it insulted Willie Mays by leaving him out of the statement.

We worked in the basement office at Kuhn's beautiful home in Ridgewood, New Jersey. We worked full days on Fridays and Saturdays for more than year, going through three drafts. It was just before the age of word processing, so I had to type each draft from scratch on my beloved IBM Selectric and had to respond to his changes in ink. But I enjoyed the process.

Promptly at 5 PM each day, his wife Luisa would appear at the top of the basement stairs.

"Bowie! Marty! Cocktails!"

So, I realized, this is how the other half does it. And it was kind of nice, although it was a different time, different sensibilities. I would

Working with Bowie Kuhn on his memoir, *Hardball*, in the basement of his New Jersey home.

never have had a drink and driven home 40 miles in the dark after we all got more responsible on the subject, largely through the grassroots efforts of MADD (Mothers Against Drunk Driving). Not that I was ever drunk, but even one drink (which is what I had) could be enough to impair.

The book was fairly well received, except by writers who could never stand him, especially Murray Chass of the *Times*, who went on to write a very nasty critique of his commissionership published the day of his funeral. Murray's column was much discussed at the church in Ponte Vedre Beach, Florida that day.

Most reviews thought it was an important work of baseball history. Some thought his pompous demeanor came through. (I was shocked one day when he told me he loved Eddie Murphy movies.) It was massive—and it was almost two years late getting finished—but his portraits of all the game's characters, while still showing his love for the players and the game, came through. The *New York Times* named it a "Notable Book of 1987" in its year-end Book Review section, and it was nominated for a Casey Award as Baseball Book of the Year. (I have won that twice—for *Slide, Kelly, Slide* in 1995 and for *Casey Stengel* in 2017.)

Nobody likes to even consider the possibility of a plane crash, let alone talk about it, but the *New York Post*'s affable Maury Allen was able to see extra gloom in such a catastrophe.

He traveled with the great Yankees teams of the early '60s, when Mel Allen was still broadcasting.

"The headline," he said, would be "Mantle, 45 Others Die in Plane Crash." Then he said, they would list the passengers in small print, and all he would get would be

"Allen, M. (2)"

I once flew with Mel Allen to a winter banquet appearance in Oneonta, New York, my college town. Oneonta has a small airport. The Catskill Airlines plane was an eight-seater. It being a typical day in Oneonta, the approach and the landing were harrowing, and it did occur to me that two

MAs, myself included, might be doomed—me and the guy who taught me baseball. But we made it.

On another winter banquet occasion in Oneonta, I drove from New York with our wonderful coach and friend Dick Howser. It was a long drive; we hit a bad snowstorm and proceeded very slowly and with great caution. I was behind the wheel.

Suddenly, in the middle of the blizzard, I saw a figure off to the left shoveling his driveway in the middle of nowhere, halfway to Oneonta. As we got closer to this hulky figure in a snow parka, I said to Howser, "You're not going to believe this, but isn't that Al Salerno the umpire?"

Dick wiped the fog off the inside of our windshield, sized up the situation, and said, "Fuck him. Keep driving."

Ballplayers never forget, although I must have laughed and said, "What's with you and Salerno?" but I don't remember his answer. Could have been a called third strike 10 years earlier.

This is a futuristic thought that runs through my mind. I even called Gene Monahan, the Yankees' longtime athletic trainer and ran it by him.

We know that a player who can throw 95 mph has a gift. You don't learn to throw 95. You either have it or you don't. Nothing you do can build up your speed more than 1 or 2 mph.

So, I wondered whether one day, whatever it is in a pitcher's arm, elbow, or shoulder can somehow be detected in childhood. Is there something in the muscle tissue? Something in the bone structure?

Can an MRI one day find the magic tendon?

If yes, that will get teams following athletes in their childhood. There may be lists of elementary students who might one day throw 90.

It's a little scary, because science hasn't yet found ways to detect stardom early. But this could be it. I hope they name it after me.

If you recognize that there were still a lot of Brooklyn Dodgers fans in New York in the decade after they left for Los Angeles...because Sandy

Koufax, Junior Gilliam, Don Drysdale, Johnny Podres, and manager Walt Alston were still there...then between 1949–1966, there was a New York rooting interest in every World Series for 18 years in a row.

In the years when the Yankees weren't in the Series, you had the New York Giants in 1954, and the Los Angeles Dodgers in 1959 (with about a dozen Brooklyn players), 1965, and 1966. You had to skip from 1948 (Braves versus Indians) to 1967 (Cardinals versus Red Sox) to find a World Series without a New York fan base. That was certainly good news for the ratings people at NBC, which televised all those series.

New York has long been the center of the baseball universe, with many of the game's very origins traced to the New York area, and then starting in 1952, it housed the office of the baseball commissioner.

It was also a hub of baseball activity when the city was home to three teams, the Yankees, Dodgers, and Giants. There were days in that era when all three teams would be in town at the same time. Schedule makers tried to work around it, but it was often unavoidable, as visiting teams liked to play the Giants and Dodgers back-to-back and not switch hotels. So, in those days, particularly before night baseball, players from six of the 16 teams would all be in town at once and could usually be found at night at Toots Shor's or Jack Dempsey's in midtown Manhattan. And where they congregated, so too did the press.

So, New York was certainly the center of the baseball universe in those days, and everybody knew everybody else in the game very well.

WMCA radio carried Yankees baseball in New York. Jack Spector (the former WMCA "Good Guy" when it was a top-40 rock station), and his fill-in and successor, John Sterling, did a call-in sports show. I came to know the people there and one day was invited to the station when John Lennon and Yoko Ono were guests. Actually, only Yoko was a guest, plugging her new album, and John stayed outside of the studio with just five of us for two hours! What a memorable night that was! (At one point, he pretended to be a caller "Johnny from Brooklyn," and in a perfect New York accent, asked Yoko if the Beatles would be getting back together. As

A night to remember with John Lennon at WMCA radio, 1971.

she was plugging her new album, it was not a question she wanted.) We all had a great laugh over that.

I probably had my worst suck-up moment ever that evening when I told John how much I liked Yoko's new album. I think he saw right through me.

Sometime later, as my budding reputation for knowing baseball trivia was growing, I had an odd but enjoyable invitation to go on the Barry Gray talk show on that station.

Barry Gray's producer, Barry Landers, invited me to a trivia night panel, with Gray hosting. I was the sports expert and, get this, Jane Fonda was the film expert. Tiny Tim was the old-time music expert. There I was with Jane and Tiny, doing live radio!

This was around the time that Jane did *Klute*, and she was absolutely beautiful. My favorite Jane Fonda era. Tiny Tim, the novelty act of all novelty acts, looked just as you would expect, and remained in character all evening.

It was actually a fun experience, although Ms. Fonda didn't ask me to keep in touch. Neither did Mr. Tim.

Barry reemerged a few years later when he was hired as the Yankees promotion director on my recommendation to Gabe Paul.

Soon after starting his job, Barry came into my office to say he had just made a tentative deal with a South Korean manufacturer to produce actual baseball gloves for less than a dollar each, which would make a spectacular giveaway day for us.

"Only thing is," he said, "I have to fly to Korea to finalize the details and see the gloves."

"Barry," I said, "can I go with you to Gabe Paul's office when you tell him you have to go to Korea?"

We never did do a glove promotion.

When we were playing at Shea Stadium in 1975, there was a day we were to honor the 200th anniversary of the United States Army. Barry set it up, and even got General William Westmoreland to attend. Hey, if he could get Jane Fonda and Tiny Tim to do trivia on the radio, I suppose getting General Westmoreland was not a big deal.

The culmination of the celebration was to be the firing of cannons in the outfield—a 21-gun salute. The cannons were placed about 40 feet from the outfield fence.

The firing began, and news footage, which survives on YouTube, shows Barry, who looked like Sonny Bono, standing next to the cannons at full attention. (Billy Martin talked exactly like Sonny Bono.)

After a few shots, the combination of the gunpowder and the reverberation suddenly set the outfield fence on fire. As the ground crew frantically headed to the scene, several panels of the wall fell backward, which I think helped extinguish the flames. But here we were, guests of the Mets in their ballpark, and we were burning their park down. There was a long delay in propping those panels back up until a more permanent rebuild could take place the next day.

When Shea Stadium closed after the 2008 season, local TV stations ran highlights of the 45 years of its existence, focusing on the Mets' two world championships there and the Beatles playing two concerts there. The only Yankees highlight shown was Barry and his cannons, burning the place down.

Our two years at Shea felt like a long road trip, and while the Mets were very accommodating, the wear and tear on the ballpark in use every day was evident by the end of the seasons. The Yankees clubhouse was the New York Jets clubhouse, and it must have been extremely cramped for a football roster, because it was tiny for us. We set up our position in the press box to be next to the scoreboard electricians, whereas the Mets' PR team set up at the opposite end. The scoreboard had a Yankee logo at the top when we were there, and we bought a few billboards along Long Island highways to read, HEY LONG ISLAND, THE YANKEES ARE AT SHEA! but we didn't draw well.

Our offices were at the one-story building in Flushing Meadow Park that had been used by Robert Moses and his team administering the World's Fair of 1964–65. Gabe Paul had Moses' office, which had its own private entrance, with a small parking lot next to it. Our scouting director was the future Hall of Famer Pat Gillick, and I remember one day we played around with a Jugs Gun in that lot, testing this new contraption to clock the speed of pitches. Joe Garagiola Jr., our in-house lawyer, and I played catch while Pat tested the gun.

We had to drive to Shea for games; it was too long a walk. The real hero of our move was our office manager, Jimmy Conte. Our move had taken place during the gasoline shortage of 1973–74, which featured long gas lines. Jimmy went to the nearest gas station on Roosevelt Avenue and bartered baseball tickets for "cut in line" privileges. I can't recall how we did that without getting battered by angry Queens drivers on line, but somehow, he pulled it off. Hooray for Jimmy.

Opening Day of 1976 marked the return of the Yankees to Yankee Stadium after two seasons as guests of the Mets at Shea. It was good to be home.

The new stadium was well received by fans and media, except for still photographers whose positions were somewhat of an afterthought and not especially safe. The ones in the "camera wells" next to the dugouts were really in the path of hard-hit foul balls, and many of them were aging and not possessed of great reflexes.

The addition of escalators, the elimination of obstructed view seating, the introduction of a new state-of-the-art scoreboard, and better restrooms, concession stands, and restaurants all made for a better fan experience, although the passage of time and the eventual closing of the new stadium in favor of the current one that opened in 2009 made many fans nostalgic for the original park, the park with Ruth, Gehrig, DiMaggio, and Mantle had played. By 2009, fans had forgotten the inconveniences of the original place, and nostalgia won out.

We really pulled out all the stops for the opener in '76. Mr. Steinbrenner had been reinstated as general partner in time for the season following a suspension, and he took an active part in the day's festivities—down to who got parking passes among the media.

His knowledge of football had him reciting the names of Giants, Baltimore Colts, Notre Dame, and Army players who had starred in Yankee Stadium, and they were all invited for field ceremonies along with Joe Louis (who seemed to draw the most attention), and the usual parade of Yankee legends—Mrs. Ruth, Mrs. Gehrig, DiMaggio, Mantle, Ford, Berra (who was back as a coach after managing the Mets), and one of my favorites, Bob Shawkey, who had hurled the first opener back in 1923.

I wish I could say it all went swimmingly, but the security people I had on the field with me were called away to help at the overflow pregame party in Mr. Steinbrenner's office and suite. So, I was alone, wrangling an enormous media corps in what surely must have looked like chaos on the field. And it was.

The Boss handpicked four especially distinguished guests to surround Shawkey for the first pitch ceremony—Pete Sheehy, our clubhouse man; Toots Shor, the celebrated restaurateur; Mel Allen, still called the "Voice of the Yankees" (12 years after he had been dismissed); and James Farley, the former Postmaster General of the United States during the

FDR Administration, who was a native of nearby Haverstraw and the longest-running season ticket holder at Yankee Stadium. Farley in fact, had unsuccessfully tried to buy the Yankees after Jacob Ruppert's death.

The day was more challenging than I would have liked, and I didn't even make it to my seat in the press box in time to see Minnesota's Disco Dan Ford hit the first home run in new Yankee Stadium, but the Yankees won and would go on to win the AL East in what felt like easy fashion. Attendance topped two million, we had the cover of *Time* magazine, and suddenly, the Yankees were big time again. It was an honor to be their press officer during that amazing year, and although I seldom wear it, I proudly received a World Series ring, which was given to league champions as well as world champions.

As good as I thought I was in the trivia department, no one could beat a college classmate of mine named John Delaney from Watervliet, New York.

If you think you know trivia, consider John—you could say "1942 Cincinnati Reds," and he would recite their whole 154-game schedule. He really could! This was before Baseball-Reference.com allowed you to look these things up! He said he loved the schedule makers, the movement of the teams back and forth across the country, and how perfectly it all came together.

John, who got two copies of the *Sporting News* each week (one to read, and one to save), could also tell you which players or coaches carried the stretcher when an injured player was hauled off the field. This really mattered to him! And the guys who carried Mickey Mantle off after his 1951 World Series mishap next to Joe DiMaggio, well they held a special place in his stretcher Hall of Fame.

John is deceased, or I would have called him at this point to remind me who the Mantle stretcher guys were. I apologize. But he was the best. I've yet to meet anyone who can tell me the results of every playoff series since baseball began division series in 1969, but John would have done it.

"John, how about 2015 postseason?"

And he'd think for a moment and then say, "Cubs over Pirates in NLWC, Astros over Yankees in ALWC, Mets over Dodgers and Cubs over Cardinals in NLDS, Blue Jays over Rangers and Royals over Astros in ALDS, Mets over Cubs in NLCS, Royals over Blue Jays in ALCS, and Royals over Mets in World Series."

I know he could have done this. He might have even known the scores or how many games.

Stretchers, by the way, have been replaced by flatbed vehicles which someone decided was more tasteful I suppose. Like changing the disabled list to the injured list.

I was editor in chief of my college newspaper, and I made John sports editor. It was not a good decision, because he usually missed his deadline and I had to replace him. That sort of ended our friendship, and I had no one else to go to get the Senators 1943 schedule.

May 31, 1974, was the day the Yankees sold Horace Clarke to San Diego. An era had ended.

The Horace Clarke Era could also have been called the Fritz Peterson Era, both of them having joined the teams after the run of pennants in the '60s was over and leaving before the pennants resumed in the '70s.

Horace had been in the Yankees organization for 17 years, eventually succeeding Bobby Richardson at second base. He was a working man's player. Not much glamour, just out there doing his job every day for a relatively small salary, barely $40,000.

But it was a comfortable living for "Hoss," a native of the Virgin Islands, and he was so easy to be with, so approachable.

I loved conversations with him where he would invoke sportswriter talk like "Fall Classic" or "speed merchant" into his sentences. Players seldom used those newspaper words.

In the Bronx, Horace was the last Yankees player to live in the Concourse Plaza Hotel, three blocks east of Yankee Stadium. He liked the convenience. It didn't bother him that the once-majestic hotel was now a welfare hotel.

He wore a helmet in the field for reasons unknown and long-sleeved sweatshirts under his jersey on the hottest summer days, explaining to me, "This is a cool snap where I come from, mon."

He roomed with Roy White, and the two of them would lug a record player and a batch of jazz records on road trips to keep them entertained.

(The soft-spoken, gentlemanly White, maybe the best left fielder in team history, once revealed that he was a member of a street gang while growing up in Compton, California. I was shocked. "What were you, the recording secretary?" I asked him.)

Anyway, Horace was dealt to the Padres while we were in Minnesota, and I got a call from Gabe Paul informing me so that I in turn could inform the press.

But before I did that, I knew that he would quietly leave our hotel for the airport so as not to be a burden to anyone. It didn't feel right.

I raced down the elevator at the Leamington Hotel to try and catch him—and I did! By seconds. He was in the lobby in his little straw porkpie hat, carrying a straw suitcase.

I was so glad to see him, to give him a proper sendoff from a Yankees "official" (me) after 17 years in the organization. At least someone was there to say, "Thank you and good wishes." We shared a warm hug.

The Padres gave him No. 7. He wasn't going to get that in New York.

The press used to get on him for occasionally "bailing out" on double plays. Once Joe Donnelly of *Newsday* devoted a whole column to why Horace must go. (He actually led the league's second basemen in double plays twice, in putouts four times, and assists six times.)

The next day Horace said to me, "Oh, in 10 years Joe will still be writing those columns, but I'll be fishing in the Islands, drinking a little rum, and enjoying the sunshine."

It was a pretty good perspective to have on life.

Horace died in 2020, and I wrote a lengthy memorial on a Facebook page called "The Horace Clarke Years." It felt like, once again, he deserved a proper send-off.

Roy White and I became friends in my very first year with the team, and he and his beautiful wife Linda were guests at my wedding. Roy should have a plaque in monument park befitting his longevity and contributions to the team over 15 seasons, but he never seemed to find his way to Mr.

Steinbrenner's favor, perhaps because he was a player inherited from the CBS years.

Roy is seventh all-time in games played for the Yankees, but he was often under the radar and only topped 20 home runs once, which was a low output for a corner outfielder and occasional cleanup hitter who choked up on the bat.

Still, when the team retired No. 6 for Joe Torre, I thought it would have been more appropriate for Roy, especially since Torre usually wore a jacket and no one really knew what his number was! (Aaron Boone's sweatshirt look recalls that.)

One year, at a sports banquet in New York, I found myself at a table with Olympic star Mary Lou Retton. She was very famous at the time, America's sweetheart. Over the course of the evening, she mentioned to me that her father had played minor league ball for the Yankees.

I had no idea. She said his name was Ron Retton and a search had me discovering an infielder named Ronnie Retton who played in the Yankees system from 1959 to '64. (Mary Lou was born in 1968.) In '64, he would have been a teammate of Roy's at the poorly named Columbus Confederate Yankees (who had a confederate flag sleeve patch on their uniforms.) Retton hit .255 and played 95 games.

Roy was seated at the dias, and I went to him with the news about Mary Lou's father. He was shocked—he never put the two names together. He came down from the dias, and had a wonderful talk with Mary Lou about that season together.

Willie Randolph and I grew closer after his playing career. When he asked me to join him for lunch to help him prepare his remarks for the day he got a plaque in Monument Park, I was really honored. Our friendship deepened around that time, and now we find ourselves frequently on the phone talking not only baseball, but life in general—the political scene, family issues, friends in common.

I met with Willie Randolph at Yankee Stadium to help outline his remarks for the day he received a plaque in monument park.

After his time as manager of the Mets, he should have had a second opportunity somewhere, perhaps with the Yankees, because he did take the Mets to a 97-win, postseason berth in 2006. The playoff run ended, Mets fans will recall, when Carlos Beltran took a called third strike in the last of the ninth in Game 7 of the NLCS against the Cardinals.

"Marty," Willie said one day, recalling the moment, "In your backyard, playing imaginary games as a kid, do you ever take a called third strike with the season on the line?" He still couldn't believe it.

Maybe if the Shea Stadium scoreboard had directed all the fans to yell "swing, batta, swing!" before the pitch, things might have turned out differently.

When Willie broke in as our regular second baseman in 1976, he was only 21, and one of the few players younger than I was. He was the big acquisition in the trade with Pittsburgh which brought Dock Ellis and Ken Brett to New York in exchange for Doc Medich. Of course, few knew that he would be the big acquisition, as his name was not well known. I remember one New York sportscaster saying, "Can you believe it? Doc Medich for two over-the-hill pitchers?"

(I once accompanied Medich to a hospital in Oakland after he had been hit in the hand while running outfield sprints. He was X-rayed and read the X-rays himself, and we left. He never saw a doctor. He was a pre-med student at the time.)

Pete Sheehy assigned Willie uniform No. 23, a pretty low number for a rookie. So, he was 23 in the 1976 Yankees Yearbook and Press Guide, and other printed information.

Came the first day of spring training, and we were both standing by the vat of "soup of the day" and hard-boiled eggs and carrot sticks that Pete put out. Willie approached me and said, "I want No. 30. It's what I had in Pittsburgh."

He was sort of demanding it. And of course, I'm thinking, *Who cares what you had in Pittsburgh; you played only 30 games there. You weren't exactly Clemente or Stargell.*

But I didn't say that, and instead I said, "Well, out of respect for Mel Stottlemyre, we'd like to keep No. 30 out of circulation for a time."

And with his Brooklyn brashness, on display at age 21, he said, "I don't give a f— about Mel Stottlemyre. I want 30, and it's available."

I guess I spoke with Billy Martin about this, because I didn't want to alienate the guy who was going to be our everyday second baseman.

"Let him have 30," he said.

And so we did, and not only did he go on to a distinguished career worthy of a plaque in Monument Park, but he was still wearing 30 as a Yankees coach in the '90s, when Stottlemyre, then the pitching coach, wore 34. And after about two months as a regular in his rookie season, Bill Kane walked right into George Steinbrenner's office and said, "Have you been watching this kid? You gotta sign him to a long-term contract!"

I suppose that second chance at major league managing isn't going to come along. Today's managers are hired because they buy into front office analytical data rather than traditional baseball thinking, and Willie is clearly old-school, having come up in that era.

And perhaps he's too famous, as well. Most of today's managers, and indeed general managers, have pretty low profiles and modest résumés.

Since I moved to Manhattan in 2003, I take the subway to Yankee Stadium. It's only 20 minutes from Columbus Circle and it can be festive, with everyone wearing their Yankees caps and shirts and getting into the mood for a ballgame. Always, there are Munson jerseys.

One day I left the stadium early to take the subway home, and I found myself packed into a standing-room only car. The well-fashioned woman next to me was reaching high to hold onto a pole. I noticed a tattoo of a rose near her elbow. Tattoos hadn't yet become "a thing," so it caught my eye. (As late as 1995, when I worked for Topps, the NBA ordered us to airbrush out Dennis Rodman's tattoos.)

Anyway, when I lifted my eyes from the rose tattoo, I suddenly realized who I was standing next to. It was Caroline Kennedy Schlossberg, who had attended the game with a friend and their two young boys. Her son, of course, was President Kennedy's grandson, Jack.

Fortunately, my sense of propriety was functioning, and I said nothing. She knew I was aware of who she was. I hoped she appreciated my silence. I wondered why she was on this subway car instead of having summoned a car and driver, but then I realized that she, like me, had figured out that this was the way to do Yankee Stadium.

Only when I got home did the obvious dawn on me—a rose! Like her grandmother, Rose Kennedy, and her daughter, Rose Kennedy Schlossberg! How did I not realize this at once?!

Tattoo accepted.

I only knew Casey Stengel a little. He was eight years removed from his tenure as Yankees manager when I joined the PR department, and he was wholly identified by now through his beloved Metsies, Metsies, Metsies. He had always turned down gestures from the Yankees to return for Old Timers' Day, and who could blame him? He had been unceremoniously dumped by the team after losing the seventh game of the 1960 World Series to Pittsburgh.

When they fired him—at a press conference, no less—they made a big deal out of giving him a handsome parting gift, a six-figure check. The problem was, it was his profit-sharing earnings, which were his anyway. It was not a bonus.

Finally, in 1970, he agreed to return. Bob Fishel put a handwritten coda on his Old Timers' Day invitation letter, which said, in effect, "If you're able to join us, Casey, we would like to retire your uniform number."

Casey liked Fishel, and he said to his wife, Edna, "You know, this is quite a thing, having your number retired." (The Mets had already retired his No. 37.)

He was right; at the time, he would be only the fifth retired Yankee number, following Gehrig, Ruth, DiMaggio, and Mantle, whose number was retired just the year before. Casey had not come back to Yankee Stadium for the Mantle Day ceremony, even though almost everyone else (except Roger Maris) associated with Mick's career had.

So, arrangements were made, and he had such a good time that when he returned home, he sent us a thank-you postcard. In his big, scrawly handwriting, he wrote, "Mrs. Stengel and I had a marvelous time, seeing old friends. We had a wonderful trip. And thank you for my prize." By prize, he meant his gift, something which cost us about $75 per player. He

Casey Stengel came back to Old Timers' Day in 1970 to have his uniform retired; the young publicist on the right was among those delighted.

addressed the card to no one in particular, just New York Yankees, Yankee Stadium, Bronx, New York 10451. I wish I had saved that one.

He continued to return until weakening health prevented it in 1975, a few months before his death. In the early summer of 1974, we hadn't heard from him, and I saw him in Texas where the Rangers were having a "former Yankees" Old Timers' Day, Billy Martin being their manager. I saw him in the visiting manager's office at Arlington Stadium.

"Casey!" I said, "I'm Marty Appel, Bob Fishel's successor with the Yankees. We haven't heard back from you, and we're hoping we can count on you to be with us in two weeks for our Old Timers' Day. Think you can join us?"

He let me have it. "Goddamn it," he railed, "I'll let you know when I let you know. Stop asking. I haven't decided."

I had been admonished by Casey Stengel, and I thanked him and hunkered out of his view. My own need to organize everything and print the program perhaps overrode my sense of giving the man his space.

I had always felt burdened by my own need to "check things off" even if they weren't ready to be checked off. It was a nasty compulsion.

By the way, he did attend the Old Timers' Day in 1974. Maybe he felt guilty about yelling at me?

Now, we fast-forward to 2015, and my agent and my editor at Doubleday approach me about doing a Casey Stengel biography.

At first, I rejected it. Bob Creamer, long a part of my monthly lunch group, had already written the definitive Casey biography, a book that was tremendously well received. Like his Babe Ruth bio, it was considered a classic.

I suggested a combined Casey-Yogi bio, but my editor said that dual biographies seldom work. "It's been over 30 years since Bob Creamer's book," he said. "Stengel is worthy of a second look. Some people just lend themselves to fresh biographies every few years."

It's true. We never get enough Lincoln biographies.

So, I agreed, and to my great joy, two things emerged that would make the book unique.

First, the internet wasn't available when Bob Creamer did his research, and now, not only was it available, but a site had appeared carrying digitized editions of the archives of hundreds of newspapers around the country. Casey played or managed in so many small towns—and there was a treasure trove of long-lost tales and adventures there. He was, as I soon discovered, a rascal even from his days in the low minor leagues, fresh out of dental college. What a find! Even as a kid in Kansas City at the turn of the century, a star 19th-century player who happened to be a neighbor (Kid Nichols, a 300-game winner) told him to listen to advice and not shrug it off.

I had met his grandniece, Toni Harsh, a few years before at a Casey seminar in New York City. She was now living in Nevada and had been a town councilwoman there. She reached out to me and said, "I have the full manuscript of a memoir by Aunt Edna [Casey's wife] written in 1958 and never published. Would you be interested in that?"

Would I! What a find that turned out to be. We could read all about Casey the baseball genius, but here was a look at the suitor, the husband, the provider, and the businessman, along with his private reactions to events in his career.

Toni became a friend and even added me to the Board of Directors of her dream project, a Casey Stengel Museum, and through her I met Bob Case, who had served as an "assistant" to Casey in his retirement years in Glendale, California and had so much detail about life with Casey.

Having Edna's "voice" in the book would mean a lot. In fact, when I was asked to read the audio book at a recording studio, I suggested that we have a woman's voice do the parts where Edna is quoted. New York radio reporter Juliet Papa, a friend and neighbor, provided Edna's voice, and I would say the end product turned out great. (I joined Juliet every opening day starting in 2014 to provide color commentary live from the press box on her station, WINS. It grew into a mini tradition.)

The book was well received, and in interviews, I was able to explain what made it different than Bob Creamer's, always being sure to honor the Creamer book with glowing praise.

Bob Creamer was a very wise man, and he once told me something I've never been able to get out of my mind. He may have heard it from someone else—I don't know for sure—but he said to me, "Suppose one day we enter the pearly gates and discover that after a lifetime of 'facts,' the only truth in the world is mathematics."

An honor out of the Casey book was an invitation to speak at the Smithsonian Institute in Washington with Paul Dickson, who had written a Bill Veeck biography at the same time. Veeck hated Casey, so it was serendipitous that the two books came out simultaneously.

An added bonus was that I was invited to Casey and Edna's hometown of Glendale to speak at the local library. I was met there by Toni Harsh and Bob Case, and they made arrangements to visit Casey's actual home.

The home was now owned by Jenna Fischer, the actress who played Pam Beesly Halpert on one of my favorite sitcoms, *The Office*. I had honored her request to not put the exact address in the book. She and her husband could not have been more gracious in letting us tour the house (more like an estate), and in turn, they wanted to learn more about the Stengels. So, it turned out to be one of the great afternoons I had ever spent, and the next day I completed the trip, visiting Casey's grave at Forest Lawn.

A few random thoughts on some accepted baseball wisdom:

Lately I have seen mentions of "Immaculate Innings," in which the pitcher gets three strikeouts on nine pitches. That's all well and good, but not as good as retiring the side on three pitches, all batted balls. Right?

I once mentioned to Larry Ritter how Mariano Rivera seems to break the bats of so many hitters—something I'd never seen before. His response: "It's not as good as a swing and miss."

Always there has been talk of hitting for the cycle—a single, double, triple, and home run in the same game. But that's not as good as four homers, or two doubles and two homers, right?

Also, I keep hearing talk of "consecutive games reached base." Really? That feels like a reach to me, almost a way of acknowledging that the days of long hitting streaks are over, for reasons unknown. (Probably because fewer balls are put in play.) In the decade of the 2010s, Robinson Cano's 23-game hitting streak in 2012 made the top 10 of Yankees streaks. It's not even halfway to DiMag's 56. But "consecutive games reached base" sounds like the 99 Cent Store version of a hitting streak to me.

By the way, it is a major league rule that a hitting streak can't carry over into a new season to be considered a record. What does that mean? It means that any run at DiMaggio's 56 has to begin by or before the 106th game of the season, or roughly the first week of August. If a player hasn't begun his streak by then, forget it. If a hitting streak starts, say, August 10—we can forget about the excitement of going after Joe. Can't happen.

Another expression from recent years is "quality at-bat." This is usually applied to a batter getting a hit or a walk after an at-bat featuring many foul balls and sometimes measuring as many as nine or 10 pitches. Anthony Rizzo had a 16-pitch walk in 2022. "That was a quality at-bat," we will hear announcers say.

This presumes that the batter has the ability to foul pitches at will until he gets a pitch he likes.

I've always found that suggestion to be exaggerated. Very few hitters are really that skilled, where they can intentionally let the ball hit the top or lower part of the bat so that it will intentionally go foul. Even a Rod Carew or a Tony Gwynn or a Wade Boggs would find that challenging. A lot of the "quality foul balls" weren't intended to be, they just were. I have a feeling if the hitter gets to first base and hears someone call it a "quality at-bat," he'd chuckle to himself and say, "If you only knew how many of those I tried to hit."

And if one believes that hitters can intentionally keep hitting fouls to stay alive, what does that do to the feeling that hitters can't beat the shift because they don't want to disrupt their natural swing. Forget it.

And while we are on the subject of the shifts, I was all for banning them and making it a rule that there had to be two fielders on each side of the infield when the ball is pitched. And most traditionalists agree.

But the more I thought about it, the more I had to admit that you have to follow the science. Once teams know of the likelihood of a batter to hit the ball in a certain direction, is it right to say, "Ignore the science, get to your positions?" The game has evolved so that knowledge is power, and to force them to go against the science is wrong. I don't like overshifting—it's a different game—but let's face it, it is a different game with analytics in place and we have to accept it or force teams to surrender runs when they have the knowledge to prevent them.

Much conversation is made from the term "on pace," as in "he's on pace to hit 60 home runs." It's an okay observation, but the reality is that very few players actually put up matching halves. If you have 30 home runs at the All-Star break, don't count on 60. And all the accompanying comparisons.

In 1969, third-year player Reggie Jackson had 39 home runs at the All-Star break. Reggie, who never hit 30 two years in a row, was the talk of the game…and then hit eight the rest of the way to wind up with 47. Since then, I've tended to tune out conversations that begin with "on pace."

Much is made, admirably, of winning a Rookie of the Year award, and the recipients are by and large worthy of such recognition, even if their careers don't quite pan out into stardom.

We think of the annual winners as almost on equal footing with MVPs and Cy Young winners but lost in the announcement is the fact that there are usually only four or five players—if that—truly competing for this honor. It's not like winning MVP against scores of players.

When I joined the Society for American Baseball Research (SABR) in the late '70s, I soon decided that this was a serious group of fans who liked research and joined because they were more than just casual fans.

So, one day in 1980 I proposed to the SABR officials that the membership vote on retroactive Rookie of the Year and Cy Young winners, before those awards were established—1947 for ROY and 1956 for Cy. I was working at MLB at the time and maybe they thought this was some sort of official directive, but I made it clear it was just me, as a member.

SABR being SABR, they got right on it, with member Lyle Spatz investigating each year's worthy candidates and preparing ballots with statistical and other notes. They did not factor in how their careers played out, and historical reputations did not matter. It was all about how people might have voted if the voting was done at the close of each regular season.

Over the course of many mailings, some 500–700 SABR members voted by decades. It was a slow process, but clearly, a well thought through one.

I loved the results—a lot of forgotten names mixed in with stars. Cy Young, the voting showed, would have won three Cy Young Awards. Each of the original 16 teams had a new footnote for their annual media guides.

SABR published the results in 1986 and a fine accompanying story, but my hope that teams would pick up on the findings and include them in team history (with a proper explanation) did not pan out at all. It was 0-for-16 with the teams, to my dismay. Still, it was a worthy project, and it was reproduced many years later in the Hall of Fame's official magazine, *Memories and Dreams*, for whom I was listed in each issue as Magazine Historian, a really nice honor.

For deep-diving Yankee historians: retroactive Cy Young winners among Yankees were Al Orth (1906), Waite Hoyt (1927), Lefty Gomez (1934 and 1937), Red Ruffing (1938), Spud Chandler (1943), Ed Lopat (1951) Whitey Ford (1955 and 1963), and Ralph Terry (1962). (From 1956–66, only one winner was named, so Ford ['63] and Terry would have won if there had been a separate American League winner.)

As for Rookies of the Year, Yankee winners would have been Russ Ford (1910), Bob Meusel (1920), Earle Combs (1925), Tony Lazzeri (1926), Wilcy Moore (1927), Johnny Allen (1932), Joe DiMaggio (1936), Phil Rizzuto (1941), and Spec Shea (1947).

The press box lavatory in the old Yankee Stadium was a wooden structure that did not look like it would withstand a high wind. If you were the official scorer that day, you needed to take care of business quickly between innings. One day the *Daily News'* Joe Trimble had to answer nature's call during an inning.

Official scorers basically had two hand signals—pointing an index finger for a hit and giving the "ok" sign with thumb and forefinger forming a circle for an error. Sure enough, Joe was in there one day and it was a questionable call. Everyone looked right, but Joe's seat was empty. Heads turned left and there was Joe's finger, sticking out of the door, signaling hit. I thought it was an error. Some player (I don't remember who) has an extra hit on his record thanks to Joe's bathroom break.

Babe Ruth died when I was just nine days old, but I'm glad I shared the planet with him for a time. His place in American history remains secure. He remains the consensus greatest baseball player ever—the GOAT— even though few are around who actually saw him play, certainly none as adults.

Think about it: the "greatest ever" conversation has pretty much moved to contemporary figures in every other sport but baseball. Whether it's Ali, Brady, Jordan, Gretzky, Woods, Federer (or Nadal or Djokovic), Serena, they are all people we can relate to. Not baseball. So large was the legend that it still carries on to this day.

My dad, born in Brooklyn in 1916, was not much of a baseball fan. But the Ruth mystique reached him. When I once mentioned that Hank Aaron was soon to break Ruth's home run record, my father said, "Yes, but I think Babe called all of his home runs."

Such is perception and word-of-mouth. And the moment was important to me, because it reminded me that not everyone is a deep fan, and some truths need to be explained each time we write them. Babe Ruth allegedly pointed to the bleachers and hit a home run in the 1932 World Series. It was the only time that ever happened. Thanks, Dad.

Ed Lucas, who died in 2021 at 82, was a blind journalist who lost his vision when he was struck by a baseball. His winning personality and self-deprecating humor made him a favorite when he visited Yankee Stadium. Phil Rizzuto in particular extended a genuine and warm friendship toward him.

One day I asked him how he was. I'll bet he was glad I asked!

"I've taken up a new hobby," he told me. "I've been skydiving. I love it, but my seeing-eye dog isn't all-in with it."

My friend Peter Bavasi, a club executive over the years with the Dodgers, Padres, Blue Jays, and Cleveland, had a special friendship with a journeyman player from Brooklyn named Al "The Bull" Ferrara. He loved telling Al the Bull stories.

My favorite was Al the Bull being traded by the Padres to Cincinnati for Angel Bravo in 1971. The story goes that in one of his first games with the Reds, he struck out at a key moment and Cincinnati lost.

After the game, he told the writers, "Hey, what did you expect? I was traded for Angel Bravo!"

Don't fact-check me on this one. Never let the facts get in the way of a good story.

I always enjoyed the company of press photographers during dinners in the press room—because very few were strictly sports photographers. At any given time, they would be out there covering all sorts of news. Ernie Sisto of the *New York Times* would be at almost all our Yankee games, and he was also the man who photographed the aftermath of the 1945 plane disaster when a B-25 American bomber crashed into the Empire State Building during a fog. That was actually the first thing I thought of on 9/11 when the earliest report said a small plane had crashed into the World Trade Center.

Phil Rizzuto used to flash a secret signal to Ernie when he was on first base if he was going to try to steal second, so that Ernie could get the shot of the play at second.

Another, Richard Drew of AP, took the horrid but historic "Falling Man" photo of a man leaping to his death on 9/11 from the World Trade Center. These guys saw a lot more of real life than the writers who covered sports did.

One senior member of the photo corps who really intrigued me was a Drew colleague at AP named Harry Harris. By the time I knew him, Harry was the dean of the photo corps, helped us plan photo areas at the new (1976) stadium, and was a very reasonable figure when it came time to solving logistical problems.

But my favorite Harry Harris story—and now, yours as well—was his tale of getting into a drunken fistfight with no less than Ernest Hemingway at a Key West, Florida saloon. Hemingway!

"What was the fight about?" I asked, fascinated.

The answer was not surprising.

"Oh, I don't remember," said Harry. "Probably over some broad."

Right from the *Guys and Dolls* days.

Hemingway is the source of another baseball story. One day, it was said, he was introduced to Yogi Berra as a famous writer. "Nice to meet you, Ernie," said Yogi (allegedly). "What paper are you with?"

I was once asked to write a biographical essay on Damon Runyan, the short-story writer whose work helped inspire *Guys and Dolls* on Broadway. I was writing a lot of essays at that time for a website called National Pastime Museum, and when it went out of business, they turned over all the columns to the Baseball Hall of Fame, where they now reside.

Anyway, at the time my desk and computer faced across West 57th Street in Manhattan and a hotel called the Buckingham.

So here I am, batting out my story, and it's time to deal with Runyon's death in 1946. I looked up the facts, and guess what—he died at his residence in the Buckingham Hotel. I was looking right at it!

A neighbor, one Tony Bennett, takes a Central Park stroll in 2017.

Whoa!

That 57th Street neighborhood also featured a neighbor you may have heard of, a singer named Tony Bennett. He was the best singer in our neighborhood. I would see him from time to time painting in Central Park or just strolling with his wife. One day I found myself in front of him on line at Starbucks on Sixth Avenue.

"Oh!" I said, "Mr. Bennett...please, step ahead of me."

"No, that's fine," he said. But I didn't want the conversation to end, so I pointed to the CDs they were selling on the counter—Adele, Kelly Clarkson, Michael Bublé—and I said, "They ought to be selling yours here!"

He smiled and said, "I do okay."

It was a nice moment.

If Tony Bennett was what you might call a mature taste, doing publicity for the auction of the original *Howdy Doody* marionettes was from, shall we say, an event that brought out the toddler in all of us.

I was an ardent viewer of the *Howdy Doody* show in the '50s, and my mother even wrote a letter to the show to see if I could get a seat in the "peanut gallery" (the audience section). Unfortunately, a letter came back with regrets, and it was signed by Dilly Dally, one of Howdy's sidekicks. That in itself was a thrill. I didn't know Dilly Dally also handled ticket requests.

The original *Howdy Doody* marionettes, ready for their auction news on the Today show.

But now it was 1997, and Buffalo Bob Smith (he was born in Buffalo, New York), the human star of the show, was auctioning off the marionettes. Bob wasn't making any personal appearances for this—he was 80—but I spoke to him on the phone to get some background, and boy, was it a kick to be speaking to Buffalo Bob himself. Naturally, I told him what a fan I was, and about the letter from Dilly Dally, and he was a total delight to talk to. He apologized for Dilly's rejection letter.

We displayed the marionettes on the *Today* show and Lester Holt interviewed the head of the auction house. I didn't think we'd get that segment without Buffalo Bob himself, but we did.

Buffalo Bob died in 1998, not long after I spoke with him, and I was so happy that I had that opportunity. He really did sound like a very nice man.

I had good luck booking guests on the *Today* show. One year the fellow who had grabbed the ball used by Wilt Chamberlain for his 100th point—an NBA record to this day—was auctioning off that very ball. We got him on *Today* and Tom Brokow did the interview. I was very proud of that one, except a few weeks later, questions were raised about the authenticity of the ball. The owner did seem totally sincere, and his story had merit, but the Philadelphia 76ers longtime executive and PR person Harvey Pollack came forward to say, "I was responsible for the balls. We went to every game with 10 and we returned from every game with 10. I never lost one in my whole career."

I immediately knew we had a bad ball. As a PR man myself who knew and respected Pollack, I knew at once that he knew what he was talking about. The item was quietly reauctioned as having been "from the game" and went for a lot less money.

I did a book in 1991 with Larry King, the radio and cable television host. It had an awful title—*When You're from Brooklyn, Everything Else is Tokyo*—but even if I didn't like it, Larry did. And it was about his pre-fame years, growing up in Brooklyn. He discovered in those years that he could enthrall an audience when, during his bar mitzvah, he spoke of his recently deceased father. He could tell at that moment that he knew how to hold an audience. His future path was set.

I enjoyed that project, although at our first meeting over breakfast at the Sherry-Netherland Hotel, he never made eye contact with me, and only lit up when he saw a real celebrity in the room. But we wound up being friends—with baseball being the common denominator. I actually lived with him in his Arlington, Virginia, apartment for a few days while we worked on the book. We worked, took a break for lunch, took another break to watch some baseball, worked a little more, and went to dinner. Not too much work.

The Dodgers were playing the Giants in a big early September pennant-race game, which we watched on TV and which certainly struck a note of nostalgia with him. He had been a huge Brooklyn Dodgers fan growing up. (He said, "One thing about the Dodgers ticket office on Montague Street—no matter who was behind the window, the name tag always said Shaughnessy. They had one name tag.")

Anyway, the game we were watching was a close one, and late in the game with a chance to win it, the Giants had Robby Thompson batting.

Larry and I looked at each other and started to laugh. We both "got it" at the same moment, and we began to recite together Russ Hodges' famous call of Bobby Thomson's pennant-winning home run against the Dodgers in 1951.

"Robby Thompson's up there swinging...he's had a single and a double and he drove in the Giants first run with a long fly to center.... Branca throws...and there's a long drive! It's gonna be it, I believe! THE GIANTS WIN THE PENNANT!"

A terrific shared moment.

Larry was later asked to write a monthly baseball column for a sports nostalgia magazine, and he asked me to write it—and told me to keep the money. Very generous, and very nice, especially as he was paying out about six alimonies at the time.

A memorable part of the book project came when he mentioned his many marriages (up to that point). I had done a little advanced research and discovered a first marriage he conveniently forgot to include (it was annulled).

A stop at Lafayette High School in Brooklyn while working with Larry King on his book. He was there at the same time as Sandy Koufax.

"Oh, that one," he said. "I think her name was Freida or Freyda, something like that. I remember something about getting hair tonic all over the couch."

I can see why he skipped over it.

He also told me that he was a chain-smoker's chain-smoker. So wedded to tobacco was he that he smoked when he showered, placing the cigarette in the soap holder when he rinsed off. But, after a heart attack, he was able to quit cold turkey.

He was married to Julie Alexander when we did the book. She lived in Philadelphia, while he maintained his residence in Arlington. "You know," he confessed, "I have to face it; when I put that key in the door at night, I just don't want anybody there."

It was an amazing piece of self-awareness, except he went on to divorce Julie and got married again, this last time for nearly 20 years.

Lee Allen was a highly regarded author and historian, a Cincinnati native and the son of a U.S. Congressman. After doing a number of well-received baseball histories and regularly contributing columns to the *Sporting News*, he became the historian at the Baseball Hall of Fame in 1959. His columns were really entertaining—a lot of "whatever became of" and "long forgotten" essays.

I was the sports editor of the weekly college newspaper at SUNY Oneonta and decided I needed to visit Lee and get know him personally. I'd already been hired by the Yankees, so I had a little something to say in a letter to him, and he responded within a few days inviting me up.

Cooperstown was 19 miles north of Oneonta, although in the snow (which was October-March), it could feel like the *Ice Road Truckers* TV series. My parents had turned over their 4,400-pound 1958 Buick to me by then, which was a good vehicle to make that journey on Route 28. (It didn't deter me from bringing a number of dates to visit the Hall of Fame.)

Anyway, by now I had some associations in baseball, and a few of them mentioned that Lee Allen was, well, a heavy drinker.

I arrived at my appointed time and was taken up a back staircase to his small office on the third floor. I was 19 and probably looked 16.

He stood up, offered his hand in a warm greeting, slid open a desk drawer, and asked if I'd care for shot of Old Forester. I declined, probably thinking of the journey back to Oneonta, or maybe just shocked by the offer.

We had a nice chat, and the Hall looked much as it did on my first visit in 1962, which is pretty much how it looked when it opened in 1939. A lot of glass cases into which you would peer at photos and documents. I remember seeing Mantle's $100,000 contract under glass and thinking, *My gosh, there is his home address for everyone to see!*

(A year later, when President Kennedy was assassinated, the network anchors reported on the shooting of Lee Harvey Oswald by stating that Dallas police identified the shooter as someone "well known in Dallas." That was Jack Ruby, but of course, I only knew one famous person in Dallas, and I said to my father, "Oh my God, I think Mickey Mantle just shot Oswald!")

I'd like to say it was the beginning of a long friendship with Lee Allen, who was certainly a writing and research hero to me, but he died of a heart attack soon after at age 54. Over the years he has become a godlike figure among baseball historians, and I am proud to be able to tell them that I not only met him, but he offered me a drink.

Not long after Thurman Munson's passing, a group for a charity called the Association for the Help of Retarded Children (now known as The Arc) came to my office to see if I could help them create a dinner to raise money in Thurman's name.

They were good people, their plans were very professional, and I of course doubled back with Diana Munson to see how she felt.

She gave her approval, and I was named to the Dinner Committee. It was a great honor to serve a worthy organization and to honor Thurman in the process. Few expected it would continue on for some 40 years, bringing together great athletes to receive a "Thurman Award" in a very classy setting. Diana dutifully attended nearly every one and gave a heartfelt speech, thanking fans for their continuing loyalty to Munson's legacy.

The most memorable of the Thurman Munson dinners I attended was the one where I was seated at a table with none other than Jimmy Cagney himself! He was about 83 at the time. I've long forgotten how he came to be included among the honorees. Still, what an honor to be with him! I did manage to tell him that *Yankee Doodle Dandy* was my favorite movie, and he said it was his favorite as well. "Mine too... *Yankee Doodle*," was his exact quote. I felt so good about that 15-second exchange.

Extra Innings

Bang the Drum Slowly, a film shot largely at Yankee Stadium (with some scenes shot at Shea when the Yankees were home), featured Robert DeNiro in his first significant role, and just a year later he was young Vito Corleone in *The Godfather Part II*. We who worked in the stadium got to witness the filming from a safe distance, and of course DeNiro, 29, was an unknown, so he attracted little interest from us. In retrospect, it would have been nice for me to strike up a conversation with him and, from that moment on, to have become his BFF.

The best part of the film for Yankee Stadium lovers was the opening scene in which DeNiro and Michael Moriarty (as sort of a Mel Stottlemyre/Tom Seaver hybrid) take a lap around the warning track, and the stadium's beauty was captured on 35mm film.

The real kick for us was that our doorman at the player/employee entrance, an older gentleman with a heavy Irish brogue named James Mahoney, was given a small part with a line. I don't remember the line, but it was something like, "This way, please." We were all thrilled that Mahoney had a star turn in the film and was listed in closing credits.

I also remember when the Jehovah's Witnesses religious order rented the stadium each year and packed it with as many as 100,000 believers, filling the stands and adding perhaps 30,000 folding chairs on the turf. The practice ended in the original stadium, and they never returned after the renovation, but I'm sure it produced a hefty rental fee for the team (and for the chair rental company). Mostly I remember that they filled our parking lots and I had to park my car about a 20-minute walk away at the Bronx Terminal Market.

I didn't like anything in the Bronx that had the word *terminal* in it.

I loved pop music of the '50s, '60s, and '70s, and it was my pleasure to form a friendship with Jay Black, lead singer of Jay and the Americans, a group that produced a string of hits led by Cara Mia, a showstopper wherever Jay performed.

Jay was a very charismatic guy, and through his work in entertainment and through one of his marriages, he grew close to mob figures. He was a big baseball fan but also a big gambler on baseball. I knew our friendship, such as it was, needed to be far apart from that world. And truth be told, he never asked for inside information on injuries or the things that would be of interest to bookmakers. Had he brought those subjects up, I would have had to walk away from the friendship.

He was also friends with Ron Blomberg, baseball's first DH and another personal friend. Ronnie, in fact, walked my grandmother down the aisle at my 1975 wedding.

So frequently, my time with Jay included Ron and his wife, Mara. At one such gathering at Jay's Long Island home, he had a guest known as Fat Andy. It turned out that Andy Ruggiano was a pretty-high-up-there mob figure and a member of the Paul Castellano crime family. He was not so well known to me. Otherwise, I wouldn't have gotten into an argument with him.

On this particular evening, Fat Andy happened to mention that Mickey Mantle was better than Babe Ruth. And while a healthy Mantle might indeed have been as good, the injury-prone Mantle was nowhere near as good, and certainly not someone who was playing the game at a level far above his contemporaries, which was what made Ruth so great.

So Fat Andy proposed that Mantle was better than Ruth, and common sense told me to take up the Babe's cause.

We argued, and it was left unresolved, but afterward, Ronnie said to me, "What were you thinking? You could have gotten killed!"

I guess I was too dumb to think that far ahead.

I invited Jay and his wife to my wedding in 1975—where Ronnie walked my grandmother down the aisle—as I felt the friendship was genuine enough to extend an invite. And he accepted.

But the wedding came, and he was a no-show. I wrote it off to the peculiarities of rock stars.

The next time I saw Jay, I told him I missed him at the wedding and was hoping he'd be there. He suddenly realized the social error and remembered that he hadn't sent a gift.

So, he reached into his pocket and handed me $47.80, which was what he had on hand. I counted it in front of him, laughed, and gave it back. I'd rather have the story to tell than the $47.80.

We lost touch over time, but I thought of doing his story as a book and met with his son Jason to talk about it in the mid-2010s. There was a lot there—rock-and-roll of the '60s, opening for the Beatles, selling out Madison Square Garden, serving as a character witness for John Gotti— but publishers said Jay would have to go on TV with me to promote it, and even Jason agreed he couldn't handle the restriction on bad language necessary to do live television. So, there was no book.

All that said, he belongs in the Rock and Roll Hall of Fame (an institution for which I did PR, but I had no voice at all in its inductions).

We fast-forward a few decades to a more modern figure in pop culture, an enormously talented singer/actress named Janelle Monáe.

I was attending 2019 Wimbledon in London and exiting the ESPN hospitality suite when I bumped into this stunning beauty, dressed exquisitely in a black-and-white dress with a high-fashion red hat. I did not know her name but knew at once she was someone important.

We made eye contact, and I said, "That's a beautiful dress."

She looked at me with disdain.

"It's called couture," she said.

I considered myself told off, put in my place, and properly educated. It was actually a good moment. I had crossed over to the other side, however briefly.

I still wasn't sure who it was, but I asked if she would mind taking a photo with my wife, who was nearby. She agreed, gave us a great smile, and moved on.

"Don't you know who that was?" asked Lourdes. "That was Janelle Monáe!"

I was again set in my place. And we returned to our seats to watch Naomi Osaka lose her first-round match. I could check Wimbledon off my bucket list and had a Janelle Monáe encounter to add to the story.

I didn't often play the "Yankees card" in my portfolio, but I made an exception in 2014 when my Philippine-born wife was approved for U.S. citizenship and summoned to a swearing-in ceremony.

Thinking that perhaps I could do better than the mass gathering in a federal building, I sent a letter to Justice Sonia Sotomayor at the Supreme Court along with a copy of *Pinstripe Empire*. Not only was Justice Sotomayor a New Yorker, but she had written the decision that ended the 1994–95 baseball strike. She was then a federal district court judge in Manhattan.

And she was a big Yankees fan who once sat in the "jury box" in right field in Yankee Stadium where select fans of Aaron Judge were seated each day.

So, I took my best shot, and she wrote back, saying, "As a baseball fan myself, I very much look forward to reading [the book]."

But she continued, "Regrettably I am unable to grant your request to participate in your wife's swearing-in ceremony. It is impossible for me to accept all of the invitations I would like to accept without compromising my obligations to the Court."

A pretty flimsy excuse, but that was her final verdict, and you can't appeal a Supreme Court decision. And she added congratulations to Lourdes on becoming a U.S. citizen.

We went to the mass swearing-in, which was actually quite touching and emotional. In a video, President Obama welcomed all the new citizens, and we would not have wanted to miss that memorable part of the day.

Oh, and on the matter of not "playing my Yankees card," I went to Yankee Stadium with my son in 2001—the World Series game in which President Bush threw out the first pitch soon after 9/11.

But I missed the first pitch. Security was very tight at the stadium, and while some of my fellow Yankees alum slipped in through the office entrance, I didn't want to set a bad example and act as though I had some entitlement. So, there we were on the pavement outside Gate 4, when the pitch happened. Thousands were with me; security just couldn't get the people in fast enough. I blew it on that one.

Even early in my career, I always enjoyed doing broadcast interviews, and later, when the opportunity arose, I loved public speaking, particularly to college students.

I would occasionally get asked where I was from, as my accent, or rather lack of an accent, made it difficult to tell.

Why no New York accent? From a guy born in Brooklyn?

It goes to the story of my mother, Celia Mann Appel. She was born in Karlsruhe, near the French border in southwest Germany, and at 12, she escaped the coming Nazi treachery by crossing the French border with her parents and two sisters, and eventually coming to America in 1937 as refugees. No one could tell the story of seeing the Statue of Liberty for the first time better than she could.

They settled in the Bronx. They went to school for the final weeks of the term in the spring of 1937. They couldn't speak English, so the experience was humiliating for my mother, who was very smart and a star pupil in Karlsruhe.

That summer, the three of them set out to learn perfect English so that come September, they would fit in at school without any language barrier. And they did it! In fact, when my mother was at Taft High School, she won the English medal at graduation. What a feat!

And that is the origin of my accent-free voice. It is the English she learned that summer of '37.

I didn't come to realize that until years after she passed away in 1994, and I wish I could have talked to her about that.

In 2015, while on vacation in Paris, I looked at a map and found that Karlsruhe was only two train stations from Paris, although several hours away in southwest Germany. I knew my mother's address and so Lourdes and I took a day trip to the city.

The actual home she grew up in was still standing, despite the city having been heavily bombed in World War II. And a very agreeable, English-speaking college student was living in my mother's actual apartment! What a find. And what an emotional day that was.

In the early 1960s, Joe DiMaggio became a spring training coach for the Yankees in Fort Lauderdale. They stayed at the Yankee Clipper Hotel on the beach. The hotel, shaped somewhat like a ship, was built in 1956. The name was kind of a coincidence, but it was perfect.

Joe married Marilyn Monroe soon after his 1951 retirement, but they were only married nine months when they divorced. Still, there was love there, and it was a connection that never went away.

In fact, Marilyn accompanied Joe to Fort Lauderdale one of those springs.

In 2004, I was visiting my father (my parents had retired to that area), and I thought, just for the hell of it, I would stay at the Yankee Clipper. I'd never been.

A bellman was in the lobby, and although by now luggage was on wheels (what took so long for this invention?) he was an older guy, and I asked him to help. I had a question I wanted to ask him.

"Have you worked here long?" I asked.

"More than 40 years," he said.

"Oh, so you were here when the Yankees stayed here? I'm asking because I used to work for them, but after they moved to Schrafft's up the beach in 1970."

"Oh, yes," he replied, as we walked down the first-floor corridor.

He pointed to his right, and said, "This is where Mr. Fishel's room was…"

And he pointed to his left, and said, "This is where Mr. [Bruce] Henry stayed, and this is where Mr. Houk stayed."

I guess they had the same rooms every spring.

We continued down the hall.

"This," he said, pointing to the right again, "was Mr. DiMaggio's suite."

A pause.

"And this," he said, pointing left, "was where Miss Monroe stayed with her hairdresser."

Well, that was a lot of information for one hallway.

I handed him a nice tip.

Like many my age, I was swept away by the charm and humor and entertainment provided by first Cassius Clay and then by Muhammad Ali when he changed his name. I seemed like we couldn't get enough of him.

When he fought Joe Frazier for the first time at Madison Square Garden, we were in spring training, and the fight was being shown by closed circuit in a theater in Fort Lauderdale. What a celebrity gathering we had in that theater! Mickey Mantle, Whitey Ford, Phil Rizzuto, Frank Robinson, Brooks Robinson, Jim Palmer, Hank Aaron, Frank Howard, all converging from Miami, Pompano Beach, Fort Lauderdale, and West Palm Beach. It was almost as glamorous in our theater as it was at MSG, though without the women in furs.

One year during the height of his fame, Ali came to the Westchester County Center in White Plains for an "exhibition." I had to be there; it was 10 minutes from my home.

The "exhibition" was his inviting small children into the ring with him so they could knock him out. He'd let them have a punch, and then he'd fall down and let their parents take pictures of their sons and daughters, standing over the KO'd champ. So it wasn't much of an exhibition, but it was great fun.

I finally met him at a sports collector's convention, long after his retirement. I rattled out the expected, "I've admired you for all these years, you will always be the greatest to me," and he looked me over and said, "You're not as dumb as you look!"

I'm sure it was a standard response from him, but I loved it. And I can always tell people that Muhammad Ali didn't think I was as dumb as I look. What an honor.

Is fame truly fleeting?

There was a time when every American, so it seemed, was either in the love or hate column when polls were taken about the sports commentator, Ali's foil, Howard Cosell. He was bigger than *Monday Night Football*—he put it on the map—and while he could be outrageous, he was also very much a social activist who was among the first to embrace Ali's political stances. Ali in turn, made it a point to do Cosell interviews, teased him, and made the Ali–Cosell interchanges memorable and controversial.

At the height of his fame, while still covering all sports for ABC, he came to Fort Lauderdale for the arrival of newly signed Catfish Hunter. This was a big deal. One of the reasons we signed Hunter was for the attention he would draw to the team. Cosell in spring training was one such example. It was a long way from Cosell's first time in camp, when no Yankees would bother with him and Bob Fishel had to round up interview guests for him.

ABC hired a Brink's truck from which Hunter would emerge for his interview, and Catfish was happy to go along with the gag.

Meanwhile, I went to the airport to personally pick up Cosell, and we had a memorable ride to the ballpark. In the car was an advanced copy of a book I had been sent—*They Call Me Gump,* the life story of New York Rangers goalie Gump Worsley. Cosell reached for it.

"Publishers keep turning out this drivel," he stated with contempt. "*They Call Me Gump,* indeed. Aren't there more compelling books we need to read?"

He was enjoying my chuckles at his comments.

"What writers will we find at camp?" he asked. "Is that inane Jim Ogle still there, eating his free Yankees food while serving as a Yankees PR man for the fabled *Newark Star-Ledger?*"

I laughed. Jim was indeed there, still batting out typewritten copy, and often, in a matter of 15 minutes, writing about the same game for the *Star-Ledger*, the *Staten Island Advance*, the *Long Island Press*, and United Press International. "I ain't great, but I'm fast," Jim would say. And yes, in retirement, he did indeed become a Yankees employee, heading their alumni association and running Old Timers' Day.

I guess Cosell did like me, at least as an audience, and over the years, I would list him as a reference on my résumé, and he would deliver a hearty endorsement.

Late in life, when he was a widower, I would see him dining alone at a small table at the Friar's Club. He seemed sad and disconnected. He certainly had outlived his fame. No one went over to say hello. Today, his name is barely recognized.

Same as Gump Worsley.

We had a ball boy in the late '60s who would commute from Washington, D.C., for home stands. His name was Thad Mumford, and he liked to point out that he was the first Black ball boy in Yankees history—and would correct anyone who said "bat boy." He stood for accuracy in the storytelling, as he later would when he went to Hollywood and was a writer and producer of the great *M*A*S*H* television series. (One thing he didn't correct was clubhouse man Pete Sheehy calling him "Tad," not "Thad," but he let that one go.)

In one *M*A*S*H* episode, he snuck me into a script, having Alan Alda read from a newspaper: "Listen to this…a Dr. Martin Appelski has discovered…" I don't remember what he discovered, but it was very cool to have my name on that hit show and for all its years of reruns.

We would often have interesting people drop by our spring training camp, and one year, the American League hired 1936 Olympic track legend Jesse Owens to tour the camps and offer running advice. He was long removed from his stardom, but what an honor it was to have Jesse Owens there, and as was often the case, the guest would join us in the press room for cocktails and conversation afterward. The Yankees coaches were regulars too, and I watched as Jesse regaled everyone with—guess what—the story of his winning the gold medal at the '36 games. That story sure had "legs."

The conversations in that press room were generally all baseball-centered, though, and one that I still remember (whenever someone gets fired) is our old pitching coach Jim Turner patiently explaining that not having one's contract renewed was not the same as being fired. The press always said "fired," but according to Jim, that was not correct usage.

He himself was made the fall guy after the Yankees finished third in 1959, relieved of his pitching coach duties by Casey Stengel. That may be where he decided he wasn't actually fired. Anyway, he signed as pitching coach with Cincinnati and had them in the World Series in 1961. He was lured back to the Yankees by Ralph Houk in 1967.

Sometimes I would be near the dugout at the end of a game to grab a player for a postgame interview. And I'd hear Jim's voice above the others, and I'd hear him using aged old expressions that perhaps only he still employed. It was like being in the dugout with John McGraw.

One day a pitcher struck out a batter with a wicked curve ball, and Jim exclaimed, "Kansas City kitty!" I guess it was a suitable expression back in the day, whatever it meant.

Jim, born in 1903, definitely had some old-school thinking going on. He lived in Nashville with his wife and two adult daughters. Long after he retired, I had reason to call him to ask some long-lost baseball fact. He was happy to hear from me, as was I to talk to him.

"How is Pauline?" I asked, knowing as I asked it that his wife would be well up there in years if she was still with us. But I asked it gently, unknowingly.

"Oh, she's fine," he said, "but she passed away some years ago."

Oops. An awkward moment.

Jim lived to be 95, passing away in 1998. Talking with him in the press rooms (he broke into the majors at 33 in 1937 and won 20 games as a rookie) was one of the delights of being part of the baseball universe.

In 2019, I journeyed to London to see MLB's first London Series, in which the Yankees played the Red Sox in two regular season games. It was

Yankees history and I needed to be there. (Besides, Lourdes and I went to London often, and it had become sort of a second city for us.)

Knowing the demand on the Yankees for tickets would be overwhelming, I asked Kevin Gregg, the Red Sox's PR director (Eric's son), if he could spare any. And he came through with great tickets right up front near first base. (The stadium configuration, however, had the seats way back from the field, more distant than at Oakland Coliseum).

Most of the fans, it seemed, were Americans visiting or living in England, and I didn't hear many British accents except from ushers and concession workers. If it was to be an example of American baseball for the Brits, well, the games were slugfests and not very artful. But Prince Harry and Meagan Markel participated in pregame ceremonies, "God Save the Queen" was played, and it was very cool to see the Yankees in their pinstripe uniforms (requested by the organizers, even when the Yankees were the "visiting" team), showcasing their baseball skills on this soccer pitch that was converted for a few days for baseball, complete with foul poles.

Unlike in the film *Naked Gun*, the Queen did not attend, and Leslie Nielsen did not umpire.

I'm occasionally asked about the greatest game I ever witnessed. There is an expectation that it would be the "Chris Chambliss homer" game against Kansas City in 1976 that produced the first Yankees pennant in 12 years. And that one is certainly high on the list, because just eight hours later, we got on a bus to head for the airport and onto Cincinnati for the World Series...and the thrill of what had happened the night before was still on everyone's mind.

I remember our trainer, Gene Monahan, taking out a pair of surgical scissors and cutting my necktie in half as I boarded the bus to the airport. And then sitting with Chambliss and explaining who Bobby Thomson was and how the home run would rank with the most memorable in baseball history.

I attended seven Super Bowls over the years, including the one in which the 49ers' Steve Young threw six touchdown passes at Joe Robbie Stadium in Miami. Most memorable to me about that game was that I was able to take my dad as a guest, and we had front-row seats behind an end zone. Dad never stopped talking about that game. But what he talked about was the ease of parking near his home, how we got on a bus and went straight to the entry gate at Joe Robbie. That was his highlight.

But the winner of my "best game ever" is...drum roll please...the high school football clash of the Nyack Indians at the Spring Valley Tigers on November 7, 1964.

Both teams were unbeaten and untied and the game drew estimates of 7,500 and up, clogging Route 59 between Nyack and Spring Valley, seven miles apart, in the smallest county by area in New York State, Rockland. (Smallest, that is, aside from the boroughs of New York City.) Rockland had gone from rural to suburban with the construction of the Tappan Zee Bridge in the mid-'50s, but its population was still relatively small.

I was the sports editor of the Spring Valley High School newspaper and I remember waking up that cool autumn morning around 6 AM and I could not wait to get to the field.

The Spring Valley field was beautiful, nestled in the backyard of the two-story brick school with bleachers on one side and on the other, a landscaped slope of stones, which by halftime was filled with students from both schools A new scoreboard oversaw the field, which we students had financed by collecting Plaid Stamps (a supermarket incentive). The memorable Sandy Lew was in her place as a Tigers cheerleader. She always knew to cheer at the right moment, even with her back turned from the field. I think every school had their own Sandy Lew, but we had the best Sandy Lew.

The Tigers coach, Jim DePasquale, wore a suit and tie on the sidelines and looked every bit like a distinguished coaching legend. He had crafted the team to be a running team; our quarterback rarely passed. Our principal running back was a tall, handsome military brat named Dave Mumme ("mummy") who also owned the New York State pole vault record. He seemed a lot more mature than the rest of us and would go on to play in the Air Force Academy backfield before a career in the service.

The Public School Athletic League (PSAL) title was on the line. Nyack scored first to lead 7–0, and then early in the second half, we got a touchdown to make it 7–6. Bobby Hooper needed to make the extra point to tie it, no small feat at the high school level. Pressure on a 17-year-old? But make it he did, and the roar of the Spring Valley part of the crowd was deafening. (I'm writing this completely from memory, 56 years later.)

The game ended 7–7, and no overtimes were allowed at that level, so we shared the championship. For Spring Valley, it was their first title in nine years. Nyack was a perennial powerhouse in the eight-team league. The *Journal-News*, the local Rockland County paper (I was its "stringer" Spring Valley correspondent for several years and later a bylined reporter before I went off to college), said 7,500 were present; the *Rockland Leader* said 7,000. An accurate count was impossible, as students eventually found ways around the entry port after abandoning their cars along Route 59. In either case, it was a county record, and it came to be remembered as 10,000 over time, which happens as the storytelling grows. (Note to self: be sure to make this 20,000 in future editions.)

The *Journal-News* headline read, "Record Crowd Sees Battle to Tie; Finest Finish in Rockland PSAL History."

The following year the two teams met again, this time in Nyack. Again, they were both unbeaten and untied, playing the last game of the season. And again, it was a 7–7 tie and a shared championship, although not nearly as many fans attended.

It is said that a tie is "like kissing your sister." Not true (although I don't have a sister, and I never kissed Sandy Lew, which would have been the real test). That 1964 contest remains the most memorable sports event I ever attended.

In 1978 I took a six-month interlude from baseball to handle PR for the New York Apples, a franchise in World Team Tennis that played its matches at Madison Square Garden.

I didn't know that much about tennis going in, but I learned quickly, and I developed the team's first media guide, falling back on my baseball training. I kept stats on each player versus each opponent in the league, including Chris Evert, Martina Navratilova, and Ilie Nastase.

Remarkably, I learned that just by watching our practices, I could become a better player myself. My mind was taking snapshots of it all, and when I went on the court, I wondered how I had suddenly become a fairly competitive player (until I developed "tennis elbow" and needed surgery—performed on me by a Dr. Apple, no kidding).

Our team was headed by the great Billie Jean King. It had been five years since her legendary match against Bobby Riggs in the "Battle of the Sexes," but already, America knew this was a formidable and historic person in American history. As someone who measures contemporary history for its place in the annals of the world, I already knew that she had a place in the books with Jackie Robinson. I appreciated knowing her, traveling with her, and forming a friendship. In fact, nearly 40 years after working with her, I was shocked to get a phone call from her inviting me to join her for lunch in New York.

She had great patience and enjoyed teaching. On a flight from New York to Boston for a match, I sat between her and her teammate Joanne Russell, who was, I believe, the No. 7–ranked player in the U.S. On a cocktail napkin, Billie Jean drew lines and angles showing Joanne where

A short foray into tennis led to a friendship with the great Billie Jean King. And yes, a few free lessons were included, but I never won a single point.

she should be after each shot she hit. (And I thought, *The No. 7 player in the U.S. doesn't know this?*)

Also on the team was Vitas "the Lithuanian Lion" Gerulaitis, a name I can still spell without looking it up because of my time with him. People thought he was foreign and spoke English slowly to him, which made him laugh. He was from Long Island and spoke pure New York. He was, in fact, a big Yankees fan and pumped me with questions regularly. One day we were in a station wagon on our way to a match, while the team coach, the Australian Fred Stolle was figuring out our lineup for the evening's match—men's singles and doubles, women's singles and doubles, and mixed doubles.

Vitas tapped me on the knee and said, "Do you think Sparky Lyle and Dick Tidrow are sitting in the Yankees bullpen right now guessing our lineup for tonight?"

For sure, I would never have made it to Studio 54 or Regine's had I not been in Vitas' company. Everyone who knew him loved him—and he was a top-four player on the international circuit as well, in the era of Jimmy Connors, Bjorn Borg, and a rising fellow Long Islander named John McEnroe.

I once asked him, delicately, if he ever, uh, stopped trying if he was losing a set, say 5–1, and just wanted to save his strength for the next set.

"You mean tank?" he said. "Of course. All the time!"

Sadly, Vitas died in 1994 at 40 from carbon monoxide poisoning while asleep at a friend's guesthouse in Southampton. It was from that death that people began installing carbon monoxide detectors in their homes along with smoke alarms.

His great sense of humor was best captured at the 1980 U.S. Open when he beat Connors, who had defeated him 16 times in a row.

"Nobody beats Vitas Gerulaitis 17 times in a row!" he told the press.

I had another foray into tennis many years later when I was asked to preside over a press conference previewing an exhibition match at the Garden in 2008 between Roger Federer and Pete Sampras, who was effectively retired at that point.

Federer was probably the most likeable figure in all of sports, and he was all charm and personality at the press conference. He was also debuting his RF baseball caps and gave me one for my wife. (He was her favorite athlete, any sport). She is rough on baseball caps and wears them out, but she still wears the one from Roger.

As for Sampras, I had told him the press conference was for 11 AM. At 11:10, we still hadn't walked out to the podium yet, which is pretty normal for these things.

He glared at me. He said, "What happened to 11? I could have slept an extra 10 minutes."

There are no PS caps in the Appel household.

Roger won in straight sets that night. And Tiger Woods was in the audience!

One good thing about working with the tennis league that one summer of '78 was that matches were played in the Madison Square Garden complex, and on this one particular afternoon, I wondered through some corridors and found myself in the main arena.

On this particular day, a band was on stage rehearsing for that evening's concert—Bruce Springsteen and the E Street Band. This was 1978, and Bruce was at the height of his career. (Not sure there has ever been a depth.)

I looked around and saw all the chairs in place for the night's concert, a few maintenance workers setting up, but essentially, I was alone. Alone to watch the rehearsal.

For almost 40 minutes, I took it all in. They played full numbers; it wasn't just a sound check. I stood in the back, expecting to be kicked out, but it didn't happen.

And then Bruce came down from stage and walked to where I was standing. I thought he was going to admonish me for sneaking in, but no; he asked me how the sound was. And there I was, standing with the Boss (a different Boss), taking it all in as the band played on.

I considered introducing myself, perhaps to nail down our future friendship. But then I remembered that his estranged manager was named Mike Appel, a separation that kept him out of the recording studio for a year. So I caught myself. (I was not related to Mike, nor to pitcher Mark

Appel, the nation's top draft choice in 2013 who made his long delayed major league debut in 2022.)

It was actually the only Bruce concert I ever attended. Does it count?

The ballpark experience.

After so many years sitting in my comfortable seat in the press box with free Cokes, free hot dogs, and free ice cream, payback came in the form of my sitting in the regular stands with regular people. And it seemed I would always be in a row with someone celebrating the Bronx Beer Olympics who needed to make 12 trips past me on beer runs during the course of the first seven innings (after which beer sales are cut off). I marvel at how sports pulled off this money-making concept when theaters couldn't.

Sometimes they say, "Excuse me," but by the fourth inning, they figure, "What the hell." That is my research on the subject.

So, if they've dropped an extra $200 during three hours of baseball and missed most of the game, so what? They did buy tickets to a beer fest, right?

Not that they've ever heard me mutter under my breath. The music pretty much drowns that out while also ending the ritual of talking some baseball to the people you came with.

I shouldn't complain, of course. They draw three times the crowds that they did when I was working there, so they are obviously doing something right.

Somewhere, perhaps at Spring Valley High, we learned the term *onomatopoeia*. It is a word that conjures up a sound as well as being just a word, like *slurp*, or *sniff*, *squawk*, or *hiss*. Not terribly important, but the word *onomatopoeia* always stuck in my brain because of its rhythm.

And not a single broadcaster, so far as I could tell, had fun with Adam Ottovino's name. But every time I heard it, I thought of *onomatopoeia*.

It wasn't, of course, a nickname. Baseball nicknames, which have pretty much receded as part of the game, seldom bordered on the intellectual, let along the obscure. A typical baseball nickname would be that used for

Johnny Hopp, who played for six teams including the Yankees from 1939 to '52. Johnny's nickname was Hippity. And in recent years, we have had Big Papi.

As editor of the Yankees yearbooks, press guides, and daily press notes, and as producer of the team's telecasts, I was in a position to invent nicknames here and there, but I honestly don't remember being clever enough to have one stick. I did resist calling George Medich "Doc," which I thought was too obvious, and he liked that I didn't do it. (Medich was a mid-'70s Yankees pitcher who was studying for his medical degree.)

I did, however, witness the worst nickname ever. We had a minor league prospect named Charlie Spikes who was tearing up the International League and seemed destined for big-league stardom. His name would be in our press notes almost daily. At the time, Mike Burke, our team president, was dating a girl whose first name was Sam.

So, one day Bob Fishel got a call from Burke during a game. He was sitting with Sam, and he told Bob, "This Charlie Spikes fellow—I'd like to have you call him Sam Spikes in the press notes from now on, okay?"

Bob hung up and looked at me and then told me what he'd just heard. The team president wanted us to nickname a player after his girlfriend.

We never did it.

George Plimpton was an erudite, well-bred, somewhat patrician New York figure who enjoyed a good measure of fame as a sort of "Walter Mitty" character, stepping into roles he was underqualified for and turning the adventure into literature. He pitched in Yankee Stadium to an All-Star lineup including Mantle and Mays and played quarterback for a few snaps for the Detroit Lions in an exhibition, turning it into his bestselling book, *Paper Lion*.

About five years later, he came up with a promotion in which the "Mickey Mantle All-Stars" would meet the "George Plimpton All-Stars" on the field at Yankee Stadium, and the selections would be accomplished by people writing in as to why they should be the chosen ones. The "game" would take place as a pregame event on Sunday, September 9, 1973.

First, however, came the selection process, and I was part of that. We gathered in Michael Burke's beautiful upper-level office on a day he was away and Plimpton, me, and a few of his assistants began reading the letters and selecting the most touching ones. The players were aged eight to 96 and a few were women.

(While the Yankees offices were sort of a blue-collar place to work, with the ground crew, the ticket office gang, and the concessionaires all having a run of the place, the Burke office evoked the upper echelon of CBS, the "Tiffany Network," including a proper 5'10" British-accented secretary for Burke, Elizabeth, who looked like a fashion model. She did not hang out with us for lunch in the press room, where Mary Collins prepared a daily spread for us at 75 cents a head, nor did she join us for the office staff photo which appeared in the yearbook. Puh-leeze.)

The Plimpton game went one inning and somehow kept going beyond three outs, and Mantle himself was captain of the Mickey Mantle All-Stars. The players got to keep their uniform jerseys, we took team photos, and they got their names on the scoreboard. I overheard someone ask Mantle if he enjoyed being famous, and he said, "It keeps me from getting a real job."

It's only significant today because we probably had the first women on the field as ballplayers that day, and because Plimpton was wonderful to work with. He was so enthusiastic about this project—he absolutely loved reading the letters and making the selections, as though this was what he was always striving to achieve. He was all-in. He turned the preparation of a small promotion into a great afternoon.

I think players need to be reminded more often what a privilege it is to be playing the game they love at the major league level. They tend to take it for granted, to think about that day's opponents. But look around, guys—the size of the ballparks, the beauty in their maintenance, the licensed products, baseball cards, the devotion of the fans, the first-class travel, the lavish postgame buffets, the free media coverage—it's all part of the experience. And it needs to be presented each spring training as the privilege it is. They might have major league skills, but remove all the noise surrounding Major League Baseball, and they would just be a bunch of gifted athletes throwing the baseball around on a high school field with no one watching. They should appreciate it and enjoy it while they are major leaguers and let the fans know they really do care. Fame is fleeting; careers are short. Bring in a retired player to explain how fleeting it all is and how to appreciate it every day. Ask the veterans on the roster to speak to the newly arrived. The extra stuff is what being a major leaguer means (and, of course, the money). Sometimes I want to grab these guys by the shoulders and say, "Look around at where you are!"

There are few things sadder on the baseball scene than a player returning to the clubhouse to gather his possessions after being "designated for assignment." No one knows quite what to say to him. He is possibly facing the end of the ride, the return to the reality of real life. Oh, players talk about "more time with the family," but that's a cliché. The day a player is released is certainly one of the saddest days of the man's life.

I was once talking to the Yankees relief pitcher Tanyon Sturtze about this, and he reminded me that he had been released and become a free agent about a dozen times in his career. At least there was always someone there with a new contract for him, until that finally ran out after seven teams in 12 seasons.

The average major league career is only four years. Tanyon beat the odds but had to hold his breath—often.

Tal Smith, who was briefly the general manager of the Yankees during the Shea Stadium sojourn, engineered the acquisition of a middle infielder named Fernando Gonzalez to replace an injured player in 1974. We purchased him from the Royals. It was the sort of deal that barely makes it into "transactions" on the statistics page (the "agate" page) of a newspaper.

Before the days when everything was available on video, you judged these players by scouting reports and statistics that were available to everyone. Fernando was considered, by that age-old scouting axiom, "good field, no hit." He had gone 3-for-21 with the Royals so far that season.

So, Bill Virdon put him at second base, and what do you know, he started off hitting fairly impressively, but his fielding was a little suspect.

I was watching him play, and after he went 2-for-2 in a game on May 10, Tal leaned over and whispered to me, "Do you think they sent us a different Fernando Gonzalez?"

Anything was possible in those pre-video days, and it did make me think that perhaps sometime in the game's history, the old switcheroo may have indeed been perpetrated on someone.

Of all the things I had to do as Yankees PR director, going with traveling secretary Bill Kane to find Ed Brinkman in spring training of 1976 to tell him he was being released (Billy Martin said he didn't have the heart to do it) was among the toughest. I'd never been in this position before, and Bill was really angry that it had fallen on him. ("It's the manager's responsibility!" he kept saying). Brinkman took it hard, cursed at us, and couldn't believe it, although no one following the team had forecast that there was a place on the roster for him. He was at the end of the line of a 15-year career, although he was only 33. Billy had managed him in Detroit and liked him but couldn't bring himself to release him.

But the thing that fell most out of the area of my responsibilities had to be the day I was told to get Oscar Gamble's hair cut. Bob Fishel had never mentioned this as part of my job description.

Oscar was 26 and had been traded by Cleveland to the Yankees for pitcher Pat Dobson in November 1975. He had a lefthand swing made for Yankee Stadium (after he homered, he would shout, "Bat boy, come get it!" as he headed for first) and would be a very popular player on the team both with fans and teammates.

I first met him when he came to our offices near Shea Stadium shortly after the trade to sign a new contract. He arrived with his agent, Haabib Jamal, and Gabe Paul rose to his feet and said, "Haabib, how the hell are you?" which was just Gabe adapting to mid-70s agent-driven baseball.

We took some photos of Oscar in a Yankees jersey, and of course, I couldn't help but notice his world-class afro. In an age when most Black players wore afros, Oscar stood out—literally—with hair that reached perhaps 10 inches beyond his skull. His baseball card was the talk of collectors, with the Cleveland cap barely sitting atop it.

Now, about two months later, we were in Fort Lauderdale for spring training. Monday would be reporting day for the position players. This was Sunday, and I was in my room watching golf at the Fort Lauderdale Inn on Federal Highway when Gabe called.

"I just saw out my window that Oscar Gamble pulled in and he still has that afro," said Gabe. "You need to get it cut today, or we won't let him workout tomorrow."

"Umm…why me, Gabe?" I asked, innocently.

"Because if he doesn't get it cut, we won't give him a uniform, and he'll file a grievance, and he'll win the grievance, and that will be the end of the haircut policy and it will be a huge PR issue," he said in one breath. He managed to get PR in there.

So, I had my marching orders, and I had to pretty much get this done by myself, since most of the coaching staff, trainers, etc., had gone off fishing following the Sunday morning workout.

As dumpy as the Fort Lauderdale Inn was, it did have a barber shop in the lobby, although it was closed on Sunday. I found the assistant manager of the Inn and asked if he could call the barber. I got on the phone and told him our situation and said I would give him $30 to come in on his day off if he would cut Oscar's hair. Of course, first I had to convince Oscar.

The barber said he would do it, and I asked if he had experience cutting a Black man's hair.

"Nope, never did it," he said.

"Well, don't tell that to Oscar!"

I gathered my courage and knocked on Oscar's door. I reintroduced myself, assuming he wouldn't remember me from the earlier meeting.

He had just driven from Alabama and was tired. I explained the situation and told him he wouldn't get a uniform the next day (but said nothing about filing a grievance), and to my delight, he said, "Okay," just as simple as that.

I called Ellie Howard's room—he hadn't gone with the other coaches on the fishing trip—and caught him up on the situation. He laughed and said something about "never seen anything like this" about the general state of the Yankees on a day-by-day basis. He agreed to meet us in the barber shop for "moral support."

The barber arrived. I reclaimed Oscar and called Ellie, and we met at the shop. The barber started cutting. I had no idea how this was going to turn out. Ellie kept laughing, which was a good thing; it was relaxing Oscar and the barber.

In the end, he had a very short haircut, and I regret not picking up the hair that had fallen to the floor. I could have sent it to Cooperstown. Or auctioned it! I regret not taking photos, but it was pre-smartphones and we just didn't always have a camera available.

Oscar smiled. He liked it! He really did.

The next day he put on his Yankees uniform, photographers had a field day, and before-and-after pictures ran all over the country.

Oscar and I had a bond from that day forward. When I was in Fantasy Camp in 2011 interviewing the retired Yankees who were coaching, Oscar and I got to relive the day, 35 years earlier, on tape. He was not only still smiling about it, but he was aware that it may have been his most famous baseball moment of a 17-year career.

With Oscar Gamble at Yankees Fantasy Camp, reliving the day of the famous haircut.

Come to think of it, maybe it was my most famous baseball moment too.

Oh, and I still can't remember how I got to the press box in old Yankee Stadium.

Acknowledgments

Special thanks to Robert Wilson; Michelle Bruton; the Appels—Lourdes, Deb, Brian, Ryan, Casey, Matty, and Tyler; the monthly Larry Ritter lunch bunch; my Yankees PR brethren; Bill Heyman; Christyne and Nick Nicholas; Leigh Montville; Ira and Dolly Berkow; Juliet Papa; Art Shamsky; Jane Hamilton; Tom Villante; Peter Bavasi; Lana Kaufman; and David Fisher.

Index

279